mi 5

po 73810

5 - 14 - 01

*Religion in the South*

John B. Boles, Series Editor

# A Genealogy of Dissent

## Southern Baptist Protest in the Twentieth Century

*David Stricklin*

THE UNIVERSITY PRESS OF KENTUCKY

Publication of this volume was made possible in part
by a grant from the National Endowment for the Humanities.

*Editorial and Sales Offices:* The University Press of Kentucky
663 South Limestone Street, Lexington, Kentucky 40508-4008

03  02  01  00  99       1  2  3  4  5

Library of Congress Cataloging-in-Publication Data
Stricklin, David, 1952–
A genealogy of dissent : Southern Baptist protest
in the twentieth century / David Stricklin.
p.    cm.
Includes bibliographical references and index.
ISBN 0-8131-2093-4 (hardcover : alk. paper)
1. Southern Baptist Convention—History—20th century.
2. Civil rights—Southern States—History—20th century.
3. Civil rights—Religious aspects—Baptists—History of
doctrines—20th century. 4. Baptists—Southern States—
History—20th century. I. Title.
BX6462.3.S77   1999
286'.132'0904—dc21         99–13977

This book is printed on acid-free recycled paper
meeting the requirements of the American National Standard
for Permanence of Paper for Printed Library Materials.

Manufactured in the United States of America

*For Sally*

# Contents

# Preface

I did not grow up in a Southern Baptist home. My hometown, Cleburne, Texas, certainly had its share of Baptists, my best friend's family among them. When we were kids, I visited his church from time to time, duly noting the differences between it and my family's church, and saw little reason to switch from our church to his. My attitude might have stemmed from the tendency I had from earliest times to side with the underdog and, in our town, the Baptists were no underdogs. They were most numerous and seemingly becoming more so. They had the biggest buildings and the most elaborate "programs," activities that occupied every age group, often creating employment opportunities for students from Southwestern Baptist Theological Seminary in nearby Fort Worth. To the Baptists, bigger was better and biggest was best, a sure sign of spiritual rectitude and divine favor. The attitude they seemed to have, as a Baptist minister I met years later said, was "triumphant." They had the sort of triumphalism that comes from belonging to a smoothly running institutional machine that set goals, engaged and trained personnel fit to achieve them, endowed those people with the necessary resources, and celebrated the results of their efforts with the unalloyed glee of those who are convinced of the divine origins of their success. Sometimes the glee turned to gloating, which prompted my Methodist great-uncles to complain bitterly about "them old Boptists [sic]." According to one observer, Southern Baptists perfected their organizational skills to an art form. Their "formula for religious success was clearcut and ultimately as measurable as the bottom line at a hardware store: keep the message simple; stir faith in the organization; expand the plant and the program . . . ; sell the product; count the results . . . . It was they who set the tone for the town, and it was not uncommon to sense their spirit at a meeting of the Rotary Club, the P.T.A., or the High School assembly."[1]

Not everyone in, as well as out of, Southern Baptist life,[2] however, appreciated the direction in which such skills took Southern Baptists. Their magnificent buildings and vast expenditures for missionary efforts struck some critics as evidence of a sense of indifference to the suffering of most of the world. Baptists countered by saying that they offered the world the greatest gift imaginable, that of eternal salvation from the unspeakable torments of hell. This fact alone served to distinguish Southern Baptists from many other Christian groups that found the old-fashioned beliefs embarrassing. I remember being amused and impressed by the remark of a southern comedian, "Brother" Dave Gardner, who summed up the principal difference he saw between the South's dominant faith and its northern counterpart. He said, "Northern Baptists say, 'There ain't no hell.' Southern Baptists say, 'The hell there ain't.'"[3] This life is but the blinking of an eye, they said, compared with the everlasting life that follows the end of one's time on earth, and it serves one poorly to ignore the threats of eternal damnation. After all, Southern Baptists added, they operated various kinds of ministries that acknowledged and tried to lessen human suffering, from disaster relief to clothes closets for poor people. Their critics responded by pointing out that such efforts often seemed to come with "strings" attached. Recipients of Southern Baptist assistance often were encouraged or even required to receive information about Baptist theological perspectives, activities, and programs. Southern Baptist ministries to the poor and bereft seemed to the critics to be awash in promotional gimmickry and self-congratulation. They did not employ Jesus' recommendation in the Sermon on the Mount that one should use discretion when performing acts of charity and not let "your left hand know what your right hand is doing."[4] When I began to become aware of the criticisms of Southern Baptists, I did not realize that many of those critics were offering their views from within the very institutions they were criticizing.

Long after I had left home for college and work, I encountered this other side of Baptist life. I learned about the Baptist tradition of insisting on religious freedom, both for themselves and for others. I read about Baptists in Britain and in the British colonies in North America who had suffered abuses, even martyrdom at the hands of coercive governments, for their nonconformist beliefs. I also began to hear stories about modern-day Southern Baptists who believed they had picked up this thread of Baptist nonconformity and gone against the grain, not just of the culture at large, but of their own triumphant denomination, and in the region of its greatest successes. They criticized their fellow Southern Baptists for concentrating so much on increasing the size and power of their organizations while doing little about the poor conditions in which so many people in the South and elsewhere lived and nothing about the causes of those conditions. These critics wondered about the changes that might be wrought if one could redirect the vast organizational talents and outright devotion that characterized so much of the work of Southern Baptists, if one could move those energies away from the enlarging of institutions and toward the alleviation of human suffering. During my time in college I heard one Southern Baptist say, "If you could find ten Southern Baptists with a social conscience for every 100,000 people, you could turn any city in this country upside down in a year. The problem would be finding those ten Southern Baptists." The same highly quotable person said in criticizing the sometimes anti-intellectual bent of Southern Baptists, "Jesus died to take away your sins, not your mind." These critics interested me a great deal because they seemed to take little satisfaction in their affiliation with the most "successful" Protestant denomination in the world. They refused to celebrate, to take pride in, many of the achievements with which other Southern Baptists were most pleased. They resisted the opposite temptation, however, to take what might have been a different sort of satisfaction, that of withdrawing from the denomination whose actions they criticized. Many people might have considered withdrawal to be taking the high moral ground, but these critics stayed within Southern Baptist life, taking the same ridicule and misunderstandings outsiders often directed against Southern Baptists as a whole, even though they agreed with many of the points made by critics from outside the circle of Southern Baptists.

I became intrigued by two questions about these people: How did they come to oppose so fundamentally the church home that had given them so much of their identity, and what became of them when they did so? With these essential questions, I began my study of Southern Baptist dissenters.

The work that led directly to the writing of this book began long before I went to Tulane University to begin my doctoral study. It began in North Carolina, where I was doing postgraduate work in theology at the Duke University Divinity School. I became acquainted with the minister of a "dually aligned" church in Durham, that is, one affiliated both with the Southern Baptist Convention (SBC) and the American Baptist Churches, the successor to the old Northern Baptist Convention. When asked the difference between the two, the minister, Bob McClernon, had an answer different from that of Dave Gardner. McClernon said, "American Baptists have realized that the Civil War is over." There were other differences, of course, but the attitude that Baptists should not be separated regionally or segregated racially was a powerful one that American Baptists embraced to a greater extent than did their southern counterparts.[5] I told McClernon of my interest in the life stories of religious people who had departed on principle from the traditions of their upbringing, and he told me about some southern white churchpeople he had known, mainly through American Baptist connections, who had been involved in the civil rights movement. These people, though native southerners with Southern Baptist backgrounds, had found their way to affiliation with American Baptists by one means or another. I was somewhat interested in the fact that they had migrated toward American Baptist life, but I was fascinated to learn that they had moved into civil rights work, having come out of Southern Baptist upbringings and, in several cases, educations. I knew enough to know that such a thing was not unheard of, but I wanted to find out more about these people and others with whom they had dealings over the years.

In 1984, I traveled to Greenville, South Carolina, to conduct the first of a series of interviews with one of the people about whom McClernon had spoken, Martin England, and his wife, Mabel Orr England. Although he was reticent about his achievements, I nevertheless learned in my interviews that Martin England's influence had extended into a remarkable network of people, many of whom I had heard about, who had overlapped and come after his career. I also learned from England that one of the great influences on his own life was someone whom I had not heard of until then, Walter Nathan Johnson. Mr. England told me he believed that "Walt" Johnson's papers were in the possession of the library at Southeastern Baptist Theological Seminary in Wake Forest, North Carolina. For reasons that will become clear in the course of the narrative, the papers were sealed and under the guardianship of the librarian at Southeastern, under the terms of the Johnson family's gift of the materials to the seminary library. The librarian allowed me to use the papers, which confirmed what Martin England had told me. Johnson had his own network of supporters, even followers, one might say, whose ranks included many of the people about whom I was learning in the England interviews and in other interviews I was conducting on the largely untold stories of southern white churchpeople who had been involved in the civil rights movement. In the fall of 1984, I went to work for the Baylor University Institute for Oral History and continued my research on these and other people who had taken their religious convictions in directions other than those of the majority of their fellow believers. In 1991, I began my doctoral course work at Tulane, concentrating in U.S. cultural history with special emphases on the twentieth century and the South. After completing the preliminary requirements for the doctorate, I began at last the task of filling in the gaps in the research I had begun almost ten years earlier and writing my description of the actions and understandings of this unusual group of Southern Baptists. The story dealt with freedom, conscience, and courage, as well as coercion, tradition, and expediency. It had deep roots and broad branches and resembled in other ways that phenomenon people refer to as a family tree.

## An Invisible Cadre

In the proceedings from a conference on civil rights history at the University of Virginia, several authorities on the subject called for new work on the role of white southerners in the civil rights movement. Julian Bond particularly called for studies on "indigenous" support for civil rights for southern blacks, including that of "the large and, to this day, largely invisible cadre of white lawyers, judges, ministers, and others who played a . . . helpful role, . . . often at great sacrifice." Bond asked for work to account for the involvement of southern whites with fairly traditional evangelical upbringings, such as Bob Zellner, a white member of the Student Nonviolent Coordinating Committee (SNCC) and the son of a Methodist minister: "[W]hy did Alabama-born Zellner, as southern as Moon Pies and RC Cola, with an accent as thick as sorghum, [and others] . . . come to SNCC? Why did they come to any kind of civil rights activity at all?"[6] Such questions needed to be asked of Zellner and others even better known, such as Will Campbell, and their experiences needed to be compared with those of that "invisible cadre" of which Julian Bond spoke. Some did only small things, but others did a great deal at great sacrifice. The same could be said of southern white churchpeople who involved themselves in other protest and reform movements in the South, such as peace advocacy and the promotion of equal rights for women. The extent of the influence they exerted for change in the South is subject to debate, but their stories are important for what they tell about religion and about the South. Much has been written, and rightly so, on the black southern churchpeople who participated in the civil rights movement and on the northern white churchpeople who went to the South to take part in the movement. Excellent studies abound of the heroic actions of these two groups of religious people who risked their livelihoods and their personal safety to act out their faiths through public protest against injustice. But they were not the only churchpeople who performed acts that set them apart from the broader culture of tolerance for injustice.

Southern white churchpeople who departed from the ordinary habits of southern social justice have seemed invisible or nonexistent to the writers of many versions of the story of the civil rights movement and from those of other protest and reform movements for a variety of reasons. One reason is a simple lack of familiarity. Many people who were involved in the civil rights struggle and in peace advocacy and women's rights efforts operated in small circles of compatriots. They had naturally limited spheres of influence and recognition, often working behind the scenes, sometimes virtually alone, sometimes for only brief periods of time. Neglect by journalists and historians of southern white churchpeople's contributions to the civil rights revolution and other protest and reform efforts resulted in part from this intentional avoidance of publicity, even occasional secrecy, with which many such participants operated, outside of the highly publicized activist networks and away from the attention of reporters who became, in many instances, household names themselves. The reputation of white Southern churches also helps explain the seeming invisibility of progressive reformers who came from within their ranks. Those churches have nearly always been perceived as bastions of conservatism, the last institutions in southern society in any age to endorse progressive changes in social relations and political expressions of them. That traditional perception largely holds true. Most churches in the South supported and many even gloried in the segregationist system of southern race relations, militarism, or traditional gender roles, but exceptions to the rule of such belief and behavior arose. Such exceptions occurred in various places in the South and produced eloquent testimony in words and deeds of the possibility of another religious response to southern racism, militarism, and sexism. Further, one should not discount the possibility of prejudice among reporters, many of whom worked for northern news organizations, some of whom did not grow up in the South. Some of them were unwilling or unable to believe that some whites in the churches of the South would go against the familiar patterns of behavior on race and other issues.

Longstanding prevailing attitudes within the scholarly community have also contributed to a discounting of the role played by some southern whites in the civil rights movement and other progressive campaigns. Progressive southern white churchpeople are poorly understood partly because they have rarely been the subjects of scholarly attention. Most scholarly treatments of the social gospel in the United States have assumed that a southern tradition of reformist Christianity was almost nonexistent until the participation of African-American churchpeople in the civil rights movement. Scholars usually concentrated on liberal pastors, congregations, and denominational leaders in the North. A southern tradition of reformist Christianity, then, is assumed by most people to have been virtually nonexistent until the 1950s and 1960s and then largely dominated by African Americans. When white churchpeople ventured into areas of concern beyond the care of souls and their immortal destinies, these concerns were usually believed to have been limited to drinking and gambling and the like, with smoking added if one came from a region of the South where the economy did not depend on the cultivation of tobacco. Carl Degler argued that the social gospel "scarcely touched" the churches of the South. Samuel S. Hill Jr. went even further, saying, "Based on the analysis that religion and regionality are both primary frameworks of meaning for white southern people with regionality predominant in the practical order of life, any semblance of a social-gospel ideology would have upset the balance and rendered impossible mutual support between church and culture. The South's particular compound for the formation of Christendom would thereby have been destroyed."[7]

Despite the apparent finality of such a judgment, and the essential accuracy of it for the most part, recent scholarship has begun to reverse the trend of denying the existence of a southern social gospel tradition. Dealing with activities early in the twentieth century and afterward, various writers have illuminated the power of reformist ideas in the South, even if those ideas exhibited northern influence or captivated only a minority of the southern population.[8] One recent general history of the South notes the rise of "a mild regional variant of the Social Gospel" that "seldom constructed a theological critique of the social institutions that produced or allowed poverty and injustice," but that nevertheless addressed more issues than the usual sins, such as drinking, condemned by most Protestants.[9] The ranks of southern Christian reformers who represented the invisible cadre of which Julian Bond spoke had limited connections to the southern social gospel tradition, as I will show, but at least one can say that such a tradition existed. That fact will make a difference as this narrative unfolds.

The manuscript that became this book first appeared in the form of a doctoral dissertation in history at Tulane University. But the work that led to the writing of the manuscript started well before I went to Tulane. I would like to thank the people who helped shape the project at each of its stages, particularly the people whose contributions are mentioned directly and indirectly in the preface and those who agreed to be interviewed for my research and for that of others whose work I was privileged to use.

It was my good fortune to encounter and to learn from Gene McLeod,

Bill Bridges, Richard Hester, and Claude Stewart, formerly of Southeastern Baptist Theological Seminary, in the course of this work. Brooks Graebner of Hillsborough, North Carolina, and *Kudzu* was a model of wide-ranging scholarly interests and gracious friendship during my work at the Duke University Divinity School, where I received a wonderful introduction to church history and historical and systematic theology from Jill Raitt, Stuart Henry, Thomas A. Langford, Frederick Herzog, and McMurry Richey. Bob McClernon, Dick Chorley, and Ken Harrell of Durham, North Carolina; Jim Pitts of Furman University; and Beverly England Williams did many wonderful things during my efforts to learn about Martin and Mabel England. William F. Bellinger Jr., Daniel B. McGee, C.W. Christian, William L. Pitts, Glenn O. Hilburn, David Hockenberg, and Rufus B. Spain at Baylor were thoughtful interpreters of the action of religion in life and history from whom I learned much. I want to thank people who loaned me materials from their personal collections, particularly Libby Bellinger, Bruce Evans, Andrew Chancey, and Twyla Gill Wright. I received various kinds of much-appreciated assistance from members of the staffs of the John T. Christian Library of New Orleans Baptist Theological Seminary, Amistad Research Center of Tulane University, Perkins Library and Divinity School Library of Duke University, North Carolina Baptist Historical Collection in the Z. Smith Reynolds Library of Wake Forest University, Denny Library of Southeastern Baptist Theological Seminary, Texas Baptist Historical Collection in the A. Webb Roberts Library of Southwestern Baptist Theological Seminary, Texas Collection of Baylor University, and Southern Baptist Historical Library and Archives in Nashville. At the last-named institution, Bill Sumners was especially helpful and hospitable. He and his colleagues richly deserve the praise they regularly receive from researchers and writers.

My work was supported in its early stages by a grant from the Ministers and Missionaries Benefit Board of American Baptist Churches. Thanks go to Bob McClernon for helping bring that support to pass and to Dean Wright for his generosity and foresight. The project received midterm help from the University Research Committee of Baylor University, in whose Institute for Oral History I worked for quite a few years. I want to thank my old friend Tom Charlton for his support in permitting me to work on a project that broke geographical boundaries for the institute and to all my former colleagues in the institute and at Baylor generally who helped shape my understandings. To continue the work into its Tulane phase, I received financial help from the Ben Williams Faculty Fellowship program at Baylor, for which I am extremely grateful. Thanks go especially to former dean William F.

Cooper for his wise counsel and rich insights over the course of a long friendship my family and I cherish. I am also grateful to the Graduate School and the Department of History at Tulane for the support of a Graduate School Fellowship and to the Lurcy Fund and Professor Samuel Ramer for assistance with the expenses of dissertation research travel. A Lynn E. May Jr. Study Grant from the Southern Baptist Historical Library and Archives was very helpful and much appreciated.

My dissertation committee, Bill C. Malone, Wilfred M. McClay, and Lawrence Powell, shared the benefits of their great talent and dedication to the practice of history. My director, Bill Malone, constantly challenged me to think and write more clearly. I tried to follow his example in these areas and benefited greatly from his extraordinary knowledge of southern culture. He and Bobbie Malone, his spouse and partner, touched my life and those of the members of my family in many wonderful ways during our time in New Orleans. Bill McClay offered very helpful criticisms of my preliminary thinking in the course of many stimulating discussions of the history of religion in the United States. Larry Powell read the dissertation with a level of care and thoughtfulness I dare say is quite rare in third readers. I am grateful as well for the suggestion each of the three of them made that I ask John Boles to read it. Thanks to another old friend and research fellow-traveler, Steve Tucker, for suggesting I head toward Tulane in the first place and for many entertaining and informative visits over the years. In a graduate student community remarkably devoted to mutual support and helpfulness, Nadiene Van Dyke stood out as a faithful friend and colleague with a boundless capacity for kindness. Ruth Barnes in the Graduate School office at Tulane and Joan Hughes of the Department of History were wise, helpful, and patient.

I want to thank John Boles for his very helpful suggestions for the manuscript. Numerous people at Lyon College have given me encouragement for this project and for myriad opportunities in that marvelous small college. Special thanks to the expert and thoughtful Peggy Weaver.

Various people have heard compact versions of the story herein at conferences where I have read papers and in informal gatherings of all sorts. I benefited from their comments, as I did from those of people who did me the honor of reading all or part of the manuscript. Of this last number, I want to mention especially my mother-in-law, Wilma Browder, whose deep devotion to Baptist life has been a constant source of inspiration. I know that some of this was hard on her to read and I value very highly the reactions she has shared with me. She and my father-in-law, Craig Browder, have shown many acts of kindness over the years to a vast number of people, myself included, giving visible expression to a faith whose best traditions they represent so admirably.

Finally, special thanks go to my mother, Betty Stricklin; my sisters, Nancy Willis and Judy Stricklin; and my brother-in-law, Jerry Willis; and to my wife, Sally Browder, and our daughters, Annie Bowyer Stricklin and Sarah Browder Stricklin, for support, perspective, and tolerance. My late father instilled in me an interest in history, but my mother proved in vast numbers of discussions the necessity for evidence in an argument. Nancy, Jerry, Judy, Annie, and Sarah stimulated my interest in books and ideas. In a very real way, however, this book originated in conversations with Sally even before we married. Many of what she graciously refers to as insights she no longer recognizes as ideas I got from her. Indeed, my first awareness of many of the people described in this story and of many of its most important issues, particularly concerning what is at stake when people act out their faith in costly ways, developed in the course of countless conversations with Sally about history, psychology, and religion. As she would say, "Life, and work, are what fill the spaces between good conversations." My life and work have been more interesting to me because of those conversations with her.

# Introduction

## Terms of Existence for Southern Baptists in the Twentieth Century

While a consideration of dissent must involve the mind of the protesters, it must also delve more broadly into the theological understandings of persons on both sides of several arguments within Southern Baptist life. These understandings grew out of the culture created by people who developed Southern Baptist norms and by those who departed from them. Much fine scholarship deals with the interrelationships of religion and culture, but the model that has most influenced me is that of George M. Marsden in his book *Fundamentalism and American Culture: The Shaping of Twentieth-Century Evangelicalism, 1870-1925*. By "culture," Marsden said, "I usually have in mind the collection of beliefs, values, assumptions, commitments, and ideals usually expressed in a society through popular literary and artistic forms and embodied in its political, educational, and other institutions." He went on to say, "In most cultures the prevailing formal religion has been an integral part of and support for the dominant beliefs, values, and institutions."[1] In the minds of vast numbers of observers, the American South has long been a culture strongly defined by the intersection of its dominant religious beliefs and concepts, however limited, of social justice. For most of the region, furthermore, the "prevailing formal religion" has been Protestantism, whose preeminent representatives in the twentieth century have been the Southern Baptists.

There is also the matter of fundamentalism. While theologically conservative, Southern Baptists as a denomination were not fundamentalists, strictly speaking, for most of the twentieth century. A distinction should be made, therefore, between fundamentalism and the broader Christian evangelicalism that gave it birth. Fundamentalism is usually characterized by scholars as a militant, often separatist, religious response to modernism, especially the theory of evolution as an explanation of human origins and the idea that solutions to problems can be found without regard to traditional religious values and understandings. Fundamentalists hold that the Bible is the final authority on matters of all sorts and that it is infallible in every way, including those details of stories that appear to conflict with modern scientific teaching. They also tend to believe that the fundamental tenets of the faith are nonnegotiable and exempt from the varieties of interpretation that members of nonauthoritarian religious bodies might place on such teachings. Protestant fundamentalists constitute one part of the larger group called evangelicals, who believe that they are bound by God to win converts to their faith, usually from both the ranks of nonbelievers and from those of adherents to other forms of religious belief, including other branches of Christianity. While not all evangelicals are fundamentalists, most fundamentalists are evangelicals. Protestant fundamentalists, furthermore, for the most part, hold a view of the end of human history called premillennialism, the expectation that Jesus Christ will return to earth, having triumphed over the forces of evil and degradation, ushering in and presiding over a period of a thousand years of heavenly peace on earth. Though there have been large numbers of biblical literalists among African American Christians, militant Protestant fundamentalism in the United States has been most often an outgrowth of white evangelicalism. Its adherents tend to be convinced of their theological correctness, determined not to enter reciprocal relationships or have fellowship with those who believe otherwise, and fully expectant that God in Christ will glorify them in the cataclysmic struggle that will mark the Endtime.

On the basis of this description, most Southern Baptists, as individuals, hold beliefs that define them as being fundamentalists. Their more highly educated leaders, however, including most denominational bureaucrats and a great many pastors and most of their seminary professors, until the 1980s, tended to hold more moderate theological views than rank-and-file Southern Baptists. One characteristic kept Southern Baptists from letting this fact tear the denomination apart for most of the twentieth century. It was the determination of the vast majority of Southern Baptists to cooperate with one another in pursuit of their common institutional goals, evangelistic for the most part, despite theological and other differences that distinguished them as individuals within the larger communion made possible by the SBC.

In Southern Baptist life, the people who felt the greatest determination to keep the convention together were those who held moderate, generally conservative theological views and tolerated a certain range of divergence within the accepted definitions of orthodoxy. They held traditional Baptist views of church order and means of association and a fervent determination to prevent dissent from spoiling the cooperative spirit that made the work of Southern Baptist institutions possible. As long as individuals did not veer "too far" off in one direction or the other, either to the right or to the left, they were welcome to associate with these moderate Southern Baptists. Such associations helped create the camaraderie and productivity that became Southern Baptist hallmarks. They also became a source of contention in the twentieth century, first in the twenties, and then in the seventies and eighties particularly, because the moderates happened to make up the core of the power structure in the SBC and its agencies and institutions. A great deal of resentment arose among those who were excluded from the alliances that the moderates assembled to reach beyond the congregational level and do the broader work of spreading the Baptist message. Radicals of the right, and the much smaller numbers of those of the left, were excluded from positions of prominence despite the fact that they represented the thinking of vast numbers of rank-and-file Southern Baptists. Fundamentalists particularly and bitterly resented the willingness of moderates to work with people who held nontraditional theological and social views and believed, quite correctly, that they represented more truly the views of the masses of Southern Baptists than did the moderate leadership.[2]

Southern Baptists worked diligently to keep theological differences from obstructing their institutional and evangelistic goals, but it would be a mistake to underestimate the influence of theological concerns on the identity and makeup of Southern Baptists, moderate or otherwise.[3] In particular, the prominence of one theological position derived from their indebtedness to Reformed theology, the perseverance of the saints, has direct bearing on any consideration of the culture of Southern Baptists. As Baptist historian Bill J. Leonard pointed out, this doctrine "was endemic to the Calvinism of early Southern Baptists." Translated into the popular Baptist catch phrase "once saved, always saved," the idea of perseverance became a great comfort to Southern Baptists. Whatever ills befell or temptations beset them, they could always count on the reliability and durability of their salvation experience. But in the absence of an active doctrine of sanctification, the focus on "growing" in the faith that John Wesley's Methodist movement stressed, the doctrine of perseverance became an excuse as well as a comfort. As Leonard said, "once saved, always saved" was a weak interpretation of Calvin's notion of perseverance, but it gained a powerful hold on the popular imagination of

Southern Baptists, creating an attitude that "Once you are in, everything else is secondary."[4] "Everything else" included serious attention to the social problems of the South. The social and political expressions of Calvinism took varied forms for different kinds of Baptists. Some took Calvin's idea of predestination to the level of opposing evangelistic and missionary efforts, believing that little could be done to alter the destiny of someone's soul, something that had been determined long since by God. The appeal of this sort of thinking among some of the poorest of southerners, especially Primitive Baptists, led some to see such theology as a tendency toward fatalism "born of a long and arduous association with their environment."[5]

Other combinations of socio-political and theological factors contributed to the relative lack of concern many southern white religious people felt for the social problems of the region. A crucial one, according to one scholarly interpretation, had to do with the need southern Protestants felt to rationalize the South's defeat during the Civil War. They "made a religion out of their history," Charles Reagan Wilson contended, through which they sought to "reaffirm their identity." This identity had suffered serious assault by the northern victory and encouraged redefinition of the vaunted southern "way of life" based on strict social hierarchies. Southern white Protestants "spiritualized" their religion—that is, they emphasized the other-worldly qualities of it—to distinguish themselves from their materialistic northern conquerors, Wilson said, as a way of trying to prove to themselves that their defeat was not a sign of God's abandonment of the South, but only an experience of testing by God, a chastisement like the Babylonian captivity of Israel. This and other ways of understanding and expressing religious beliefs set southern Protestants, particularly Baptists, apart from their northern counterparts. In contrast, in the early nineteenth century, New England Congregationalists, who had deep roots in Calvinist soil, subsumed potential influences of the concept of perseverance and other Reformed doctrines to support the social status quo within their broader determination to reform society in the image of the more activist idea of the old Puritan Commonwealth. In fact, their willingness to use the power of the state to achieve the ends of reform in a land under "divine judgment" constituted one of the chief differences between them and Baptists, north and south.[6]

Political changes in the twentieth century worked to upset the traditional Southern Baptist dedication to corporate harmony. The fundamentalist sentiments of vast numbers of rank-and-file Southern Baptists became aroused and mobilized by a determined leadership with great appeal to broad segments of the public, especially those with conservative political orientations who were willing to sacrifice denominational harmony for the sake of their convictions.[7] Dismissed by many observers as backward-looking, anti-intellectual, and dangerous, fundamentalists in the South, for approximately the first thirty years of the century, waged a form of religious warfare against the cultural and educational changes associated with modernism. They waged intellectual, political, and legal battle with their modernist opponents, especially with the goal of winning control of religious institutions and using the apparatus of secular governments to stamp out modernist influence. The most famous example of such efforts was the trial of high school teacher John Thomas Scopes, who was convicted of violating laws of the State of Tennessee that prohibited teaching the theory of evolution in the public schools, a struggle in which Southern Baptists took part on various levels. Southern Baptists gave the nation one of its most remarkable fundamentalist leaders, Baptist pastor J. Frank Norris of Fort Worth, Texas, and other strong Southern Baptist states provided homes for some of the nation's best-known fundamentalist institutions and movements.

As the century wore on, fundamentalists in general attracted and sought less public attention. They realized they were unlikely to win control of mainstream religious organizations or achieve their most fervently longed-for changes in society through legal channels. During the middle third of the century they followed a strategy of separating themselves from people who disagreed with them on the fundamentals of the faith. Most of their efforts during this period went toward the establishment of their own schools, publishing concerns, and broadcast media facilities devoted to halting what they saw as the nation's turning away from the message of Jesus and embracing that of secularists. These actions often led fundamentalists who were Southern Baptists to stop calling and considering themselves Southern Baptists because of their dissatisfaction with the moderate leadership of the SBC. They began separating themselves from the denomination and forming their own groups. Southern fundamentalists participated enthusiastically and publicly in anticommunist activity in the 1950s and 1960s. They helped build an evangelical subculture during these years that later took on a highly visible role in national debates over public policy and personal morality, making the South a focal point in the last third of the century for the merger of right-wing politics and traditionalist religion.[8]

In the latter decades of the twentieth century, then, fundamentalists in the South resurrected many of the methods they had employed in their public and institutional battles in the first part of the century. This last period also saw the rise of modern methods of persuasion and marketing by fundamentalists determined to restore "traditional" values to prominence in the United States. Their reemergence in the major denominations from which they had separated in earlier years reflected a national trend back to the kinds of intrachurch conflict aimed at ridding denominations of suspected liberal influence that had characterized fundamentalism's beginnings. At this point, from 1979 on, fundamentalist Southern Baptists began a concerted effort to increase their involvement in SBC organizational and political activities and exerted massive efforts to redirect Southern Baptists, denominationally, by gaining administrative control of the convention and removing moderates from positions of authority and leadership.[9]

In the battles that led to what moderates called the fundamentalist "takeover" of the SBC, the architects of the fundamentalist resurgence invoked the specter of "liberalism" within the structures of Southern Baptist leadership. A progressive, reformist tradition did in fact exist among Southern Baptists, first the one dating back to the days of the social gospel movement and then the one that is the subject of this book. But this progressive tradition never had as much power in the SBC as the radicals on the other end of the spectrum contended. Southern Baptist progressivism functioned in a small but somewhat subversive subculture within the religious culture of the South, and it criticized many of the political and economic practices of the region and the nation as a whole, as well as the dominant Protestant leadership that supported most of those practices. It also created several ironies and curiosities.

First, the progressive dissenters sometimes seemed to have more in common with their fundamentalist counterparts than with the moderate, "establishment" figures in convention leadership positions. The progressives operated in almost continual tension with the moderate power structure of the SBC, at least as much as and sometimes more so than with the fundamentalist subculture in Southern Baptist life. In the 1970s and 1980s, the fundamentalists found themselves in increasingly frequent conflict with the moderate leadership, culminating in the closest Southern Baptists ever came to open warfare. Another irony, though perhaps a less surprising one, was the fact that much of the involvement of Southern Baptists in the strand of reformist Christianity in the South began during a time when it had fallen out of style for the most part in the northern part of the country and among the small numbers of southern churchpeople who had embraced the social gospel in the early years of the twentieth century. From the 1920s through the 1950s, when such theologians as Karl Barth and Reinhold Niebuhr were questioning many of the assumptions of liberal Christianity, those very ideas entered the thinking of a growing number of religious people in the South.

In another twist, race relations, which had been a relatively minor issue in the old northern social gospel, became a principal concern of these reformist Christians in the South. Prompted by this central issue of life in the South, such people spoke and acted out of theological and intellectual demands that were out of step with the majority culture in which they lived and worked. In some cases, their ideas ran counter to the newly arising assumptions of neoorthodox or "crisis" theology that criticized those of the social gospel, even when they branched out into peace activism or advocacy of women's rights.[10]

A network of persons with personal ties to Southern Baptists picked up this thread of activist Christianity, put their own peculiar Southern Baptist tint to it, and moved far beyond the positions taken by most advocates of the social gospel idea, north or south. They created and sustained a subculture within Southern Baptist life that offered a voice of protest against traditional southern and Baptist ways of understanding and behaving. This network developed, of necessity, by means of personal influence and informal communications and relationships, in direct contrast with the highly structured Southern Baptist denominational system. It posed personal and institutional threats to the mainstream power structure of Southern Baptists and helped prompt the rise to power of a fundamentalist faction within the SBC.

If any group epitomizes the vital interrelationships of religion and culture, most observers probably would agree it is the Southern Baptists.[11] Southern Baptists became the preeminent examples of the symbiosis of faith and the setting in which it flourished largely because of social and cultural factors, but also because of factors of a theological and political nature. One must sort through such phenomena to account for people who went against this powerful tradition.

# Religion and Culture in the Baptist South

## 1

### At Work in the Fields of the Lord

*Oh who will come and go with me? I am bound for the promised land.*
—Samuel Stennet, *On Jordan's Stormy Banks*

Born in 1845 of the conflict that tore apart several Protestant denominations in the United States, the struggle between North and South over the issue of slavery, the Southern Baptist Convention (SBC)became the ecclesiastical structure, if a loose one, with which many of the South's most conservative Christians affiliated. Baptists, though, had not always been conservative. They had, in fact, deep historic roots in dissent against state-established religion and coercive expressions of religious belief, actions that set them apart as radicals during their beginnings in early seventeenth-century Holland and Britain. Southern Baptists inherited several strains of theological and ecclesiological understanding from their forebears, with periodic flights of intense antiestablishment or antiauthoritarian feeling. Baptist historian Walter B. Shurden said that the founders of the Baptist tradition "cut their teeth" on civil disobedience and that "in the records of court proceedings, search warrants, and prison records[,] Baptist names are writ large . . . . Baptists were born in the bosom of radicalism!"[1]

## From the Bosom of Radicalism to Ease in Zion

Such radicalism consisted primarily of resistance to coercive governments that established one faith community in preference to others with tax revenues and other forms of support or attempted to impose regulations on members of dissenting religious bodies that violated their freedom of conscience. Baptists fought such government interference in religious life on behalf of themselves and others, helping in the process to inspire some of the statutory and constitutional guarantees of free exercise of religion that emerged in the early days of the United States. Baptists' devotion to freedom also inspired and reinforced their fierce congregationalism. These people "who called one another brothers and sisters, believed that the only authority in their church was the meeting together of those in fellowship."[2] They were no more eager to accept the ecclesiastical domination of a bishop than they were that of the local magistrate. When they sought to cooperate with each other on such efforts as missionary activities, they kept in mind their common devotion to noncoercive forms of affiliation. Thus they adopted voluntary missionary associations, then missionary societies that raised funds for the appointment of foreign missionaries as their first methods of allying churches with one another. Subsequently, a voluntary missions organization structure authorized by representatives of churches meeting in conventions functioned as a central clearinghouse for funds given to support missionaries, theoretically without creating a ruling ecclesiastical structure. Even though it had the effect of centralizing ecclesiastical authority, the new convention structure did not extend to having any real disciplinary power over individual congregations. Conflicts emerged, of course, over the kinds of missionary enterprises to support. Some even questioned, depending on the degree to which they had been influenced by Calvinism, the theological necessity of fielding missionaries. But Baptists were virtually unanimous in their belief that they should be free of coercion from any source except the Almighty. In the tradition of the Protestant Reformation, Baptists relied solely on Scripture for sources of inspiration regarding God's will on any subject and agreed that each believer should be free to interpret Scripture as he or she saw fit.[3]

There were other sources of Baptist devotion to freedom. Of the two predominant traditions that informed and molded Southern Baptists before the Civil War, one stressed order and a more dignified approach to church life, while the other emphasized intensity of feeling surrounding the salvation experience. The first tradition originated in Charleston, South Carolina, in the late seventeenth century and stressed an orderly form of church conduct and governance, preferably led by an educated clergy, a strict Calvinist theology, and a determined approach to evangelism. The Charleston tradition's influence was felt principally in the urban areas of South Carolina, the Tidewater and Piedmont regions of North Carolina, and eastern Virginia. The other key tradition for Southern Baptists came out of the frontier, specifically the Sandy Creek Baptist Church in western North Carolina, and reflected the exuberance and freedom of much of the experience known as the

Great Awakening. The Sandy Creek tradition spread with the frontier into Tennessee, Kentucky, Arkansas, Louisiana, and Texas. It often manifested itself in the form of a deep suspicion of extracongregational alignments and authority, "too much" education, and theological formulations that did not come essentially verbatim from the Bible. Partly for this reason, these Baptists, who were part of a larger group called Separate Baptists, were less rigidly Calvinistic than those in the Charleston tradition, who were part of the group called Regular Baptists. The difference became important particularly with regard to the experience and assurance of salvation. The Regular Baptists contended that no one had the free will simply to choose to "accept" Christ and receive salvation. Ministers preached as though anyone could be among those elect whom God had chosen for salvation. Those who were so chosen would receive God's "irresistible" grace and likely, in some way, would be aware of their salvation. The Separate Baptists had a more revivalistic orientation, believing that persons who heard enthusiastic and convincing preaching could choose to accept Christ, thus demonstrating that they had been elected by God for salvation. Not as openly Arminian as the Methodists, Separate Baptists certainly allowed more room for the idea of free will in their theology than did their Regular Baptist counterparts, especially those in the Charleston tradition. They both held tightly, however, to the Calvinist idea of perseverance of the saints, the doctrine that a genuine experience of salvation cannot be lost, no matter how frequently the believer strayed from the paths of righteousness onto those of temporary sinfulness.[4]

These two traditions in which much of Southern Baptist life was rooted, along with other less powerful but important ones, created many differences and disagreements among Baptists in the South. After the SBC formed, Southern Baptists representing the two primary traditions frequently found themselves in conflict with one another, particularly over charges of elitism and snobbery brought by Sandy Creek partisans against Charleston traditionalists. No precise east-west divergence developed within Southern Baptist life, but other potential rifts emerged, irrespective of geography, between those who felt that they had an influence over denominational affairs and those who did not. Those who exercised some power among Southern Baptists usually came from the larger, urban churches in the Southwest and the Southeast, which usually had pastors with more education than did the pastors of smaller, rural churches. The Sandy Creek tradition lived on in the hearts of the majority of Southern Baptists, both pastors and laypeople, but what power that existed in the decentralized system of Southern Baptist governance usually belonged to pastors in the Charleston tradition. A sort of populist rhetoric developed that many denominational figures used to gain a significant appeal within the SBC, even if the speaker happened to be a member of the Southern Baptist elite, and in many other ways Baptists continued to appear to be democratic, hardworking people of modest means and attainments. But despite their internal conflicts as a denomination and frequent setbacks as individuals, and the persistent appeal of an easily understood preaching style unadorned by elaborate theological arguments, Southern Baptists as a whole were on their way to a form of respectability that took them far from their modest, even rustic, origins in the antiestablishment fellowships of the colonies and the camp meetings and brush-arbor revivals of the frontier.[5]

Southern Baptists had many reasons to feel "at ease" with the southern way of life. As the nineteenth century wore on, few events offered them reasons to want to change. Between the end of the Civil War and the turn of the twentieth century, particularly, Southern Baptists continued the process of becoming more prominent in the religious life of the South. They became more respectable and more powerful as they became more numerous in southern society, becoming in the process also a subculture of accommodation to the larger culture of southern life. Baptists preserved their determination not to allow government interference in matters of the faith. But now, instead of conflicting with the power structure as they had during the colonial period, in many communities they constituted its core. They abandoned virtually any trace of their former critical stance toward coercive political and economic forces and instead focused their criticisms of society on untoward personal behavior. They came to stand for a determination to defend the status quo, not just in racial matters but in other political, social, and economic issues and concerns as well. As a society built on rigid racial, socioeconomic, and gender hierarchies, the South bothered most Southern Baptists not at all. They had contributed greatly to the ways that society was structured, the ways it operated, and the ways people understood it. They had done much to create that society, and they liked it the way it was. To them, the South was the "Baptist Zion," the promised land. By the last decades of the nineteenth century, Southern Baptists had become more than predominant in and representative of southern religious life. They had become the archetypal southerners: racially and sexually hierarchical, suspicious of "modern" viewpoints, complacent about the exploitation of the economically disadvantaged, militaristic, nationalistic, and generally hostile toward the reformist (and northern) social gospel.[6]

Before the rise of the civil rights movement, therefore, and in large part afterward, most churchpeople in the South, white and black, devoted most of their religious energies to the institutional goals of the churches and focused especially on evangelization of the populace. They worked diligently, faithfully, with the utmost sincerity, preparing themselves and others for the afterlife. None worked harder than Southern Baptists. Some critics interpreted this activity essentially to be membership recruitment, and certainly it could be said that the church rolls grew as a result of the efforts of professional and lay evangelists, both preachers and common members, who invited people to go along with them on the great journey they planned to make one day to the promised land of heaven. No doubt there were ministers and members who delighted in the addition of other members for a great variety of reasons, from the most genuine to the most crass. Some enjoyed the feeling of belonging to an organization that was popular enough to attract other persons, validating their own decision to unite with it. Some looked forward to the resources, especially money, that new members might bring with them in helping the churches grow even more in numbers and influence or advance other sorts of agendas. Apart from the institutional aggrandizement that accompanied increased membership rolls, however, Southern Baptists were engaged in a work they considered to be of the gravest seriousness. They concentrated on what they believed to be the saving teachings and work of Christ, helping to lead others toward the bliss to be enjoyed in heaven, while usually ignoring the ethical teachings of Jesus in the Gospels that often challenged the social and economic status quo. They spent their lives as most southerners are often thought to do, getting "ready to be dead."[7] In this way, as in many others, Southern Baptists expressed the dominant religious view of the culture with its "emphasis on personal sins and vices and . . . enthusiasm for otherworldly theology."[8] Any progressive reform movement within Southern Baptist life had to struggle against this predominant attitude.

In the twentieth century, W.A. Criswell embodied the standard Southern Baptist attitude as well as anyone. The longtime pastor of the SBC's largest congregation, Criswell once said of his First Baptist Church of Dallas, "This place in the eye of God is more favored than any other. It is from here, from our dear church, that we are all going to heaven."[9] His views should be contrasted with those of Carlyle Marney, also a Southern Baptist minister but one who was a fervent critic of much Southern Baptist practice. Marney called the thought of Southern Baptists such as Criswell "the heresy of the South." Marney did not discount the need for a personal experience of regeneration, of turning away from sin and devoting oneself to the demands of faith, but he decried the widespread belief that the rescue of the individual soul from damnation constituted the sum of Christianity. According to Marney, "Religion in the South has kept Jesus in the heavens. Because if he ever gets in our alley, we'll have to be like him. . . . A person who keeps Jesus too godlike doesn't have to be responsible as a human being." In Marney's view, "Any religion that reduces my responsibility for this earth is a cop-out."[10] Historically, most of Marney's fellow Southern Baptists, however, held a view closer to or identical with Criswell's, viewing personal sin as the evil to be combated, the individual soul as the battlefield, and salvation as the sign of victory. For many Southern Baptists, conversion was an experience so dramatic that they regarded it, as one writer said evangelist James Robison did, "with the relief of a man who has just escaped from a galloping terror."[11]

Southern Baptists have believed and behaved more often like W.A. Criswell and James Robison than like Carlyle Marney, a fact that can be illustrated by countless life stories. True to their heritage as southerners, Southern Baptists traditionally have been great storytellers. They have created a particularly rich body of narrative material focused on conversion experiences, joining their personal life stories to the stories of the faith experiences of persons through the ages.[12] The experiences of one Southern Baptist help explain the ways many Southern Baptists blended their understandings of themselves, the theological underpinnings of the particular ways they chose to live out their sense of God's requirements, and their resultant prospects for an afterlife of eternal bliss with God in heaven. His life provides a microcosm of the probable mentality of the majority of Southern Baptists. This individual's experiences illustrate the power of the conversion experience among Southern Baptists and, almost as important, its limitations. They also demonstrate the extent to which Southern Baptists focused on the requirements of "soul-winning," without feeling a great need to address the earthly problems of the people whose souls were the prizes at stake. These experiences also serve as an example of the safeguards against extremism that Southern Baptists maintained for most of their history.

Otis Strickland grew up a nonbeliever in some of the rough neighborhoods of Fort Worth, Texas. After his conversion to Christianity and affiliation with a Southern Baptist church, Strickland moved into that pattern of life that southern evangelicals called "full-time Christian service." According to his own account, his identity as a Christian and Baptist took over every aspect of his life. It led him to the presidency of a small Baptist college and caused him to cross paths with some of the most remarkable figures in Southern Baptist life in the middle decades of the twentieth century, including the legendary fundamentalist firebrand J. Frank Norris. Strickland described his conversion experience, which came upon him suddenly at the age of twenty-two after he had been persuaded by a friend to attend Fort Worth's Travis Avenue Baptist Church. It was the early 1930s. The church's pastor was C.E. Matthews.

> As a result of that I got under conviction and my brother, who was a catcher on the Fort Worth Cats baseball team—that was a professional team in the Texas League—witnessed to me one Sunday night and I was convicted more deeply and was saved there at home, by myself, sitting on the divan. . . . So I ran out of the house and ran a mile to . . . the church and found the usher and . . . told him I wanted to tell Brother Matthews I'd found Jesus. Well, I'd been hiding from Brother Matthews for years and years. I would see him come down the street and I'd run down the alley and get behind a privet hedge where he couldn't see me. . . . So the usher said, "You go upstairs and sit down and Brother Matthews will give you a chance." . . . I sat down there and I don't remember what Brother Matthews preached, but I remember what Mrs. Anna Harrington, a missionary to Brazil, sang. She sang, "Some through the water and some through the flood, some through the fire but all through the blood." I don't have a very good memory, but she just had to sing that once for me to remember it. I went down there and made my profession and a layman came by, Mr. Jess Redford, . . . and he pulled out a little tear-stained black book and he had two columns of names written, one on one side and one on the other. And he had the word "lost" written at the top of one column and there was my name at the top. . . . And then on the other side he had the word "saved." . . . So he took a little stub of a pencil out of his shirt pocket and marked my name out. . . . I said, "Brother Jess, what're you doing?" And he said, "I'm marking your name out of this list of the lost and putting you over here on the saved. And I'll pray for you that you'll be a great witness."[13]

Otis Strickland soon found himself at work in the fields of his new Lord. Two weeks after making his profession of faith, he went with Jess Redford to visit a family Mr. Redford had been concerned about for quite some time. They lived in a ramshackle house in a pasture in an undeveloped section of the city. Mr. Redford, who "had no formal training and . . . could just barely read and write . . . just pulled out his New Testament and said, 'I'm Jess Redford. I'm a child of God from Travis Avenue Baptist Church and this young man was saved just two weeks ago. And we're out here to talk to you about the Lord.'" Some of the people resented the presence of the uninvited visitors and resisted the entreaties of their Baptist message, which prompted

Strickland to ask Mr. Redford what was wrong with them. He replied, "Son, you were just like that two weeks ago."[14]

The young convert reverted to his rough background and offered to take one of the reluctant men in the family "out here behind the house" and "work on him," but Mr. Redford said, "No, son, that's not the way you do it." Strickland recalled,

> Well, I didn't know any other way to do it. I'd just lived in that world so long. So [Mr. Redford] went on and laid out the plan of salvation, so beautifully, and I was convicted of my wrong attitude toward that lost man. So then he said, . . . "Now son, . . . you're going to lead us in prayer." I'd never prayed in my life except when I thought I was going to be killed, when I was living in a certain gang there in Fort Worth. He got down on his knees beside me and I said, "Brother Jess, do you think I can do this?" He said, "You're saved, aren't you?" And I said, "I surely am." And he said, "Well, now, you can pray." . . . And he started me off and pretty soon the words were flowing and I had to ask for forgiveness for having the wrong attitude toward those lost people and began to pray for them and so on. I didn't know to say "amen" when I stopped and Brother Jess just said, "Amen." And we got up and walked away. He didn't say another word. And I had to look back; I just had to. So I looked back and the grandmother and grandfather—tears just coursing down their faces. And those people were just sitting there in awe, some of them with their mouths open.
>
> We went to the car and I got in the back seat and got down in the floor and Brother Jess drove along down the street. And I said, "Brother Jess, I ruined everything, didn't I?" And he said, "No, son, we gave them the word of God, and we prayed." I never could get enough courage to go back anymore to that particular place. And Brother Jess went back until Brother Matthews baptized nineteen of those people.[15]

C.E. Matthews, Strickland's pastor, had come from a very modest background and had never finished high school. He was converted in a "crusade" held by the great revivalist preacher Billy Sunday and baptized "into" the First Baptist Church of Fort Worth by its pastor, J. Frank Norris, who made a national reputation by attacking Southern Baptist leaders for their alleged modernism. Matthews became Norris's close associate, working with him on the staff of the First Baptist Church until Matthews came to feel that he should obtain some seminary training and become a pastor himself. Matthews went to see Norris, as Strickland recounted it, and said, "[T]he Lord's called me to preach." Norris said, "No, you stay with me, Matty, and I'll . . . make a great man out of you." Matthews persisted in his plans to go into the ministry on his own, however, and made an enemy of Norris, virtually for life. Norris revoked Matthews's preliminary credentials as a minister, his "license," usually the preliminary step leading to ordination by a Baptist church, which had been granted by First Baptist, Fort Worth. After Matthews became a pastor, according to Strickland, Norris sent Matthews a telegram "every Saturday night for ten years, saying, 'I'm after you, Matty. I'm going to hang your crepe on the door.'"[16] Norris apparently intended for such threats to anger Matthews and cause him to retaliate in some way, bringing embarrassment to himself and repudiation to his work. "Ten years, every Saturday night," Strickland said, but added, "Well, Brother Matthews loved him, said, 'He baptized me.' I'll never forget that. And the harder Norris fought him, the more Brother Matthews loved him and prayed for him."[17] The threats had added significance because of Norris's reputation for violent acts, including the shooting death in 1926 of an angry, but unarmed, visitor to his office.[18]

Otis Strickland was not alone in his great admiration for C.E. Matthews. Although Matthews had limited formal education and only the most rudimentary seminary course credit, some of the members of the Southern Baptist professorial elite from Fort Worth's Southwestern Baptist Theological Seminary greatly appreciated his preaching. Strickland recalled one instance when Walter Thomas Conner, a highly respected theology professor from Southwestern, went to hear Matthews preach and found himself beset by students. "Matthews preached one of his typical warm, evangelistic sermons—must have had about ten or twelve people saved . . . . So the next day in school they said, 'Dr. Conner, why would you go to hear Matthews preach? He has no formal training.'" Conner replied, according to Strickland, "He does something for my heart. He makes me feel good. He makes me feel like the sinner that I really am."[19] There was another facet to the story of C.E. Matthews, however, one Strickland mentioned almost in passing. In an interview with Baylor University church historian Glenn O. Hilburn, Strickland described Matthews's early pastorate in the Fort Worth-area community of Hurst:

> STRICKLAND: So Brother Matthews was called down here to Hurst; it was just a village church then. And Brother Matthews was a member of the Ku Klux Klan.
>
> HILBURN: Are you serious?
>
> STRICKLAND: He really was. And he was a strong member, too. I might add, he didn't know what the word fear meant; he never heard of it. He just didn't have any fear in him, of anything or anybody.

Strickland then went on to describe, as evidence of Matthews's fearlessness, an incident in which he persuaded the highly regarded Dallas pastor George W. Truett to raise money for financially strapped Southwestern Seminary.[20] After several minutes of the interview, Hilburn brought Strickland back to the subject of Matthews's possible Klan membership.

> STRICKLAND: And he was great in wisdom; he had wisdom from God. . . . And he was about . . . the most respected preacher in Tarrant County and I judge in the state of Texas. So I'd sum him up as a man of wisdom, of faith, of courage, a great worker, and a super soul-winner.
>
> HILBURN: Well, since it came as such a surprise to me, I would like to know a little more about the Klan. That is such a surprise to me, with Dr. Matthews. . . .
>
> STRICKLAND: Well, he got into that in Missouri, out in the mountains of Missouri, a little ways out of St. Louis. You know, they were strong up there. And he just continued that when he was down here. And he'd go to the meetings and he would have part. Some man in the community who wasn't treating his family right, they'd have a little meeting with him. And they'd put it on him; they'd do whatever they had to do. And Brother Matthews was right in the midst of it. He just brought that right down with him and just continued it here. Then when he got so busy in a larger church, well, he dropped out of it and didn't have anything else to do with it.[21]

If C.E. Matthews was a member of the Ku Klux Klan, he was not the only minister, Southern Baptist or otherwise, north or south, who belonged to that organization. Many prominent individuals of a perfectly respectable public appearance, north and south, belonged to the Klan, including professionals and political figures, as well as members of the clergy.[22] In fact, according to the noted Southwestern Seminary ethicist T.B. Maston, W.T. Conner himself was one of several Southwestern faculty members who had been members of the Ku Klux Klan.[23] Many members in the 1920s and 1930s claimed to have joined the Klan out of a genuine concern for the well-being of various powerless members of society, including abandoned or abused women and children, not necessarily because of the racism for which the KKK is so well known.[24] To Strickland's interviewer in 1972, nevertheless, it was a jarring experience to learn that a well-respected minister of the gospel might have had anything to do with an organization so identified with sordid, hateful activities.

Matthews's possible Klan membership is surprising, however, only if one overlooks moral and theological consequences of Otis Strickland's narrative.

Partly, such a thing might demonstrate the extent to which racial and other prejudices can compromise religious beliefs and values. But there are other realities present in Strickland's story. His fellow believers could celebrate the simple, earnest faith of Jess Redford, whose compassion for the family living in the pasture kept him awake at night praying for their souls, and that of his pastor C.E. Matthews, whose simplicity and dignity earned the respect of those far more highly educated, and that of the seminary professors themselves, who reminded their students of the heartwarming capacities of pure faith in the saving God. They could understand how someone could say that hearing a preacher who "makes me feel like the sinner that I really am" could also say that such a thing "makes me feel good," how being reminded of the continual need for God's forgiveness, because of one's continual lapses into sinfulness, serves as a reminder of the constant availability of God's grace. These same Southern Baptists, for most of the period from the 1930s to the 1980s, admired the resistance that C.E. Matthews and other mainstream pastors put up against the bullying of J. Frank Norris, even if they agreed with Norris on most points of theology. Most Southern Baptists viewed Scripture as the inerrant word of God, without error of any sort, scientific, cosmological, or otherwise, as Norris did. Most probably viewed modern education with suspicion, especially Darwinian ideas of natural selection and the relatedness of species in the evolutionary process, as Norris did. Most Southern Baptists, however, had a high view of the autonomy of the local Baptist congregation, the "competency" of each person's soul to seek its own salvation, and the need for Baptists not to permit any individual, such as Norris, to assume dictatorial powers over churches, their members, or the denominational structure they supported to make the larger work of their faith possible. They held traditional Baptist views of the nature of the religious experience and the ways it should play itself out in dealings among believers, especially among those affiliated with the SBC.

In addition to holding traditional Baptist views, most Southern Baptists also held other views that were identifiably southern. They were not likely to ostracize a faithful pastor for belonging to the Ku Klux Klan, which stood for many of the core values that Southern Baptists had helped implant in the South. Few would have found any contradiction at all in Otis Strickland's assessment of C.E. Matthews as "a man of wisdom, of faith, of courage, a great worker, and a super soul-winner" while almost dismissively mentioning what Strickland believed to be Matthews's membership in the Ku Klux Klan. Likewise, few would have questioned Jess Redford or anyone in the Travis Avenue Baptist Church of Fort Worth regarding their views of the degraded living conditions of the family living in the field, the "unchurched" objects of Mr. Redford's evangelistic efforts. Such questions would not have occurred to them in the context of their prayerful considerations of the immortal perils of living and dying apart from a saving relationship with Christ.[25] The connections between the salvation experience they prized so highly and the ethical demands of the Jewish faith of Jesus or their adaptation by the early Christian church simply did not occur to most southerners or to most Baptists. Otis Strickland's experiences and memories demonstrate that, for many people, the "Baptist Zion" that flourished during the period between the end of the Civil War and the end of the nineteenth century was still alive after the passage of more than one hundred years.

## Ill at Ease in Zion

There were those, however, who could sense the contradictions of a faith that cared so much for the afterlife and, it seemed, so little for earthly existence. In the twentieth century, dissent began to appear in Southern Baptist life as exemplified by small, but growing departures from the Southern Baptist norm, especially between about 1920 and 1990. The people who committed these acts of defiance against normative southern and Baptist ways of thinking and behaving were never very numerous, but they are historically significant nonetheless. They demonstrate the failure, if a small one, of hierarchical southern society to keep its hold on all of the religious people in the South. If not a large-scale collapse, such a rebellion is significant because it occurred not solely as a result of the ministrations of outsiders such as northern civil rights workers or the rising of the righteous oppressed such as southern African Americans, but also through the efforts of the sons and daughters of the very institutions that created and sustained the culture of the Baptist South. Southern Baptist dissenters, in fact, came in most instances, if not from the ranks of privilege, then at least from the ranks of opportunity. They had some connections to the small social gospel movement in the South. Mainly, though, for many and varied complicated reasons, they simply did not find it possible to be, as Rufus Spain said, "at ease in Zion."

A "genealogy of dissent" developed among Southern Baptists, for this small group of protesters functioned in many ways like a family. Dissent among these people unfolded along several pathways of influence much the way the branches of a family tree develop, especially in the lives and actions of a network of dissenters that arose in the middle decades of the twentieth century. This network grew out of the influence of a remarkable, and virtually unknown, radical Baptist, Walter Nathan Johnson, who harked back to a time when the expression "radical Baptist" was not a contradiction in terms. A pioneer racial integrationist in the 1920s and 1930s, Johnson also challenged the corporate "captivity" of Christianity in the United States. He created a network of supporters and sympathizers from the 1920s through the 1940s from which came civil rights advocates, labor organizers, advocates of women's rights such as ordination to the ministry, and proponents of disarmament and abolition of capital punishment, all Southern Baptists. As this network unfolded, people who were influenced by Johnson became influences on the lives of other people, who influenced others, and so on. Among their numbers were people who challenged some of the most fundamental aspects of southern society and of Baptist ecclesiastical structure and practice. Some eventually departed from Southern Baptist life altogether. Others remained as faithful as they could to the "church home" that had helped nurture their most personal spiritual yearnings and had given them a crucial part of their theological and psychological heritage. One does not have to claim that the people in this genealogy of dissent never would have rebelled against traditional Southern Baptist ways if it had not been for "Brother Walt" Johnson. Some of them drew apart from Johnson, while many others never even knew who he was. This network of dissidents was not the only one within Southern Baptist life, but its evolution represents a telling example of a culture of indigenous protest within a highly traditional society.

These dissenters formed themselves into several loosely organized groups, three of which will be considered for the insights they offer into the interrelationships of religion and culture in the southern United States. One branch of the genealogy, or pathway of influence, grew out of concerns about the central problem of the southern United States: race relations. This branch included people who found their way into the civil rights movement or at least into situations of taking stands, sometimes at some personal danger and often at great risk to their professional well-being, in favor of better treatment of and opportunities for African Americans. Their interests often widened to encompass other issues growing out of southern racial dynamics, particularly questions of unequal economic opportunity, access to justice in legal matters, and the general oppressiveness of poverty in the South. A second core group of dissenters arose around questions of peace and justice, both within and among nations. A third group arose around the struggles of women for equal political and economic rights in society at large and for equal vocational opportunities within churches and denominational organizations and institutions. Because of overlapping membership and activities, some persons show up in all three groups. Their activism arose from many wellsprings, but all drew inspiration, in part, from sources that ultimately can be traced back to Walt Johnson. Some of these people achieved heroic status among large numbers of Southern Baptists; some even held positions of leadership in Southern Baptist educational institutions and agencies. But many suffered for their actions and beliefs, losing jobs, experiencing physical danger and injury, or suffering various forms of character assassination. In the end, many found themselves held up as examples of denominational drift into liberalism and took on powerful roles as symbols in the political struggle that culminated in the fundamentalist resurgence within the SBC and its affiliated agencies and institutions in the 1980s and 1990s.

The lives and actions of progressive Southern Baptist dissenters provoke several questions concerning the culture of dissent among Southern Baptists in the twentieth century. How did persons who protested or rebelled against the usual southern and Baptist ways of behavior and belief manage to transcend their culture? How did they understand what they did? How powerful was the effect on them of such presumed southern values as the sense of place and of history? How were their beliefs and habits challenged or fulfilled by radical rebellion against so much that is commonly considered quintessentially southern? If Southern Baptists have played central roles in the formation of southern values, did dissenters view their beliefs and actions to be the fulfillment, or the repudiation, of their identities as southerners, as Christians, and as Baptists? Did they consider themselves the heirs of the old Baptist tradition of radical protest against religious coercion and moral complacency? To what extent did they direct their efforts for change toward Southern Baptist institutions, and to what extent did they give up on the possibility of such change, if indeed it even occurred to them? What did their goals have in common with those of their counterparts on the far-right end of the Southern Baptist political and theological continuum? Carlyle Marney and W.A. Criswell and their compatriots seemed in some ways to be on parallel tracks, both offering visions of a different Southern Baptist manner of religious life from that embodied by the moderate leadership of the SBC, which turned out to be the conservative center against which radicals on the right and left alike rebelled. Did the prospect of challenging the moderate Southern Baptist leadership hold any allure for dissidents the way it did for fundamentalists? Were fundamentalists the natural enemies of the progressive dissidents or, in a strange way, potential allies in a struggle against the common moderate foe within Southern Baptist life? If Southern Baptists embraced the model represented by W.A Criswell and rejected that of

Carlyle Marney, did the Baptist family of dissidents leave any lasting mark on the life of faith in the South? Finally, did the presence of progressives in Southern Baptist life energize fundamentalists to begin their ultimately successful campaign to wrest control of the SBC from the centrist or moderate group that had held power for most of the twentieth century?

These Southern Baptist dissidents offer a window through which one can gaze into a subculture that many have said represents southerners at their most traditional, but that contains surprising instances of discomfort with, even active opposition to, the traditions of hierarchical southern society. To understand their experiences, it is necessary to begin with the ways the network was assembled.

# Fellowship of Kindred Minds

## 2

### Foundations of a Genealogy of Dissident Southern Baptists

*Blest be the tie that binds*
*our hearts in Christian love;*
*The fellowship of kindred minds*
*is like to that above.*
—John Fawcett, *Blest Be the Tie*

Precursors of the genealogy of dissent among Southern Baptists were small in number, but rich in variety, nature, and motivation. Furthermore, as was true of support in the South for the social gospel itself, the origins of progressive dissent among Southern Baptists were never purely indigenous.[1] Many dissenters had embraced northern ideas, some from actual periods of study in northern colleges and seminaries. They departed, however, from both northern and southern social gospel advocates in some significant ways, most especially in the matter of race relations. Southern religious progressives from the 1930s and 1940s on stressed the centrality of race relations, a subject on which the northern social gospel was frequently silent. For instance, pioneer social gospel and Northern Baptist leader Walter Rauschenbusch's manifesto for the social gospel, *Christianity and the Social Crisis*, originally published in 1907, scarcely even mentioned slavery, something that many people alive at the time could still remember. He was not alone. While not ignoring the situation of black people, Washington Gladden and other prominent social gospel figures felt a greater sense of urgency regarding the plight of industrial workers. As many social gospel leaders understood it, "a major step had been taken for the Negro with the abolition of slavery; now it was the turn of wage-slaves to be freed."[2] Few persons in the South who favored a more activist form of Christianity during the social gospel period in the early part of the twentieth century went so far as to advocate widespread changes in race relations in the South. Further evidence that the network of progressive religious dissenters among Southern Baptists departed from the social gospel, north and south, arises from the fact that their network developed at about the time the social gospel idea was passing out of favor, withered by the criticisms of Karl Barth, Emil Brunner, and Reinhold and H. Richard Niebuhr. In an odd way, the development of this particular Southern Baptist network of dissenters may have been aided by the decline of the social gospel. Though it had penetrated the South, the social gospel was seen by many people as a northern phenomenon. Even many of the most progressive southerners were ambivalent about following northern examples. Whatever the extent of northern influence on southern churchpeople who felt called toward a more activist expression of their Christian principles, religious progressivism in the South developed into a phenomenon all its own, with an agenda and methods all its own.

Among Southern Baptists, the closest thing to a form of the social gospel found expression in formal institutional structures fairly early in the twentieth century, though its conceptualization reflected traditional Southern Baptist views and its organizational entities worked under severe limitations. The SBC established an organization to research and make statements on various "moral" issues in the years just before World War I, in partial response to the nationwide attention being given to social issues during the Progressive Era. The Social Service Commission issued some statements calling for changes in traditional race relations, specifically targeting lynching, and a handful of other issues. It was an important voice for some Southern Baptists, but because of the lack of ecclesiastical authority within Baptist polity, it lacked any power to instruct Southern Baptist congregations and individuals as to their behavior. It also labored under the limitation of the prevailing preoccupation with alcohol. In 1914, the Social Service Commission was combined with the SBC's standing committee on temperance to form the tellingly named Temperance and Social Service Commission. Southern Baptists were not likely to depart greatly from the traditional views that they had held through more than half of the previous century just because persons in other denominations were embracing the day's social interpretations of the gospel. Such thinking characterized even the early leadership of the commission, embodied in the towering figure of one individual, A.J. Barton, the commission's director for more than twenty-five years and a thoroughgoing conservative. Largely because of Barton's presence,

Southern Baptists resisted the societal meaning of the gospel that moved to the center of many Christian group agendas in the early years of the twentieth century. While Southern Baptists from their earliest years stressed religious liberty, temperance, marital fidelity, acts of compassion, and good citizenship, they were leery of the social gospel. They saw it as the resort of Christians liberalized by modernism. They believed God's grace in the human heart was the starting place for Southern Baptists, and A.J. Barton, the first chairman of the Convention's Social Service Commission, said all social and civic responsibilities began there.[3]

After the triumph of Prohibition, the Temperance and Social Service Commission went back to being called the Social Service Commission and turned its efforts to crime, "the divorce evil," immoral influences of motion pictures, Sabbath disrespect, pornography, gambling, and other matters reflecting Southern Baptists' more traditional concerns about personal behavior. Though dancing attracted some of its sternest criticisms, the Social Service Commission also visited some nontraditional issues, including "injustices in industrial relations" and the "growing unrest among minority groups." A lack of institutional support from the convention, however, hampered the work of the commission. Off and on, from 1921 to 1932, commission members proposed that the SBC create a permanent office for the commission and employ "a qualified man to have charge of the social service ministry of Southern Baptists." Tiring of inaction, but hopeful for the potential good he believed the commission might be able to accomplish, Edwin McNeill Poteat Jr. called in 1933 for Southern Baptist support of the Social Service Commission and was named to chair a committee to make recommendations regarding the Social Service Commission. Poteat's committee's report was offered in 1935, but action on it was deferred until the 1936 meeting of the convention, at which the report was tabled altogether. Depression-era financial difficulties assuredly played a role in the convention's decision, but its failure to support the Social Service Commission beyond the level of subsistence also reflected the probable lack of interest most Southern Baptists had in the work of the organization. One Southern Baptist writer in 1935 derided the recommendations of Poteat's committee as "socialistic wares" that Poteat should "peddle" in the North and that would create a "smelling committee that would go around meddling with . . . everybody's business," especially on behalf of "mendicants and dead-beats." One of the key reasons Poteat's plan failed to win convention support was his own reputation for liberalism, which had gotten him into trouble in earlier Southern Baptist institutional affiliations and which earned him the fearsome opposition of none other than A.J. Barton, who "helped defeat the very thing he had been advocating for fifteen years."[4]

The Social Service Commission also faced limitations because it lacked any sort of power to effect changes in Southern Baptist life. This absence of power derived from the historic dedication of Southern Baptists to carry out the congregational/free church traditions of their Baptist forebears. In the nonhierarchical, non-"connectional" polity of Baptists, local congregations cooperate voluntarily with other congregations through local or county "associations" of churches and through state conventions and the SBC, which during the twentieth century has far outgrown the boundaries of the old Confederacy. Each of these three levels of Baptist denominational structure supports a professional staff that establishes voluntary guidelines for projects and promotional emphases congregations may adopt, mostly having to do with evangelism techniques. Occasionally, offices issue literature and offer pronouncements bearing on social issues of the day. Well into the twentieth century, such positions usually stayed close to those to which Southern Baptists had traditionally limited their focus, such as godly behavior on the Sabbath, proper relations between young people of the opposite sex, and other matters associated with circumspect conduct. Even these pronouncements, let alone others of a more controversial nature, were strictly advisory. No churchly authority moved upward or downward through any levels of denominational structure to enforce congregational conformity except in the most extreme cases of divergent conduct that threatened the ability of churches to cooperate with each other. The most common example of a congregation's noncooperation is the withholding of funds given to the work of the convention, a nominal payment of which is necessary to qualify a congregation to participate in Southern Baptist activities. Unlike Methodists, the other predominant white denomination in the South, Baptists insisted that ecclesiastical discipline was something that took place within churches, by which they meant local congregations, not something that impinged on them from outside their memberships.[5]

Congregational church discipline had a much more vivid life in Baptist churches in the nineteenth century. Along with the usual reasons for banishing someone from membership, usually for behavior offensive to the community's moral sensibilities, churches also took other causes under consideration. Depending on how well organized or functioning the civil authorities were, Baptist congregations might investigate and mete out punishment for public offenses such as theft or settle disputes between private citizens. But such actions seldom reached beyond the congregational level of involvement, concerning either community or churchly matters. A Baptist church's association, which corresponds mostly closely to the Methodist "district," has no power to cause changes in the practices within a local church. It can only "withdraw fellowship" from an offending congregation, as the Tarrant County Baptist Association did to J. Frank Norris's First Baptist Church of Fort Worth. A "disfellowshipped" congregation cannot send "messengers," representatives other groups would refer to as delegates, to association or convention meetings. In recent years, congregations have been dismissed from associational affiliation because of involvement in charismatic activities—faith-healing and speaking in tongues—and in the ordination or employment of women ministers. Such an action can have the effect of enforcing a measure of behavioral or doctrinal conformity by putting pressure on the church's leadership, which likely would be sensitive to the reluctance of traditional Southern Baptists within the congregation to risk alienation from other Southern Baptists. In actual practice, most Baptists who care about such matters as associational fellowship would be unlikely to belong to a church that would take the kinds of actions that would cause it to lose favor with the association in the first place. Such drastic punishment as the withdrawal of fellowship from a congregation has been a very rare thing among Southern Baptists and, when it has taken place, has nearly always occurred on the associational level. Usually, it simply has not been necessary.[6]

Lacking any disciplinary power, therefore, as an agency of the SBC, the Social Service Commission could only influence the hearts and minds of individual Southern Baptists through exhortation. It published pamphlets and other materials to aid pastors and lay leaders in discussions of some of the pressing public issues of the day, though it did little beyond calling on church members to examine themselves in light of the timelessness of Christ's moral teachings amidst the changing requirements of modern times. But the commission created a pattern that was full of portent, one in which nonbinding, moderately progressive statements of opinion from national or state denominational Christian Life Commission (CLC) offices constituted practically the only expressions of concern about social conditions in the South that came from Southern Baptists. Ministers of local congregations seldom preached on the need for a more just South during the period from the establishment of the Social Service Commission until well into the 1950s. Those who were inclined to do so may have felt relieved of the duty by the issuance of statements from the Social Service Commission. In this way, denominational efforts on behalf of a more "Christian life" actually may have impeded the growth of social gospel sympathies among Southern Baptists, if inadvertently.[7]

Another institutional expression of reform sentiments among Southern Baptists, however, may have had more of an impact on ministers and grassroots Baptists. It came through the teaching of certain professors at SBC-supported seminaries and at a growing number of colleges and universities supported by state Baptist conventions. These professors usually offered course work in Christian ethics or in other fields that explored connections between faith and the context in which it is lived. Most courses of this sort dealt with the imperatives within the teachings of Jesus for humane treatment of all people, regardless of condition or characteristic. One of the best known of these professors was T.B. Maston, long affiliated with Southwestern Baptist Theological Seminary in Fort Worth. Maston, a layperson, gained a national reputation for his challenging positions on racial justice. Several professors at the oldest SBC-supported seminary, the Southern Baptist Theological Seminary in Louisville, Kentucky, earned reputations for calling on students and pastors already in the field to forgo racist sentiments and actions. One was T.B. Maston's counterpart in Christian ethics, Henlee Barnette. Using various pretexts, he and other Southern Seminary professors held up an example that was different from ordinary Southern Baptist practice on social relations. Some professors called for different ways of behaving and believing as the logical extension of their teaching on missions. W.W. Barnes, for instance, made eloquent entreaties for students to realize the illogic of supporting missionary efforts among the people of Africa while also supporting discriminatory treatment of African Americans. Some Southern Seminary professors and students participated in the work of the Fellowship of Reconciliation (FOR), which had an active chapter in Louisville, and other progressive organizations.[8]

As the century went on, a third form of denominational support arose for a fairly mild form of reformist thought among Southern Baptists. It was the "Christian life" initiative, which began in the 1950s when the Baptist General Convention of Texas created a social-concerns agency, the Christian Life Commission. The CLC model came to be duplicated on the SBC level and followed by several other state conventions of Southern Baptists through the creation of agencies of the same or similar names. In many ways, the Southern Baptist and state CLCs operated on the same order as the old Social Service Commission. Lacking any coercive or disciplinary power, the commissions worked diligently to influence thought and practice and won the admiration of persons within and outside the SBC, including many secular and religious activists in the South. The pronouncements and programs of the CLCs usually had little effect, however, on the entrenched conservative majority of Southern Baptists, who used materials the commissions generated in the most noncommittal ways, if at all.[9]

## A Gospel for the Here and Now

Another group of supporters of progressive change among Southern Baptists drew on all the sources already mentioned, but also forged its own identity, activities, and self-understandings. It was a network of dissidents that operated in many respects like a family tree, with various members exerting varying levels of influence on other members as they "came along" within the family network. In a great many respects, the founder of this network was Walter Nathan Johnson, known to his associates and admirers as Brother Walt. Once widely known among Southern Baptists, Walt Johnson wrote and spoke so extensively and persuasively on the subject of stewardship, the practice of church members to make "sacrificial" gifts to the work of their churches, that in the early decades of the twentieth century his name was almost synonymous with Southern Baptist stewardship education. Johnson wrote several widely circulated books on the subject, published by the Southern Baptists' Broadman Press. He served in high denominational office in two state Baptist conventions, gave hundreds of addresses in Baptist settings throughout the South, and authored dozens of articles in state denominational papers and other publications. Upon his death in 1952, that year's *North Carolina Baptist Annual* was dedicated to his memory, but scarcely a mention of his name appears in Southern Baptist histories. No mention of him appears in the *Encyclopedia of Southern Baptists* entry on stewardship, with which he was once so identified among Southern Baptists, or in the entry on the history of the Southern Baptist Stewardship Commission. Apparently, the only published account of his life in Southern Baptist sources is a one-paragraph entry in the *Encyclopedia of Southern Baptists* that simply cites his schooling, professional positions, and publications. It mentions nothing of his contributions to changing race relations in the South, his radical vision for churches, or the undercurrent of controversy that characterized the latter years of his life and career and may help explain his absence from so many works on Southern Baptist history.[10]

Born in 1875 in North Carolina, Walt Johnson grew up in a Southern Baptist family and committed to a life of "full-time Christian service" as a teenager. He assumed his first pastorate in 1899 upon graduation from Wake

Forest College. The early years of his career in the ministry progressed fairly typically for someone of his background and training, serving in pastorates in North Carolina and Louisiana. In both states, however, he also became involved in positions of statewide denominational leadership, where he showed noticeable promise. He served as Secretary of Missions for the Southern Baptists of Louisiana from 1907 to 1909, the highest executive position in the state convention's paid staff. In a similar position in North Carolina, he won ever-increasing amounts of respect and responsibility, particularly in the area of stewardship education. Johnson took to the highways and railroads of North Carolina and beyond with a message of single-minded devotion to the task of building up the Body of Christ by means of supporting the various agencies and outposts of Southern Baptist institutional life—congregational, associational, statewide, "Southwide," and worldwide. It would be difficult to imagine a more devoted denominational worker than Walt Johnson in the years before, during, and immediately after World War I. What began his departure from the Southern Baptist mainstream was an effort that began in 1919 and that embodied, in a way, everything to which he had previously devoted himself. It was the epitome of institutional aggrandizement, a large fund-raising program called the Seventy-Five Million Campaign.[11]

Walt Johnson's complaint against the Seventy-Five Million Campaign, an effort to raise that many dollars for Southern Baptist work, stood on a simple philosophical point, but it gave voice to a remarkably complex series of responses that marked the rest of his life. He disagreed with the campaign's premise that large amounts of money should be directed through central SBC offices, which theretofore had not operated as transfer points of local church offering proceeds. Johnson came to be increasingly suspicious of all ecclesiastical "federations," including voluntarily cooperating conventions, taking a determinedly free-church, congregational position on matters of church governance and accountability.[12] In his resistance to the creation of a powerful centralized church structure for the convention, Johnson set himself on a collision course with his denomination. It was only a matter of time before large, central agency offices, typical of most growing institutions, evolved out of the very work Johnson and others were doing in stewardship education.

The Seventy-Five Million Campaign aimed to establish a pattern of financial giving to which most Southern Baptist church members had not been accustomed. In the early stages of the campaign, Johnson supported the effort. However, in 1920, after state quotas were set and a highly organized publicity and solicitation system put in place, Johnson resigned from his position with North Carolina Baptists, citing his disappointment with the direction Southern Baptist stewardship was taking. He later referred to the Seventy-Five Million Campaign, which never achieved its fund-raising goal, as a "religio-military organization" that had committed an "egregious blunder" by concentrating on raising money instead of revitalizing churches through spiritual discipline.[13]

A period of reassessment and realignment followed Johnson's departure from positions of high denominational visibility. It resulted in a two-pronged development that characterized the rest of his career. First, he methodically continued the logical extension of his earlier thinking and working on matters of stewardship, especially a highly developed conceptual distinction between religious organizations and institutions and the church of Christ. Second, he began, as an outgrowth of this conceptual framework, a process of seeking to give programmatic expression to his ideas that took on increasingly radical appearances. He took the basic idea of stewardship to its most dedicated, if not extreme, forms, advocating an attitude toward church involvement that moved beyond support for the institutional manifestations of Christian life to a more personal level of commitment that affected one's entire lifestyle. He never turned against the local congregation as a setting for the embodiment of the gospel. Indeed, he based his entire hope for the future of the propagation of the Christian message on it. He proposed, however, a program of church "vitalization," a drastic series of measures intended to produce followers of Jesus prepared to live, think, and act in ways that required increasingly costly discipleship.[14] Johnson did not consider these measures drastic, though he did not shy away from using the word "radical." He said in 1942, "Yes, we say *radical* Christians. We need to restore the original meaning to this shocking word—it means 'going to the root of everything'—and then use it freely among ourselves as witness of Christ in us."[15] But, to the culture of his time and place, the measures Johnson advocated were drastic and more.

Johnson's vehicle for expressing his ideas was a newsletter he began in the mid-1920s, called for most of the next twenty-five years *The Next Step in the Churches.* In its pages Johnson promoted his positions and announced methods by which churches might become more faithful to the tasks of the gospel. Those tasks went far beyond the traditional preoccupation with adding people to the church rolls and encompassed what came to be called "peace and justice" issues, concerns that are usually associated with the social gospel. Johnson student Robert Alfred Melvin said that the social gospel movement played a major role in the development of Johnson's thought and cited the large number of books in Johnson's personal library that had been written by social gospel figures. According to Melvin, Johnson was particularly influenced by the work of Harry F. Ward, cofounder of the Methodist Federation for Social Service, and was one of the few southerners with a deep appreciation for Walter Rauschenbusch.[16] Citing the judgment of church historian Robert T. Handy that few southern churches during the social gospel era coupled pronouncements on social conditions with action, Melvin said, "Johnson's career proves him to be one of the few exceptions to this general rule."[17] *The Next Step* carried articles and quotations on a wide variety of matters, giving expression to Johnson's evolving thinking. Many items dealt with concerns peculiar to churches, but a great many concerned the broadest matters of national and international political and economic relations, especially something of growing concern to Johnson, the excesses of big business. In 1949, for example, he said, "War is only the recurrent Spasms of Competitive Business."[18]

Alongside peace, Johnson gave his most fervent and eloquent attention to economic concerns and to race relations in the South. In the 1920s he began promoting in the 1920s a series of meetings of ministers and laypeople that became in time overnight retreats in various settings in North Carolina. The goal of all of Johnson's educational efforts remained church vitalization. Nevertheless, economic justice was touted as a vehicle for improving the lives of the people who attended the meetings, who were encouraged then to work to improve the lives of others in their communities. Meeting first in mountain communities in the western part of the state and in mill towns in Gaston County, the Schools of Applied Stewardship dealt with practical business and technical skills and personal improvement, as well as biblical principles of lay devotion.[19]

In his writings, Johnson developed increasingly critical opinions about the economic system of the United States and capitalism in general. While never going so far as to embrace socialism, Johnson nevertheless endorsed many of the criticisms of capitalism found in socialist thought and practice. He said, for instance, that there was much that was "worthwhile" in Josef Stalin's policies in the Soviet Union in the early 1930s. He also showed enthusiasm for the views of Mohandas K. Gandhi of India.[20] As the Great Depression wore on, Johnson became convinced that society was witnessing the collapse of the "competitive economic order" and that churches and churchpeople should move quickly to "withdraw their sanction from ownership of property as the central motivation" of life to begin the process of establishing an economic system based on Christian teachings of self-sacrifice and mutuality.[21] Johnson believed, in fact, that true Christianity was "subversive of capitalism in its present habits of life."[22] He was particularly critical of the company towns in the South, likening their practices to feudalism and saying they were "thoroughly doomed."[23] He also offered harsh criticisms of agencies and institutions of the SBC that had "sold out to business" and attributed the terrific indebtedness of Southern Baptist churches and institutions to faulty concepts of stewardship that were based too closely on the ideals of the secular business world.[24]

By the 1930s, Johnson had begun to speak and write extensively about the shame of race relations in the South. He had a broad view of worldwide racial exploitation, especially citing the traditional designs of white colonialists on Africa as evidence of the failure of Christianity to exert a moral influence on the leaders of European and North American businesses and governments.[25] Closer to home, however, he saw the involvement of churches in the segregationist system as an impediment to justice for African Americans in the South and as a moral poison in white southern churches that would prevent their ever being able to advance the cause of Christ. In the 1940s, he began holding interracial retreats, probably in violation of local ordinances forbidding such gatherings. In 1944 he announced in 1944 that a small number of Native Americans were expected to attend the next retreat at Mars Hill College in western North Carolina along with a few African Americans. In *The Next Step*, Johnson said, "And we are going to treat them all as brothers, neither our inferiors, nor our superiors, but utterly our equals in the fellowship of Christ dwelling in us."[26] Johnson intended for the interracial conferences and retreats to have a twofold purpose, as he described it years later in an attempt to define "the next step": "SPIRITUAL LABORATORIES In Which The New Testament is *Re*-read, *Re*-tested and *Released Into Demonstrations* of The Spirit That Jesus *Still Comes Alive* among Us in *Quickened* Persons, in *Disciplined* Groups, in *Worshipping* Churches Will Put Us On THE NEXT STEP IN THE CHURCHES."[27]

Put another way, Johnson believed, first, that local churches would be revitalized by a new kind of devotion that focused attention on the ethical demands of Jesus and away from the corrupting demands of the culture, including those that prompted people to engage in racist behavior. Second, Johnson believed that such revitalization would infuse the Holy Spirit into the work of transforming that culture in the "here and now."[28] Such a transformation would come about when Christians stopped worrying about trying to make certain they were "going to" heaven and started behaving as radical, critical participants in the life of this world for the purpose of changing it.[29] Radical Christians of the type Johnson sought to invigorate with his intense vision for the gospel, he said, would turn to Christ in their churches and respond to him "through their state, through their schools, through corporate capital, through organized labor, through art and literature, through power machinery, through all the channels of publicity and public opinion, through a world organization." The result would be "universal worship," the placing of all levels of society under the guidance and authority of God in Christ.[30] Such beliefs, including his faith that the actions of churchpeople would provide a setting for the Holy Spirit to do its work, expressed decades after the publication of Rauschenbusch's *Christianity and the Social Crisis,* are found in nearly every extant statement of the social gospel. To Johnson, however, unlike his northern counterparts, one of the key problems holding churches back from becoming settings for the appearance of the Holy Spirit on earth was their enslavement to racism.

In *The Next Step,* Johnson developed his rationale for the training meetings and recruited participants in them. By the mid-thirties, with a mailing list of several hundred in a dozen states, *The Next Step* had reached some of the most influential of progressive Southern Baptist ministers and pathbreaking laypersons in the denomination. Johnson's retreats had achieved a great deal of attention as well among Southern Baptists of a progressive or at least somewhat nontraditional bent.[31] Participants and speakers included presidents of several Baptist colleges and universities and several professors from Southern Baptist seminaries, including W.W. Barnes of Southern Seminary and the same W.T. Conner of Southwestern Seminary who had spoken so highly of C.E. Matthews's preaching.[32] Johnson also maintained some ties with more traditional mainstream Southern Baptist leaders and carried language on the masthead of his newsletter saying that its purpose was "not to destroy any denominational organization."[33] He enlisted the aid of several officials of North Carolina's Baptist-affiliated Mars Hill College, who risked the ire of the people of their area by providing space for the interracial retreats, which also took place in churches and other sites in Salisbury and Raleigh over the years. Johnson also maintained relationships with a number of officials of the Baptist State Convention of North Carolina, some of whom helped him promote and, occasionally, lead training meetings. But as the 1940s wore on, Johnson's circle of influence became smaller and smaller. In the postwar period, attendance at the retreats declined, and leaders became more difficult to recruit. Six weeks before his death in 1952, Johnson pleaded in a letter for a minister in High Point, North Carolina, to try to recruit white ministers to attend an upcoming interracial retreat.[34]

One of the sources of Johnson's declining influence may have been the nature of the stand he took against plans to move North Carolina Baptist-related Wake Forest College from the town of Wake Forest to the city of Winston-Salem. He had many reasons for opposing the move, but the basic objections centered on the fact that a major denominational decision was being made on the basis of financial expediency and that the college's relocation was being financed by persons with direct ties to a major corporation, the R.J. Reynolds Company. Though the move to Winston-Salem and establishment in a more spacious campus were actually financed by members of the Reynolds family, Johnson hammered relentlessly at the move of the college as an example of the selling of church work into the bondage of dependence on corporate patronage. Johnson was particularly galled that the company in question had founded its riches on the manufacture and sale of products made from tobacco.[35]

Johnson apparently received little public criticism for his positions on the moving of the college or for his caustic remarks about the state's agricultural lifeblood. The fall after Johnson's death the messengers to the 1952 Baptist State Convention of North Carolina passed a resolution of tribute to him.[36] In fact, most North Carolina Baptist leaders seemed to have held a deep respect for Walt Johnson. An article in the state Baptist newsmagazine, for example, called him "a modern saint."[37] But his many years as a gadfly, along with the scathing criticism that marked his latter years, especially that related to the move of the college, surely contributed to his isolation. He never despaired of the potential of the individual Baptist congregation, but his contempt for the otherworldly theology of most Southern Baptists, expressed from the 1920s until the end of his career, certainly did not serve to make him universally popular among the leaders of Southern Baptist agencies and institutions.[38]

Though the decline of his influence seems to have paralleled his intensifying attacks on the state denominational leadership for moving Wake Forest College, another factor may have contributed more. If Johnson's story had ended with the Wake Forest College controversy, it could have been summed up as that of a visionary within a fairly small circle of progressive churchpeople who themselves went on to make significant contributions to the ethical modernization of churches in the South. Johnson could have been viewed the way his contemporary admirers described him, as someone ahead of his time, especially on matters of racial justice. But his story took a strange turn, one that the publicly available sources do not acknowledge[39] and that probably contributed to the lack of awareness of his contributions to the reformist tradition in the South.

Johnson became increasingly preoccupied in his later years with eugenics, a subject that he presented as the logical outgrowth of his increasingly radical commitment to discipleship. In his newsletter and personal correspondence he began to call for a system of artificial cross-fertilization of radical followers of Jesus with the intention of creating a "new breed" of Christians. Coming during and after World War II and the horrors of the Nazi period, this proposal could not have occurred at a worse time. In 1940 he published something of a capsule prototype of his ideas on the relationships between spirituality and sexuality, saying,

> The sexual impulse and religious emotion are said to be centered so close together in the human brain that they are warmed up together. Sex among God's worshipers must be rescued from animal debauch and restored to spiritual significance.
>
> The falling birthrate among civilized people is a disaster. Only militarists are now working to increase the number of babies among their people: litters of victims for the gods of war, crossbreeds of Venus and Mars! . . . We perilously need among true Christians a series of studies that link up spiritual churches with monogamic families in an increase of breeding and rearing of children among regenerate people. While the state sterilizes the unworthy, let the worship of God fertilize good families in our churches.[40]

Johnson circulated questionnaires designed to measure lay familiarity with such procedures as in vitro fertilization, carried on correspondence with medical researchers, and wrote an allegorical novel titled "The Lighted Couch" dealing with these matters. The novel's plot revolved around the relocation of a fictitious church-related college, one clearly based on Wake Forest, a move financed by a large corporation. The expression "lighted couch" referred to the setting of a vision Johnson described in the manuscripts; the couch was in his study that to which he had retreated as his health declined and that he said was illuminated as if by divine visitation during one of his dreams.[41]

Johnson got a variety of responses from his circle of associates and admirers to the new direction his thought was taking. His son, Falk Johnson, encouraged him to proceed with plans to publish the manuscript and said, "As I read *The Lighted Couch,* I found myself most frequently reminded of two other books, Sir Thomas More's *Utopia* and Karl Marx's *Das Kapital*— the first a stimulating and thought-provoking book; the second a manual for action, or a blueprint for a crusade. I still am not sure which I believe it will turn out to be." Wayne Oates, the pioneering Southern Baptist pastoral care professor, said,

It was a refreshing experience to be permitted to be one of the first to read this very important dream of yours. The New Testament says that the old men shall dream dreams and the young men shall see visions. Your dream has given me a vision. I am amazed that the thing you are suggesting is so closely parallel with a new area of research in the field of counseling and psychotherapy. I am speaking here of group counseling, group psychotherapy, and group teaching. . . .

I thought at first that your idea of eugenics might be out of proportion to the rest of the book. . . . But at this time I feel that it has been woven very nicely and appropriately into the total context of the groupal idea which you are setting forth, and in no wise do I feel that it is offensive. Rather I feel that it is a challenge to the understanding of the meaning of human reproduction.

One negative response, among several, came from W.R. Cullom of Wake Forest College, who read a draft of the novel and chided Johnson for "trying to accomplish spiritual results through fleshly means. If you bring to pass a super race," Cullom said, "it seems to me that you will still be very far from the ideal of Jesus."[42]

In his last years, Johnson suffered from a series of health problems and financial difficulties derived in part from his long years of depending for maintenance on small newsletter subscription revenues and donations. He had always operated on a shoestring budget. He no doubt faced periods of great discouragement, especially as he became more isolated near the end of his life. His involvement in activist Christianity began during a time when it had largely fallen out of style elsewhere in the country. He spent the bulk of his speaking and acting from theological and intellectual demands that were out of step with virtually every aspect of the majority culture in which he lived and worked. He wondered himself about visions he had in his later years, titling a long description of one of them "Inspired or Insane?"[43] Whether his ideas on eugenics simply carried his thought to its logical, if radical, extremes, or whether Walt Johnson was, in fact, mentally unstable may not be possible to ascertain.

It is clear, however, that Johnson thought his understandings of the nature and purpose of Christian teaching in the South came directly from God and that they had appeared to him over the years in natural progression of ever-increasing purity and costliness. His wide-ranging reading had a vast influence on him. His thought and behavior, for example, strongly reflected the teachings of Stanley Jones and other writers quite removed from the traditions of Baptists in the South. Furthermore, he had some foundational study that could have had an influence on his views of the South and of a liberated view of the gospel such as that of Rauschenbusch and Gladden. His brief postbaccalaureate theological education consisted, according to Robert Alfred Melvin, of "a period of study for several months in 1905 at Southern Baptist Theological Seminary . . . and a summer term of study at the Divinity School of the University of Chicago during the summer of 1911."[44] He probably came into contact with social gospel concepts in Louisville and in Chicago, if not in North Carolina, though there is little direct evidence that he only came to hold a radical vision of the claims of Christianity after studying so briefly in the North. His departure from mainstream Southern Baptist positions of ministry, for instance, came well over a decade after his brief time in Chicago. It is true that his scalding criticisms of his fellow Southern Baptists, whose denomination he once said seemed to be on its way to becoming "little more than a folk religion under ecclesiastical control,"[45] frequently corresponded with the views of northern critics of southern religion. But the closest Johnson ever came to trying to account for his views appeared in an article in one of his last newsletters describing one of his dreams or visions. Fittingly, for someone so often called a mystic, he recalled a "directive" he believed he had received from God in October 1932 during a period of disability caused by arthritis and intense anxiety caused by dwindling financial resources for his work.

> [O]ne afternoon . . . , I was lying on a couch nearly asleep. My logical faculties were so relaxed that Experiential Reality could get immediate to me. Was I awake being spoken to or was I speaking to myself? Was I asleep dreaming? I can't tell you which it was. But I do know that with the instant clearness of a pistol shot, or a flash of light, It came:
> "Identify yourself with the Underprivileged and your Health and your Finance will be cared for till your job is done."
> My arthritis was not cured. But something beyond me happened in me.[46]

The source of Johnson's thought may have been what he believed it to be: his own experiences as an intense seeker after spiritual guidance who received direct communications from God, not necessarily his reading or other contacts with northern thinkers. Unlike them, Johnson offered his criticisms of southern religion from a position of identification with the South and determination to remain within it. Though he expressed discouragement about the immediate effects of his work, he held to the belief that it would show results at some future point. Speaking of his writings in *The Next Step*, he said in 1946, "I am deeply assured that some of the views in these obscure columns, all but ignored now in many places, are going to have a posthumous value in the general crackup less than a generation from now."[47] Furthermore, he seems never to have despaired of the potential for growth and change in the churches of the South. He had labored for almost half a century to create a fellowship of kindred minds within the churches of the Baptist southland and continued to hope that, even in their flawed conditions, they yet would take "the next step."

## Branches of the Family Tree

Two of those who sought to take some of the very steps Walt Johnson hoped churches or churchpeople might take were Martin England and Clarence Jordan. Jordan read a letter from Martin England in the July 1941 issue of *The Next Step in the Churches* that determined the course of his career and resulted in the creation of a ministry and reform effort whose effects are still unfolding more than fifty years later. Inspired in part by Johnson's repeated encouragement of interracial alliances for the sake of the gospel, England wrote Johnson with an idea for the creation of an experimental interracial community. Jordan read the letter and sought out England, saying that he had long dreamed of helping establish a place where people of different races and classes could live and work together based on the "economics of Jesus" and demonstrate that it was possible to "live out" the gospel in a prophetic yet pragmatic way. With their wives, Florence Kroeger Jordan and Mabel Orr England, they bought some land in southwest Georgia and established Koinonia Farm as a "demonstration plot for the Kingdom of God."[48] England and Jordan inspired many Christians in the South, including many Southern Baptists, with the possibility that southern society could be changed. Their influence manifested itself particularly in the area of race relations. While Jordan stayed at Koinonia, which attracted worldwide attention as an island of racial harmony in a sea of segregation, England quietly became known among Baptists in the South as a minister to the civil rights movement. Throughout the 1950s and 1960s, England showed up in various places and times to help people who found themselves in trouble, especially southern white churchpeople, because of actions they took or statements they made for the cause of racial justice in the South.[49]

England and Jordan became two of the principal links between Walt Johnson's vision of the South brought under the leadership of Jesus and other branches of the Southern Baptist dissident family tree. The two, particularly Jordan, had a special effect on Foy D. Valentine, a Texan who had studied Christian ethics at Southwestern Seminary and become involved in the Christian Life initiative among Southern Baptists. He heard about Jordan as a student and went to live and work at Koinonia Farm in the late 1940s to learn firsthand about the interracial experiments under way there. Valentine became a mentor for several generations of Southern Baptist progressives, especially regarding civil rights for blacks in the South. By virtue of his service as director of the SBC Christian Life Commission, he was known for many years as the "conscience" of Southern Baptists. Younger CLC figures in several states and on the SBC level point to him as their inspiration. Valentine is also known as one of former President Jimmy Carter's "heroes" as a result of Carter's longtime lay involvement in Southern Baptist affairs and attempts to translate his convictions as a Baptist and a Christian into influences on public policy. Carter acknowledged two influences on his thinking about more equitable race relations as a young person growing up in Sumter County, Georgia, people who "ignored the strict social separation of the races." One such person was his mother. The others were Clarence Jordan and his fellow members of Koinonia Farm, which was located less than ten miles from Carter's hometown of Plains.[50]

England played a particularly persuasive role in the life of Carlyle Marney, one of the most powerful, and one of the most liberal, preachers in Southern Baptist history. Marney had a tremendous admiration for the ideas and actions of Walter Rauschenbusch. He also drew heavily from the example of Martin England, whose humility and commitment to social justice Marney admired tremendously. As pastor of the First Baptist Church in Austin, Texas, during the 1950s, Marney had a great influence on several generations of University of Texas students, including a number of Southern Baptists who became involved in or supportive of the civil rights movement and the call for equal rights for women, particularly their fitness to serve as ministers in Southern Baptist churches. Marney had a colleague and fellow "troublemaker" in Austin named Blake Smith, pastor of the University Baptist Church and someone with ties to several different groups of progressives within Southern Baptist life.[51]

As pastor of the Myers Park Baptist Church in Charlotte, Marney also influenced Southern Baptists in North Carolina. Some of these people became involved in struggles for racial justice and against the death penalty. After Marney retired from the pastorate in the 1970s because of problems with his health, he began a retreat center in western North Carolina for pastors. Marney sought specifically to help those who had become exhausted or demoralized by efforts to get "permission" from their congregations, by which they and he meant, in some cases, the moral courage to address social issues in sermons and other expressions of concern. At Martin England's suggestion, Marney called his retreat center Interpreter's House, after a place mentioned in Bunyan's *Pilgrim's Progress*. It was open to pastors from all denominations, but "burned-out" Southern Baptists were said to be some of its most needful participants. Marney was the subject of a nationally broadcast television profile by political figure and journalist Bill Moyers, who grew up Southern Baptist and was himself influenced by people within the genealogy of dissent.[52]

Many people in Southern Baptist life traced progressive influences to Marney. One of the Texans he captivated was Martha Gilmore, who met Marney while her husband was a law student at the University of Texas at Austin. She became a pioneer Baptist woman minister in Texas and an example and mentor to other women who sought credentials and employment as Southern Baptist ministers.[53] Inspired directly by Marney, an entire network of moderate or "alternative" Southern Baptist churches in Texas created a covenant relationship with each other through an association known informally as the "camping churches." This network included congregations that ordained women deacons and ministers, observed "open" communion and membership policies, and maintained other practices that departed from standard Southern Baptist methods of conduct and order. Membership in the network of camping churches spread beyond the boundaries of Texas to include nontraditional Southern Baptist congregations in several nearby states.[54]

In North Carolina, those influenced by Marney included Bob McClernon, who served with Marney on the staff of the Myers Park Baptist Church in Charlotte and who participated in a number of civil rights and other social justice and peace activities. After he became pastor of the Watts Street Baptist Church in Durham, McClernon held membership in a group called the Wranglers, moderate and progressive Southern Baptist pastors and professors in the Raleigh-Durham-Chapel Hill area, which included in its early period some former associates of Walt Johnson. Great numbers of other Southern Baptist ministers and laypeople felt the influence of Carlyle Marney's critical and eloquent voice.[55]

In the broad field of Baptist and Christian activity, Clarence Jordan became much better known than Martin England, partly because England left the United States after a few years at Koinonia to continue a period of service as a missionary in Burma that had been interrupted by World War II, while Jordan stayed at Koinonia Farm for the rest of his life. England's lesser celebrity also resulted from the nature of his work after he and his family returned to the United States and he began serving in the South as a minister to people involved in the civil rights movement. England traveled around the South with an intended anonymity. Jordan, from his base at Koinonia, served as a mentor to progressive Southern Baptists and others who visited the interracial community. Some, such as Foy Valentine, stayed for long periods. Others were moved by Jordan's folksy translations of the New Testament, known as the "Cotton-Patch Gospels," and other writings that stressed the "economics of Jesus," his term for the injunctions he found in the Gospels and in various texts from the Hebrew Bible against the economic exploitation of the poor and powerless. Many people learned of Jordan because of the role Koinonia Farm played in the creation of Habitat for Humanity International, the house-building work with which Jimmy Carter became closely associated.[56]

Jordan and Koinonia inspired the creation of several other "intentional" communities, communal experiments devoted to various programs of social justice. One was the Jubilee Community, also in Georgia, which became involved in ministries to the "eastern stream" of migrant farmworkers in southern states on the Atlantic seaboard. People at Jubilee also became involved in the work of assisting undocumented immigrants, partly because of their experience with Hispanic laborers and partly because of their revulsion toward U.S. policy in Central America. Jubilee became part of the Sanctuary Movement during the Reagan administration, aiding El Salvadoran and other refugees in this country illegally in their attempts to avoid arrest and deportation and to cross the United States in hopes of reaching safety in Canada. Another intentional community inspired largely by Koinonia Farm and one that drew heavily on Southern Baptist membership was the Open Door Community in Atlanta. Open Door, in alliance with Oakhurst Baptist Church in Decatur, became one of the most vigorous centers in the South for advocacy of support for homeless persons and for opposition to the death penalty.[57]

Open Door and/or Oakhurst Baptist Church members included several young people who became involved in a number of other social justice efforts, including the creation of *Seeds* magazine, devoted to hunger issues. Out of this group as well came Ken Sehested, founder of the North American Baptist Peace Fellowship, and husband of Nancy Hastings Sehested, a Southern Baptist minister who had been associate pastor at Oakhurst Baptist Church before becoming a pastor in Memphis. Nancy Hastings Sehested became probably the most visible woman minister in Southern Baptist life. Her church, Prescott Memorial, in Memphis, was "disfellowshipped" by its association when she was named pastor.[58]

One of the most famous Southern Baptists who stood in the influence of Jordan and England was Will D. Campbell, the iconoclastic preacher and author. Campbell was an inspiration for numerous Southern Baptists who chafed at the southern status quo. Through his articles, including those published in his coedited newsletter, *Katallagete* (Greek for "be reconciled"), and later through several widely selling autobiographical and fictional works, Campbell became a voice for compassionate treatment of powerless blacks in the South and for honorable regard for almost equally powerless poor whites. The first message was sometimes more easily received than the second.[59]

Jordan, England, and Campbell had a strong influence on a small but vibrant number of Southern Baptists who did the lonely work of labor organizing among pulpwood cutters in Mississippi. Growing out of this labor union work was an affiliation of a small number of Southern Baptists with the Industrial Areas Foundation, a community organizing effort. One of the leaders of IAF, operating in several cities in the South, was a Southern Baptist named Perry Perkins.[60] Perkins, his wife Patricia Perkins, and a college friend named Francis Marion King had been members of the Sojourners intentional community in Washington, D.C., in the early 1970s, working on race relations and peace and justice issues. Sojourners established a national reputation as a community of "prophetic" voice in the inner-city Washington neighborhood where its members lived. Its magazine, also called *Sojourners,* combined an orthodox evangelical theological stance with progressive political and economic reform positions, attracting some of the country's best-known theological and political figures as contributors of articles and editorials and as subjects of profile articles. The magazine highlighted many of the leaders among Southern Baptist dissenters.[61] Patricia and Perry Perkins and Francis King had spent time in Chicago doing inner-city ministry work and community organizing where they met Sojourners founder Jim Wallis, then moved to Washington with Wallis and the other original members of the Sojourners community.

Chicago had a pull on white Southern Baptists, though in smaller numbers, in much the same way it attracted southern blacks; it served as a magnet pulling them toward an expectation of a better life. Other Southern Baptists who acknowledged the influence of Will Campbell and who felt a pull toward Chicago included Joe and Nancy Gatlin, who became involved in inner-city housing and other ministries, she as a pastor of a storefront church. They later lived and worked in Waco, Texas, in similar occupations and belonged to an intentional community called Reconcilers Fellowship, which included several other members with Southern Baptist backgrounds and Campbell and Sojourners influences, including particularly its founder, Jimmy Dorrell. Reconcilers was similar to Sojourners in combining an orthodox theological stance with a number of radical political and economic practices, including, in several cases, the "common purse," the ownership in common of all monetary assets, and tax protests, the withholding of federal tax payments in proportion to the percentage of military spending in the federal budget. Dorrell established a reputation as an effective teacher of college students who were interested in gaining some understanding of poverty through simulated experiences in homelessness and other degrading conditions. Waco was the setting of another intentional community created largely by a group that split off from a charismatic Southern Baptist church. The separated community called itself the Church of the Prince of Peace and had fraternal ties with a similar community that was based in Chicago, as was true of Reconcilers Fellowship. Prince of Peace was also influenced by Sojourners and Jubilee elements. It was involved in refugee smuggling and other nontraditional activities for Southern Baptist churches, despite being composed almost entirely of members with very orthodox, even ultraconservative theological views.[62] Another Chicago connection, as well as one with organized labor, involved more Southern Baptists with various ties to the dissident network, Richard and Barbara Cook. Former Peace Corps volunteers in Panama, they used their command of the Spanish language in a longtime involvement with Farmworker Ministries, a companion organization of the United Farm Workers, with which Francis King was also affiliated for a time.[63]

Walt Johnson's influence moved in other directions besides the Jordan-England "branch" of the family tree, for Jordan and England were only two of Walt Johnson's devotees. Others who acknowledged his influence included Olin T. Binkley, pioneer Southern Baptist social ethicist and one of the early presidents of Southeastern Baptist Theological Seminary (Wake Forest, North Carolina), and Wayne Oates, pioneer professor of pastoral care at Southern Baptist Theological Seminary and the University of Louisville.[64] Binkley became a leading light among reform-minded Southern Baptists in North and South Carolina. Some of them founded a church in the 1950s in Chapel Hill, the Olin T. Binkley Memorial Baptist Church, that was devoted to open membership policies and to advocacy of equal rights for blacks and women. One of the people in this realm of influence was a South Carolinian named Robert E. Seymour, who pastored a church in Mars Hill, North Carolina, one of Walt Johnson's favorite places, and who served Binkley Memorial for twenty-five years, getting involved in a number of public protests during the days of the civil rights struggles. A number of younger people came under the influence of the heritage of Olin Binkley and the Binkley Memorial Church, moving particularly into various advocacy positions in women's issues. When Seymour retired, the church selected a woman as its next pastor. Another person in this line of influence was Warren Carr, who preceded Bob McClernon as pastor of the Watts Street Baptist Church in Durham, North Carolina, and who was pastor when it became the second Southern Baptist congregation to ordain a woman deacon and the first to ordain a woman minister.[65]

Walt Johnson also had an influence on a prominent family of Southern Baptist educators active in North and South Carolina, the Poteats. They became quite well known in both the North and the South for their liberal outlook and hospitality toward students and faculty who were inclined toward challenging the Southern Baptist cultural and theological status quo. Edwin McNeill Poteat Jr., in fact, was "tried" for heresy at Mercer University, the Southern Baptist-affiliated school in Macon, Georgia, early in his career. The influence of the Poteats was felt in particular at Furman University, which gave rise to several generations of Southern Baptist students that included a number of progressives who went on to seminary studies and other enterprises preparing them to engage in advocacy and action of a dissenting nature. These students were especially involved in civil rights and women's rights, and several were women who became ministers. Toward the end of Martin England's life, Furman University, his undergraduate alma mater, acknowledged its indebtedness to him and its ties to the reformist traditions in Southern Baptist life by awarding England an honorary doctorate.[66]

Another educational conduit for Johnson's influence was McLeod Bryan, an associate of Martin England, biographer of Southern Baptist progressive W.W. Finlator, and longtime faculty member at Mars Hill College and Wake Forest University. These schools became centers for varying levels of dissident activity. When Warren Carr left the pastorate of the Watts Street Baptist Church in Durham, he accepted the pastorate of the Wake Forest Baptist Church on the campus of Wake Forest University in Winston-Salem.[67] Mars Hill College was one of the sites of Johnson's early interracial retreats, sponsorship of which earned the college a great deal of criticism.

Various persons in the line of the genealogy had a dramatic influence on women who desired places of service within Southern Baptist life, especially as ministers. A major center of activity for such women was Southern Baptist Women in Ministry, a support and networking organization headquartered in Louisville. That city also became important for Southern Baptist women who desired careers in ministry because of the presence of Wayne Oates, the well-known Southern Baptist pioneer in the field of pastoral care and an associate of Walt Johnson's. Oates corresponded with Johnson toward the end of Johnson's life and drew from his ideas on racial and economic justice. Oates's leadership in the creation of hospital chaplaincy and other extracongregational service venues for ministers opened ministry opportunities for many Southern Baptist women who felt called to full-time Christian service but who had great difficulty finding churches that would ordain or employ them.[68]

Southern Baptists who felt drawn toward a vision that the South could be something more than it was knew the influences of many bold thinkers and actors for change. One should not link such people exclusively to Walt Johnson and his genealogy of dissent. They drew heavily, though, on Johnson's example, either directly or from the heirs to his tradition who mediated it to others who came after them, many of whom never knew or even knew about Johnson. Indeed, another small progressive network, with some members who overlapped with Johnson's, had no discernible connections directly with Johnson. It was one of the most interesting and powerful, though short-lived, efforts at fomenting liberalism among Southern Baptists and came, like Walt Johnson's work, out of North Carolina. It arose at about the time Johnson's influence was fading and took the form of an organization with an unimposing name, the Baptist Book Club, which, also like Johnson's work, generated a publication, called *Christian Frontiers.* Founded just after World War II by an increasingly disaffected graduate of Southern Seminary named Das Kelley Barnett and headquartered in Chapel Hill, the Baptist Book Club and *Christian Frontiers* advocated civil rights causes and offered biting criticisms of the one-party, segregated South. Barnett's supporters included such Johnson associates or admirers as Garland Hendricks, W.R. Cullom, W.W. Finlator, Claude Broach, Wayne Oates, Warren Carr, McLeod Bryan, and L.E.M. Freeman. They also included people who were not directly connected with Johnson but associated with those who were, people such as Blake Smith, Sara Lowrey, and J.C. Herrin. One historian said that the short-lived Christian Frontiers movement failed because "its causes were too unpopular, its criticisms too radical, and its aims too far advanced to develop strong support from a basically conservative denomination." Low on money and numbers of supporters, Barnett also despaired of changing Southern Baptists because of the intractable nature of the congregational autonomy Johnson prized so highly. In a move that foreshadowed events long in the future of the dissident network, Barnett and two other key members of the Baptist Book Club left the Southern Baptist denomination.[69]

Other dissidents stayed and made significant departures from mainstream Southern Baptist attempts to fashion a modest, modern-day form of activist Christianity, desiring themselves to bring about more dramatic change, particularly in the area of race relations. Johnson wrote more about economics than he did about race, but his ideas had their greatest effect on people who first sought change in the area of race relations. In many ways, it was natural that concerns for peace and justice, which Johnson and many others in the dissident tradition saw as inextricably linked, flowed out of the work of the civil rights movement. If some people acknowledged that U.S. society, or at least the South, posed problems for the fulfillment of the blessings of liberty for people of color, it became easier in many cases for them to see other problem areas of society. Those problems needed the attention of people who could couch them in terms that embraced central tenets of Christian teaching on peace, charity, and reconciliation. These tenets found expression among Southern Baptist dissidents who tried to break down hostility between people, who addressed the causes and results of poverty, and who sought to end conditions that limited the full realization of ministerial vocations by women. But in many cases, the awareness of problems and determination to do something about them began in the context of race. Much of the other work by people in this genealogy of dissent, therefore, grew out of the struggles for civil rights for African Americans. Other causes and activities that attracted these Southern Baptist dissenters flowed very naturally from their awareness of race relations. The evolving consciousness of those Southern Baptists who advocated and worked for changes in race relations in the South, therefore, must be examined in order to understand the story of this family of dissenters.

# "Who Is Their God? Where Were Their Voices?"

## 3

## Southern Baptist Dissenters and Civil Rights

> *Where cross the crowded ways of life,*
> *Where sound the cries of race and clan,*
> *Above the noise of selfish strife,*
> *We hear Thy voice,*
> *O Son of Man!*
> —Frank Mason North, *Where Cross the Crowded Ways of Life*

In direct contrast to the denomination as a whole, Southern Baptist dissenters took their boldest, riskiest stands on issues of civil rights for southern African Americans. Their expressions of how they understood themselves and their relationships with each other tell a great deal about the modern South and the role of religion in the makeup of this most storied region. The experiences of these people, especially those of one most remarkable but little-known person, form the body of testimony that makes this illumination possible. All through the network of dissident white Baptists in the South, an attitude and a manner of difference arose, a way of being, thinking, and acting that diverged from the norms of the South as a whole and Southern Baptists in particular.

In the minds of many people, racism is the quality that always defined the South most clearly. This belief about the South has taken on special significance in the intersection of the religious values and racial views of white evangelical Protestants. To many observers, religious values have been used as an excuse to turn a blind eye to racial inequalities or, worse still, have served as an impetus to engage in acts of racial bigotry. Martin Luther King Jr. was one of the people who held this opinion of many religious white people in the South.

In April 1963, King was being held prisoner in the city jail in Birmingham, Alabama, when one of the most famous public utterances of the "benign" form of racial insensitivity ever made came to his attention. The statement was an appeal by eight white clergymen of Birmingham who asked African Americans to be patient in their pursuit of the full rights of citizenship. The clergy, seven Christian ministers and one rabbi, felt sympathetic toward the goals of the civil rights movement and had tried publicly to distance themselves from their colleagues who openly supported the segregationist system prevalent throughout most of the southern United States. By the standards of their time and place, these eight clergymen were quite progressive on the issue of race relations. But they were concerned that the civil rights movement, especially "outside" agitators, would breed such dissension within their community that the movement's own goals would suffer, along with the general peace of their city. King had no patience for their calls for more suffering in the face of injustice and longer postponement of the fulfillment of the promises of liberty so long withheld from black Americans. He turned aside their concerns for civic harmony and pointed instead to the need for protest that could not wait until a time when goodwill would grow more widespread on its own. In his famous response, an open letter to the clergy of Birmingham, King described his travels around the South:

> On sweltering summer days and crisp autumn mornings I have looked at the South's beautiful churches with their lofty spires pointing heavenward . . . . Over and over I have found myself asking: "What kind of people worship here? Who is their God? Where were their voices when the lips of Governor Barnett dripped with the words of interposition and nullification? Where were they when Governor Wallace gave a clarion call for defiance and hatred? Where were their voices of support when bruised and weary Negro men and women decided to rise from the dark dungeons of complacency to the bright hills of creative protest?"

The eight clergymen never responded.[1]

If King had asked who the God of most of his fellow Baptists was or where their voices were, at least for the majority of white Southern Baptists, he could have answered his own questions easily. For the most part, their God was the God of John C. Calhoun and Nathan Bedford Forrest, and on the subject of freedom for blacks, their voices were silent or raised in opposition. Some of the most prominent figures in the southern power structure with many different kinds of vested interests in maintaining the status quo were Southern Baptists. Most of the members of traditional Southern Baptist congregations, like those of most other white religious bodies in the South, followed their leaders on this as on other questions. They either acquiesced in the southern system of race relations or gave active support to it. People in a second, smaller group gave well-meaning but essentially unhelpful verbal assent to the need for eventual change in southern race relations.[2]

Other southern white ministers and their congregations made different responses to the civil rights movement. They departed from the paths most southerners followed, confronting racial injustice openly and calling into judgment those who practiced or permitted it. They were the least numerous of the three groups, but they included Southern Baptists among their numbers. One of them had a personal relationship with Martin Luther King, Jr., received one of the first copies of the Letter from the Birmingham Jail, and helped arrange for it to appear in one of its first published forms.

## A Context of Civility

Those southern whites who practiced the third form of response to racial injustice had precursors, of a sort, among Southern Baptists, although most of these forerunners offered only partial responses to the breadth and depth of southern racism. Concerns for denominational unity and the maintenance of a selective sort of civility far outweighed the willingness of most Southern Baptists to accost their peers because of differences in views on race relations. They fought quite fiercely on matters of program planning and allocation of financial resources, but resisted most temptations to call traditional modes of conduct into question. A diversity of attitudes existed among Southern Baptists, but racism was so fundamentally ingrained in their thinking that the statements of their leaders sometimes contained the most outrageous racist hyperbole, even when expounding on the need to spread the gospel of a loving God among people of color. Such was the context in which Southern Baptist attitudes and expressions on race relations developed in the twentieth century. In 1920, for example, J. Franklin Love, executive secretary of the Foreign Mission Board, argued that Southern Baptist foreign missions should be targeted at white people, who would then take the message of Christ's love to people who were not white. Love's rationale was that God had not given the "instinct and talent" to spread the gospel "to the yellow, brown or black races. Only the white race has the genius to introduce Christianity into all lands and among all people." Of these statements, Bill J. Leonard said, "Naturally, Love based his ideas on the Bible."[3]

Institutionally, Southern Baptists in the twentieth century made some responses that gave more of a promise of moving toward a higher view of their African American neighbors. In 1906, they passed a resolution at their convention disapproving of the practice of lynching, although unlike many reformers, they did not describe it as the cornerstone issue of race relations. Lynching, they believed, was mainly a threat to the orderly functioning of society, and they tempered their condemnation of lynching "with equal emphasis, and in many cases with even greater emphasis, against the horrible crimes which cause the lynchings."[4] By the mid-to-late 1940s those introducing resolutions at the SBC had moderated their language quite dramatically. Southern Baptist leaders had made efforts to move the denomination toward becoming, or at least appearing to be, less racist. Such statements of the majority of Southern Baptists voting at the annual convention and other expressions of denominational leaders reflected these efforts. One of the most dramatic moments in the evolution of Southern Baptist declarations on race relations came during the 1947 convention, which accepted the statement of principles of a special study committee appointed at the previous year's convention. The statement called on Southern Baptists to eliminate prejudice from their actions, speech, and thoughts; to acknowledge the rights of blacks to experience political and economic equality; and to seek opportunities to develop goodwill between the races. The convention approved the publication of a series of educational materials to aid pastors and congregations in their consideration of the issues involved in the relations of blacks and whites.[5] Another notable resolution of the SBC affirmed the 1954 *Brown* decision of the U.S. Supreme Court as being consistent with both constitutional and Christian principles. Southern Baptist Sunday school literature in the 1950s occasionally included admonishments against racial bigotry.[6] Several state Baptist conventions commended Southern Baptist Brooks Hays, a member of Congress who lost his seat after seeking to mediate the Little Rock Central High School desegregation crisis, which took place in his congressional district, and openly advocating the goals of the civil rights movement. For every Brooks Hays, however, there was an Orval Faubus, the architect of the Little Rock crisis as governor of Arkansas, an ardent segregationist, and a Southern Baptist, as was Ross Barnett, whom Martin Luther King Jr. mentioned in his Birmingham letter.[7]

Statements approved by those several thousand in attendance at the annual convention did not always translate into changed behavior among the millions of rank-and-file Southern Baptists. With respect to race relations, one could be assured that progressive resolutions would be ignored almost uniformly across the Baptist southland. Evidence in the early 1950s indicated that few of the recommendations of the Southern Baptist Social Service Commission on race relations had been put into practice "by Southern Baptists, either by the denomination, the churches, or by individuals." CLC positions in the 1960s, furthermore, alienated many Southern Baptists who either opposed desegregation of southern society or at least disapproved of any SBC agency's involvement in the public debates over the issue.[8] Some denominational officials claimed that welcome changes were occurring within Southern Baptist life. The public relations office of the Baptist General Convention of Texas, for instance, boasted that 234 congregations in that state had indicated in a survey in 1963 that their policies provided for admission to church membership for blacks and whites equally. In light of the fact that the survey was sent to four thousand congregations, however, such policies were in place in fewer than 6 percent of Southern Baptist churches in Texas, a figure hardly likely to impress integrationists. In addition, highly publicized instances in which churches denied admission to black prospective members continued to suggest that Southern Baptists were not ready to give up their identity as a white body of Christians.[9]

Other Southern Baptists offered hopeful forecasts of changing attitudes among the people of their denomination. In 1969, a prominent Southern Baptist pastor and former president of the SBC, Wayne Dehoney, bemoaned news accounts of white churches that refused to accept black worshipers and gave rise to the image of "an apostate Southern church with barefoot red-necked segregationists in the pews and an illiterate prejudiced brush-arbor revivalist in the pulpit!"[10] Without denying that many Southern Baptist churches practiced exclusive membership policies, Dehoney countered that there were also stories of southern churchpeople, including Southern Baptists, who stood up to the dominant racist culture, advocated "open membership," and engaged in other acts of subversion, sometimes with costly effects. Dehoney cited the examples of several prominent conservative Southern Baptists, including W.A. Criswell of First Baptist Church, Dallas, who Dehoney contended had repented of his long-held support for the restriction of African Americans from membership. Criswell explained his advocacy of a change in membership policy in the summer of 1968 as an outgrowth of his fear that the church would be embarrassed by demonstrations seeking to take advantage of his recent election to the presidency of the SBC.[11] Dehoney also cited the example of James L. Monroe, who said, "I'm as Southern as grits and hush-puppies, as turnip greens and corn pone, . . . Born in Alabama, I am unashamedly and without apology a Southerner . . . . My love for the South is inborn. My parents and grandparents . . . were not Southern aristocrats, but I am honored to be of their lineage—the lineage of farmers and mountaineers." He offered a confession, however, that "Like many of my fellow Southerners, I grew up with a guilty conscience." He then described how he became aware of contradictions between his professed faith in Jesus in light of his feelings of superiority toward African Americans. In the same way, his profession of political and philosophical beliefs in freedom and equality fell by the wayside as he considered his attitudes toward his black fellow southerners.[12]

Other mainstream Southern Baptist pastors whose hearts and minds changed and whose views on the race question became more progressive faced the growing realization that the South had to face the problem or be destroyed, that the region had to confront recalcitrant congregations and communities. The context in which Southern Baptist civility usually played itself out was becoming cluttered with new challenges. Cecil E. Sherman exhibited a direct form of anger when, in April 1968, as pastor of the First Baptist Church of Asheville, North Carolina, he preached a sermon the Sunday before Martin Luther King Jr. was buried. He addressed his congregation on the subject of the need for leadership in the black struggle to take up the mantle of the fallen King. He said, "[T]he NAACP is the very essence of evil to some of the people in this room. . . . You don't like the NAACP. You don't like the Southern Christian Leadership Conference and Dr. King." But Sherman said of King, "He spoke for the poor. He was shot down while helping garbage men register their complaints. He was in the Jesus pattern." Speaking of blacks, he told his congregation, which still had at that point an exclusive membership policy, "We are part of their pain. . . . Today there will be no invitation [to visiting nonmembers to join the church]. Since the doors of this church are not open to some people simply because they are black, the doors of the church will be open to no one."[13]

Brooks Ramsey, pastor of Second Baptist Church, Memphis, had been actively involved in efforts to integrate First Baptist Church, Albany, Georgia. In Memphis, he invited an African minister to preach in his place on Race Relations Sunday in the tension-filled spring of 1968 that culminated in the murder of Martin Luther King Jr., then publicly sided with the sanitation workers in their strike demands against the City of Memphis. A group within the deacon body of the congregation began efforts to have him removed as pastor. As Dehoney says, "To avoid 'splitting the church,' Dr. Ramsey offered his resignation to the congregation. But the congregation responded by rejecting the pastor's resignation and 'firing' the deacons." The sermon was preached the week before Race Relations Sunday, in preparation for the congregation to be addressed for the first time by a black person.[14]

For the most part, however, Southern Baptists, especially denominational leaders, were unwilling to risk controversy or acrimony within the denomination for the sake of challenging southern views of African Americans. In the early 1970s, for instance, officials of the SBC Sunday School Board withdrew from publication 140 thousand copies of a Sunday school lesson booklet called Becoming. Written by Twyla Gill Wright, the materials were intended to help young people become more aware of the need that Wright and her editor at the Sunday School Board agreed existed for "A Ministry of Reconciliation" and featured a photograph of a black male teenager talking to two white female teenagers. The only thing worse than the negative national publicity that resulted from pulling the material, from the denominational standpoint, was the firestorm of criticism the leadership of the Sunday School Board expected would ensue if they distributed the lessons across the churches of the SBC. The majority of Southern Baptists, so they reasoned, were determined that they would not care to see the changes in southern life proposed by the leaders of the civil rights movement.[15] Some acted militantly to prevent those changes from coming to pass, in both private and public ways. Their devotion to civility did not extend to their African-American neighbors.

## The Third Way

Into this segregationist landscape, several Southern Baptists appeared who managed to escape the gravitational pull of the traditions and practices of normative white southern experience and embrace a conciliatory conception of race relations. They did not accept the racial status quo or content themselves to issue vague statements about the need for greater justice for southern African Americans. One of the most remarkable and least well known of the people who adopted this third view of race relations was a southern white minister, Martin England, the South Carolina Baptist who had been influenced so greatly by Walt Johnson. England had not only responded to King's "Letter from the Birmingham City Jail," but had also visited King in jail. He was given a copy of the letter by a member of King's entourage and arranged for the letter to be published by the Ministers and Missionaries Benefit Board of American Baptist Churches, the sponsor of his work in the South.[16] Martin England was one of the people who provided Martin Luther

King Jr. with very different answers to the questions, "Who is their God? Where were their voices?" from those King no doubt had in mind for the masses of southern white churchpeople. England participated in two dramatic events that defined many of the aspects of the third way of conceiving race relations. One was the founding of Koinonia Farm in the early part of World War II. The other was the civil rights movement, with which he was involved in the late 1950s and the 1960s.

Born in a South Carolina mill town in 1901, Jasper Martin England determined at an early age that he wanted to be a Southern Baptist foreign missionary, preferably in Africa, and made his decision to do so public while attending Furman University in Greenville, South Carolina. England's antisegregationist attitudes, unusual for a young man growing up in his circumstances, were inspired by events within his own family and nurtured by his experiences in school. He traced his desire to be a missionary to Africa to a story his grandmother had told him when he was a young boy about her husband's experiences at the beginning of the Civil War.

> My grandfather, Jasper Wilson, was drafted into the Confederate army and was at Fort Sumter in the early stages of the war and was badly wounded and thought he was going to die and his tent mates thought he was going to die, too. And he wanted to die at home, which was a good many miles away from Charleston, back up in the mountains of western North Carolina. And his tent mates put him on a train, sewed up a lot of Confederate money . . . in the lining of his coat so he would have enough money for his needs on the way home. Train crews lifted him off of one train onto the next when he had to change. Finally he got to Walhalla, the county seat town of Oconee County, that was the end of the railroad. It was about forty miles, I suppose, further on to his home in the mountains. And he lay on the station platform in Walhalla two whole days, begging anybody who could to take him to his home in the mountains and also, if anybody could, to get word to his family, that he was there.
>
> Finally, a black man who had a horse and wagon, hauled freight from the station to the stores in town, picked him up and put him in his wagon and took him home. When they . . . got to his home, the road crossed a little creek, below the house on the mountainside and he called out to Jeanette, my grandmother, his wife, "I'm home" and "Bring clean clothes and towels and soap, but don't come near me." From his wounds, the pus and the blood, and from insects that all soldiers in most wars . . . know about, he said, "I'm lousy and don't come near me, but bring these and throw them across the creek." She did that. The black man very gently undressed him and bathed him there in the creek and dressed him in clean clothes and then took him carefully up to the house.[17]

England's grandmother coupled her telling of this story with admonitions that a white person should never speak ill of or behave badly toward black people. In his mind, there was a direct line between his hearing the story of the black man who had shown such kindness toward his grandfather and his desire to be a missionary to Africa. The story had even further-reaching effects on him, however, later in his life, leading him to broaden its lessons into a wide-ranging conciliatory view of race relations.[18]

England's schooling reinforced his inclinations, but redirected them in some unforeseen ways. At Furman University, he especially appreciated his contacts with a handful of professors and administrators who had gone to school in the North, including members of the Poteat family, and who had an attitude that deemphasized "the sectionalism that had prevailed." To England, the feeling in this immediate post-World War I period was, "We're Americans now, . . . and let's put that back in the background."[19] It was logical that Furman graduates who sought a career in the ministry should go to Southern Seminary. Southern had started in Greenville and many Southern Baptist educators and students moved back and forth between the two schools. Few seminary-bound Southern Baptists from the Carolinas went to Southwestern Seminary in Fort Worth, and England began his ministerial training long before Southeastern Baptist Theological Seminary was founded in nearby Wake Forest, North Carolina. England's studies at Southern Seminary did not make a profound effect on him, although he had a great appreciation for W.O. Carver, the professor whose attitudes about missions and race presented a challenge to many Southern Baptists, seminary students and laypeople alike. England also appreciated being exposed to the large number of foreign students at Southern, a presence that reinforced his sense of church as something transcending national and regional boundaries. He went north to receive his seminary training only after hearing of a scandal involving the disappearance of a sizable amount of money in the care of the Southern Baptist Foreign Mission Board that made it unlikely that they would be able to give him an overseas appointment. He thus abandoned his childhood dream of becoming a Southern Baptist missionary, but felt a strong sense of identity as a Baptist and went north to school in the hope of securing appointment as a Northern (later known as American) Baptist missionary. To this end, he enrolled in one of the seminaries affiliated with Northern Baptists, Crozer Theological Seminary in Chester, Pennsylvania.[20]

Between the end of his studies at Southern in 1928 and the start of his course work at Crozer, England made the first of three formative encounters that reinforced the bent toward conciliatory race relations he had received from his grandmother. First, and most important, he met Walter Nathan Johnson. For a time after finishing at Furman, England taught at Mars Hill College, where he encountered Johnson, who had his headquarters there in the late 1920s and early 1930s. Johnson captivated England, particularly with his views, an "obsession" England called it, of how churches had "missed the mark of what it meant to be church. A class church, for example, church of only well-to-do people, he felt was a denial of the basic spirit and teachings of Jesus. . . ." His general orientation away from powerful, worldly churches and toward sacrificial communities gave Johnson an ability to listen to pastors from out-of-the-way churches who wielded little power in the Baptist State Convention of North Carolina. The retreat settings Johnson created gave them a sense of freedom and acknowledgment that was missing from their encounters with the larger groups of Southern Baptists. Johnson also impressed England with his concerns for Southern Baptists' positions on racial issues and his attempts "to discover the mind of Christ with regard to race relations and economic questions." England became aware of Johnson's overtures to black Baptist denominational leaders in North Carolina and of his invitations to black Baptist ministers to meet in retreats on an equal basis with white participants. Out of this growing awareness of Johnson's advancing views on race, England wrote him the letter outlining his vision of a community of mutual responsibility that cut across racial and socio-economic lines.[21]

England had two more formative encounters. One was with George Stoll, a Methodist layperson and the owner of an oil refining company headquartered in Louisville. Stoll had an interest, partly humanitarian, partly paternalistic, in the operation of community centers in Louisville for low-income people. While England never came to feel completely at ease about Stoll's motives, he shared some of his ideas about experimental Christian communities with Stoll, who wrote him in September 1932 offering England some suggestions. Stoll praised England's ideas about an "ungraded educational institution" for low-income students and took the idea a step further, adding elements from his readings in the current literature on grass-roots development projects in the South and his theories on the empowerment of working-class people through the abolition of their virtual enslavement to the retail-credit cycle.

> Such an idea has gripped me—has grown on me for sometime. Every now and then comes a new impetus—the last a reading about Schweitzer—but more reading about Denmark. Have you ever visited Brasstown and the J.C. Campbell Folk School? Have you read Mrs. [Olive] Campbell's "The Danish Folk School" . . . ?

Tell me more of your ideas—dreams—plans.

Let's give imagination a little freedom—not to soar—just to jump around a bit. Suppose—situated in a place where the world tours by—say in the Lincoln area, or in one of the Carolinas—there were a farm of a few thousand acres—a modern Utopia. To it could come the oppressed to find the easy yoke, the light burden—physically—and every chance to learn about Him who offers another kind. You see an easy yoke makes for work—perhaps more work accomplished. Easy in being without debt, buying only what can be paid for. . . . A laboratory farm, cannery, factory, that might, like the pioneer, provide most of our own needs and buy from the rest of mankind what it could buy with its products or services but having what the world today so sorely lacks—buying resistance. Buying resistance creates buying power—rapidly![22]

Ten years passed before Martin England acted on the ideas he and George Stoll had shared in the early 1930s and only after he had had the third of his crucial, formative encounters. In the meantime, he and his wife, Mabel Orr England, had received appointments to serve the Northern Baptist mission field of Burma.[23] When the Japanese conquered Burma at the start of World War II, the England family was in the United States on their first furlough and was unable to return to Burma to begin their second term in the mission field. Attracted partly by the presence of George Stoll and partly by that of the Southern Baptist Theological Seminary, the England family settled temporarily in Louisville. During his time at Mars Hill, England had become aware of the FOR. While working on an early-day form of community-development project in Wakefield, Kentucky, near Louisville, England became involved in the FOR and reacquainted himself with the work of Walt Johnson. England particularly appreciated the developments in Johnson's thoughts on the interrelationships of people's views on property and on race.[24] He attended some of Johnson's Mars Hill retreats, at which "The Negroes, Whites, and Indians all slept under the same roof and ate together at the same table."[25] During this period, in 1942, England wrote the letter that attracted the attention of Clarence Jordan, who was a member of the Louisville chapter of the FOR. At a meeting of the Louisville Fellowship, England had his third formative encounter when he met Jordan, a fellow southerner of Baptist heritage and a fellow devotee of Walt Johnson. Jordan was a subscriber to *The Next Step in the Churches,* which had just published England's letter to Johnson describing his vision for an interracial community set up along the lines of early communal Christian groups as suggested in the Acts of the Apostles. Upon meeting England, Jordan, who had just read his letter, said, "We've got to talk!"[26]

Over time, it became clear to Martin England that his grandmother's story had inspired more than his inclination toward service as a foreign missionary. That story also bore the origins of his departure from southern norms regarding race relations. To Jasper Martin England, who was named for his grandfather, there was one clear lesson to be learned from the story his grandmother had told: that he was never to do anything unkind toward a black person. He became mindful of the story whenever he found himself in the presence of behavior that exhibited a demeaning attitude toward people of color. It also became clear in his mind that he had been led by an odd series of unanticipated developments, thwarted expectations, and new opportunities put in their place into a once-in-a-lifetime alliance with a soul mate. Clarence Jordan had the same vision for an interracial agricultural community that England had. They began immediately to lay the plans for what became Koinonia Farm.[27]

## A Witness in the Dirt

Jordan had been working as the administrator of a community center for blacks and of one for low-income whites in different parts of Louisville and had many concerns about the disadvantages with which both groups lived. He was deeply concerned about the deprivations rural southerners, black and white, experienced as they came "crowding into Louisville." With his rural Georgia background, a university degree in agriculture, and sympathies for the downtrodden, Jordan fairly naturally turned toward the idea of some sort of farming community as an improvement over the degraded existence of most poor people in large cities such as Louisville. His interests were reinforced by his reading of Walt Johnson on the virtues of cooperative learning ventures and experiments in group interactions. Compared with Jordan's vision for the possibilities of dynamic new forms of community, the centers where he was working in Louisville seem hopelessly ineffective.[28] He had absorbed a strong sense of service from his mother, focused on a desire to devote his life to some form of Christian ministry. Like England, Jordan had a story in his past that had helped turn him from the path most southerners traveled with respect to race relations. At the age of twelve shortly after he became a Christian, in his hometown of Talbotton, Georgia, theologian James McClendon wrote, "one summer night . . . he heard terrible groans coming from the nearby chain-gang camp, and realized that a Black prisoner he knew, Ed Russell, was being tortured in the stretcher—the stretcher being a Georgia version of the ancient rack—used in disciplining convicts. What added irony was the boy's knowledge that the administering torturer was the same Warden McDonald who only hours earlier had been lustily singing 'Love Lifted Me' in the Baptist revival choir." The experience did not disillusion Jordan against Christianity as a whole, but it gave him a sense that he should direct his life toward helping people "at the very bottom."[29]

Sumter County, Georgia, was an especially unreceptive area for the ideas and practices Koinonia represented. It had a reputation for a high degree of racial prejudice among the county's minority white population, especially later, after the civil rights movement became a force in southern life.[30] The Jordans and Englands had little in the way of a plan for how their experiment would operate, only that "[W]e'd go and settle down on a farm as farmers first, and then bit by bit, as we could financially and otherwise, add to our activities, making a witness in the dirt, as real farmers, not as professionals or as ministers going in to tell people how to live on a farm in Georgia." They knew they had to be taken seriously as farmers if they were to have any hope of reaching people with "the underlying philosophy, theology, commitment" of Koinonia,[31] but they worked from the outset to develop the farm as an educational center. One of the first activities they added was a practice of hosting college students who came for short terms of work and study at one of the few "intentional communities" formed up to that point in the South. They took their meals at the same table with the black farmworkers whom they hired to help them make a viable agricultural operation out of the played-out Southwest Georgia farmland. They attracted little notice at first, except for occasional reference to the fact that the Koinonia people ate with the black farmworkers and gave black schoolchildren rides to their school instead of passing them by on the way to the white school. With his own family, some of whom already doubted his wisdom in going off to Burma to do mission work and most of whom had not been affected the way he had by his grandmother's story, Martin England had an even more delicate task in explaining Koinonia. He deemphasized the racial aspects of the experiment and concentrated on describing the advantages he expected to derive from learning about agricultural methods, knowledge that would help his mission work. Similarly, England's and Jordan's wives dealt with their work in a gingerly manner where family was concerned. When Mabel England's mother came from Alabama for visits, Florence Jordan would invite the black farmworkers to take their meals at her house. When Florence Jordan's mother came, Mabel England fed the workers. They were both concerned about scandalizing their mothers, who had traditional attitudes toward "mixing" of the races. Martin England's mother, however, had a "sympathetic and friendly" reaction during her visit to the farm.[32]

England's assessment of Koinonia was based largely on his view of the influence of Walt Johnson:

> We believed we had a call. We believed that it was the will of God that some-body make a demonstration of these applications of the teachings of Jesus, not only to life in the church and on Sunday morning, but to all of life. And this was something that Walt Johnson widely preached, that Jesus is Lord of the whole house, of all the life, of all relationships, race, economic, family, nation-ality, that is that there was no human relationship that could say, Well, the Bible teaches so-and-so, but you can't expect to let a Hitler walk all over us. And the Bible doesn't say anything about a good income for a tenant farmer. We felt we had a mission to challenge that kind of thinking that life could be compartmentalized and that there were some decisions that could be made disregarding the teachings of the New Testament.[33]

Martin and Mabel England left Georgia in 1944 to receive additional training in New York that would assist them after their return to Burma. Clarence and Florence Jordan remained at Koinonia and formed the core of the community that became an outpost of racial tolerance and reconciliation amidst a hostile world. After new permanent residents came to the farm in 1949, the world of Koinonia began to be more hostile. In 1950, the people of Koinonia, who numbered about fifty at middecade, began to have trouble with their neighbors, first with the church most of them attended, Rehoboth Baptist, in nearby Americus. They were expelled from membership because of their practice of bringing non-Caucasians to worship services, in violation of church rules and customs.[34] More serious trouble developed in 1956 as Clarence Jordan took an increasingly visible role in helping two African-American students enroll in Georgia State University, which was then an all-white institution in Atlanta. Koinonia held interracial children's summer camps and continued to hold regular interracial worship services, social gatherings, and other events, despite persistent tension with Americus and Sumter County residents. Jordan received threatening telephone calls. Legal harass-ment from county officials who devised charges against the farm followed, along with a boycott of Koinonia produce, bombing and shooting incidents directed at Koinonia property, and arrests and beatings of Koinonia resi-dents. Koinonia attracted a considerable amount of state and national atten-tion and support during its time of greatest crisis. It found little but criticism in its home county, however, except for some statements of support from the ministerial association in Americus and quiet expressions of encouragement from persons such as the future governor of Georgia and president of the United States, Jimmy Carter, of the Sumter County town of Plains.[35]

Koinonia survived, continuing its "witness in the dirt," while Martin England moved into a different form of testimony to the need for new forms of "living out" the Christian message in the South. His contributions to the changing face of race relations in the South would have been great if only because of his role in the founding of Koinonia Farm. But an unusual turn of events placed him back in the South after World War II and put him in position to do more for the cause about which he cared so deeply. In 1944, the Englands were asked by Northern Baptist foreign missions officials to attend a training program at Cornell University for missionaries in rural areas. They and their children left Koinonia in that year and later returned to Burma for two more terms of service after the war. For reasons related to Mabel England's health, they gave up the mission field and came back to the United States in the early 1950s. England went to work in New York City for the American Baptist Ministers and Missionaries Benefit Board, visiting American Baptist pensioners, helping them with the occasional problems of retirement. He never lost his dream, however, of helping bring about changes in the South. With the civil rights movement well under way, England suggested to Dean Wright, his supervisor in New York, that American Baptists "ought to have something to do with that." Under the auspices of the "M&M Board," England returned to South Carolina in 1962, ostensibly to establish an office to assist pensioners who had retired in or to the South. Some were American Baptist retirees who had made their homes in the South. Others were persons in other Baptist bodies or churches that had "dually aligned" with the American Baptists, establishing two sets of denominational affiliations. Most such persons worked with National Baptist churches, one of the major African-American denominations in the South. But a few served a growing number of moderate, predominately white Southern Baptist congregations whose members felt the need to affiliate with their northern Baptist counterparts. Part of the impetus for dual alignment came from informal networks that grew, for instance, out of ties Southern Seminary graduates had with former Southern Baptist classmates and friends who had gone to the Louisville seminary but taken jobs with churches in northern states near or contiguous with Kentucky. England and Wright, however, both understood that England's main reason for being in the South was to serve as a minister to the civil rights movement. England traveled around the South quietly and often anonymously, appearing seemingly out of nowhere on various occasions to help black Baptist pastors, many of whom were affiliated with the old Northern Baptist Convention, and a growing network of ministers and laypeople in Southern Baptists churches who were sympathetic to the civil rights movement and who were in varying degrees of trouble because of their sympathies. England tried particularly to help those persons who went to jail, sometimes encountering the threat of violence to himself. He was personally acquainted with several civil rights workers who lost their lives, including Martin Luther King Jr.[36]

He moved south and began building a network of contacts, first among black Baptist churches in the South that were dually aligned with their own convention of churches and the American Baptist Churches. He also established ties with the Southern Regional Council, a progressive umbrella organization linking smaller ones to each other, and with such local organizations as the Human Relations Council of Greenville, South Carolina, one of whose key supporters was Tom Poteat of the liberal Southern Baptist family that had ties to Walt Johnson. Another network England interacted with was that of the Christian Action Council in South Carolina. It was headed by Howard McClain, a friend of England's and of Clarence Jordan's who had met them as a student at Southern Seminary during the period when both were working in and around Louisville. McClain led a transformation of the Christian Action Council from essentially a temperance organization to one that worked for a number of changes in race relations in South Carolina.[37]

When Martin England began his work in the South, he set up an office in Greenville and immediately hired an African-American woman to do clerical work. Local landlords would not rent office space to him because he had a black secretary. Some of the members of the First Baptist Church of Greenville, the Southern Baptist church he and his family had joined, were suspicious of his activities. First Baptist had a significant history of involvement with moderate Baptists through its ties to Furman University and such figures as members of the Poteat family and progressive pastor L.D. Johnson, who attracted the ire of certain members of his congregation with periodic sermons on bringing race and labor relations under "the Spirit of Christ rather than . . . the prevailing standards of the community."[38] The church included among its members, however, individuals who resented the civil rights movement and the interference of federal authorities and northern activists and journalists in the traditional ways of the South. England's response to such people was, "There was no reason for our coming to Greenville except that this area had been my home. I'd grown up here and maintained contacts all through the years with people, and it was just home."[39] England's absences created a great deal of anxiety in the England household because of the danger involved with the civil rights movement. But England felt he had no choice about the matter. "This is where I belonged. . . . The racial conflict was beginning to heat up and I saw no way that I could escape being involved and I felt to be involved in the South was for me, a white southerner, the proper place." The choice to stay in New York was one he felt he could not make: "I couldn't have lived with myself."[40]

During his Ministers and Missionaries (M&M) Benefit Board work during the 1950s and early 1960s, England received a "steady stream" of letters from friends and associates working in white southern churches who had suffered professional and other repercussions because of stands they had taken on behalf of the civil rights struggles of southern blacks. Throughout the South, such ministers were fired or refused employment by churches. Others were pressured to curtail preaching or other measures to promote racial justice. England had few guidelines for and no restraints on his work among such people. His job was to help in any way possible, including to put white ministers in trouble in touch with other churches in the South that might be friendlier to their viewpoints.[41] England also received letters from other people doing pioneer interracial work in the South and kept in touch with some in or near the South, including Wayne Oates of Southern Seminary, who had an interest in short-term experimental interracial communities or retreat centers.[42]

England also tried to assist black Baptist civil rights leaders, including Martin Luther King Jr. England knew King's parents because of the affiliation of the elder King's church with American Baptists and had some common ground with him because they both had graduated from Crozer. He also had had a number of conversations with the younger King about his need to join the M&M pension fund so he could get life insurance. England went to Birmingham for a meeting of ministers, shortly after which King was put in the city's jail in April 1963. He visited King in jail to express his support and that of American Baptists. King had completed his work on the written response to the moderate clergy of Birmingham and, knowing it might not see publication if jail officials confiscated it, arranged for his associates to determine ways to distribute it. England was one of the few people to whom the letter was entrusted. Before it was published in any other form, he sent his copy to Dean Wright, "and he published it fast," according to England. England was impressed by King's positive and hopeful attitude in jail, and King was grateful for England's visit.[43] England went back to Birmingham on

September 16, 1963, the day after the Sunday morning bombing of the Sixteenth Street Baptist Church that killed four young girls. He encountered a white man who was observing the damage from the wrecked church building. The man told England that he planned to kill King, who was scheduled to speak that evening at a rally protesting the bombing of the church and the killing of the girls. England warned persons associated with King of the threat the man represented, then spoke again with King about the need to insure his life, recounting the conversation with the threatening man earlier in the day. After much pressure from King's associate, Ralph David Abernathy, whom England had enrolled for M&M benefits some time earlier, and England's declaration that the M&M board itself would fund King's contributions to the program, relieving his church of the expense, King signed the application form. England, who kept a stamped envelope in his pocket at all times, pushed his way through the crowds assembling for the rally, and mailed the application to the M&M board.[44]

A number of King's associates, including Samuel D. Proctor, the noted pastor of the Abyssinian Baptist Church in New York City, called England's persistence in pursuing King remarkable. Proctor said that he helped England get through to King after England had expressed his frustration at the protectiveness and suspicion King's entourage showed toward him. Proctor promised to try to intercede: "I said, 'I'm going to tell the fellows to let you see him when you get near him.' Martin asked, 'When will that be? I keep a record.'" Proctor was astonished that England "had a list of all the places King was going to go. He spent money out of his own pocket going from place to place. I couldn't believe it—a man born and raised in South Carolina, a white man, sixty-five years old, following King all around to sign him up for a pension and death benefit plan!" "Anybody who felt the climate in the South . . . would be forced to conclude," England believed, that King would suffer death at the hands of an assassin. Less than five years passed before exactly that happened. In April 1968, England rode from Greenville to Atlanta on a chartered bus with many of his black friends to attend the funeral of Martin Luther King Jr.[45]

England participated in a direct way in some of the activities of the civil rights movement. He walked several segments of the March from Selma to Montgomery and heard the jeers and saw the gestures of derision of hecklers along the way. Mainly, however, England worked behind the scenes. In his view, if there "was a Baptist minister in trouble, . . . that was all I needed to go see him." He offered whatever help and encouragement he could. England believed that, more than anything else, a minister in such a situation "wanted assurance that everybody in the world wasn't against him."[46] He participated in the building of an informal network of people who had similar views and needed to know that like-minded ministers and laypeople were continuing to live out their beliefs amidst great critical pressure and that there were people who could offer them moral support and encouragement. No formal denominational structure provided support for ministers in trouble. England believed that Southern Baptist officials stayed removed from the civil rights struggle for the most part because of the threat it represented to their institutional strength, as well as the threat it posed to them as individuals, because unlike the situation for leaders of Baptists in the North, the troubles were often taking place where they lived. England and others in the informal network usually stayed in touch by telephone, letting each other know if someone needed help. They established a pattern that sustained their own associates and even people they never met who went through similarly trying times in the struggles that were raging throughout the South.[47]

## A Service of Influence

Martin England said of his former Koinonia partner, "Clarence Jordan set out to be a farmer, and he wound up being one."[48] Jordan was much more than a farmer, however. His popularity as a speaker helped spread the word about Koinonia and attracted many short-term residents to the community. Foy Valentine, for example, heard Jordan speak at Baylor University in Texas and later spent the summer of 1944 at Koinonia. Well-wishers, admirers, and the curious came from many different parts of the country, including quite a few northern states. Some came from overseas.[49] Jordan's popularity spoke to a reality, though, that was deeper than the pleasure many people took in hearing him speak about the experiment of Koinonia or that of seeing it for themselves. Jordan's appeal, like England's, though more flamboyant, gave evidence that southern white churchpeople, including Southern Baptists, were starting to fret about their region and its traditions in race relations. These reassessments were prompted by many different experiences and insights, but significant numbers of people began their questioning after coming in contact with persons such as Jordan and England, as the two of them had with Walt Johnson. Their roles as practitioners of a new moral and ethical stance within the Baptist South were complemented by their service influencing others to try to be the same. They inspired many of the activities and attitudes of people who dissented from the ordinary southern and Baptist ways.

Jordan and England were not the only people with ties to Southern Baptists who did and said courageous things. In December 1956, Paul Turner, pastor of the First Baptist Church in Clinton, Tennessee, was beaten by a segregationist mob for advocating integration of the local public schools. The following Sunday, in nearby Knoxville, Charles A. Trentham preached a sermon at the First Baptist Church condemning the assault on Turner. "[W]ithin the shadows of our own city, only twenty miles away, a Baptist minister of the gospel has been beaten for trying to protect the constitutional rights of Negro children. Some said that he was out of place, that he should have confined his ministry to preaching the gospel. I personally feel no more heroic act of practical Christian courage has been seen in Clinton, Tennessee, than this."[50]

G. Avery Lee, though a pastor whose service took place for the most part in traditional Baptist churches, was considered a liberal on the subject of race relations. In 1954, he publicly supported the *Brown* decision while pastor of the First Baptist Church in Ruston, Louisiana, and survived criticisms to go on to preach in support of Autherine Lucy's rights to enroll in the University of Alabama, which she attempted to do in 1956. That sermon was published as a pamphlet by the CLC of the SBC. Like most white southerners, both liberal and conservative, Lee viewed southern race relations as a problem that should be solved by southerners. Though he considered himself a liberal, he doubted that many others did so, because in his mind liberals on race relations usually welcomed the involvement of northerners in the issue. He was adamant in his belief that the southern churches should take the lead in presenting a model of the "worth and dignity" of all people as the way the South should change, and that outsiders had not as much to offer. "We are closer to the problem," he said. "We understand it better. I honestly believe we are more sympathetic. The Southern white and the Southern Negro have a kind of love for each other, although there has been too much white paternalism and too much black subservience." As pastor of the St. Charles Avenue Baptist Church in New Orleans, a congregation that later came to embrace many features of Southern Baptist dissidence, Lee tended to a church that had an open membership policy toward blacks.[51]

Pastors at fairly traditional Southern Baptist churches, such as Ralph H. Langley at Houston's Willow Meadows Baptist Church, took unpopular stands and made ties within the minority communities. Willow Meadows operated a program in the 1960s called Heart of Houston that established relationships between middle-class white church members from outlying areas of the city and low-income inner-city black residents. The people on either end of the program visited each other and became involved to some extent in each other's lives. In some cases, the results included having somewhat more powerful whites take on advocacy roles on behalf of blacks who felt powerless to address the degraded conditions in which many of them lived. The program also put whites in uncomfortable situations on a number of occasions, as their motives and attitudes were challenged by the recipients of their attempts at reconciliation. Heart of Houston put quite a few white Southern Baptist laypersons and several of their ministers in positions of some risk.[52]

Many people who departed dramatically from the normal Southern Baptist ways of race relations, though, drew more heavily on the examples and encouragement of the nontraditional ministers and laypeople in the genealogy of dissent that grew out of the work of Walt Johnson, Clarence Jordan, and Martin England. One of the key sources of spreading progressive ideas, including his own, was Carlyle Marney. The powerfully eloquent Marney moved within a circle of churches in Southern Baptist life that had many connections with different kinds of dissent. He was attracted to and attractive to a network of progressive congregations that had histories of involvement with social issues. He was sought out, recruited, so to speak, by nontraditional Baptists who felt overwhelmed by the burdens of living in the South as it was in the 1950s and 1960s. They felt a great sense of despair about whether their denomination could or would provide any real leadership that spoke to the crucial matter of race relations and about what Baptist Christians might have to offer in response. Before Marney came to North Carolina, Martin England had heard of his preaching, and he went to hear him after Marney moved to the pastorate of Myers Park Baptist Church in Charlotte. England became acquainted with Marney and eventually suggested that Myers Park might want to be dually aligned with the American Baptist Churches and with the SBC, in the same way that increasing numbers of black Baptist churches in the South were aligning with American Baptists, National Baptists, and other black Baptist communions. Marney was intrigued by the idea. He had long felt that Southern Baptists had cut themselves off from helpful and enlightening alliances because of their fervent refusal to affiliate the SBC with the National and the World Councils of Churches. The American Baptist Churches belonged to both ecumenical organizations, which advocated progressive positions on race relations and other questions and offered the possibility for white Baptist churches in the South to establish ties with black Baptist churches through common affiliation with American Baptists. Early in their relationship, Marney told England he was concerned that the people of Myers Park were reluctant to become involved in the racial conflicts in Charlotte. Marney persuaded the church to support peaceful integration of facilities and institutions in the city and worked to create an atmosphere of fairly open dialogue about the various situations that were developing as the civil rights struggle came to a head.[53]

Marney hosted interracial meetings at his Charlotte church so that speakers could address the need for changes in race relations and the ways communities and churches might help bring about those changes, an example that was followed in several Baptist churches around the South. One such meeting took place in 1964 in Baton Rouge, Louisiana, at a church that was formed from a split in a congregation over the civil rights positions of its pastor, Bruce Evans. Evans was fired by a segregationist-dominated faction in his former church and hired to lead a new congregation of people who had left the church that had fired him. They held a public meeting to discuss civil rights issues, a meeting called in part as a response to the refusal of the recent SBC meeting in Atlantic City to pass a CLC-sponsored resolution calling for Southern Baptists to support the claims of African Americans for equal rights. Fellowship Baptist Church, which later dropped the word "Baptist" from its name, had Carlyle Marney as the principal speaker for the meeting. Marney likewise became a source of inspiration for Baptists at such North Carolina congregations as Pullen Memorial in Raleigh, Binkley Memorial and University Baptist in Chapel Hill, and Watts Street in Durham; Oakhurst in Decatur, Georgia; Northminster in Jackson, Mississippi; Prescott Memorial in Memphis. Texas churches influenced by Marney included Seventh & James and Lakeshore in Waco; Second in Lubbock; Austin Heights in Nacogdoches; Calder Memorial in Beaumont; and Highland Park and University Baptist in Austin.[54]

After suffering a heart attack, Marney gave up his pastorate at Charlotte's Myers Park Baptist Church. He and Martin England had discussed the need for a center for ministers to visit if they got into trouble over their advocacy of civil rights for African Americans or if, for other reasons, they became "burned out." England arranged for support for Marney's efforts through Dean Wright, England's boss at the M&M Benefit Board of American Baptist Churches, and suggested the name Interpreter's House, taken from John Bunyan's Christian allegory *Pilgrim's Progress.* Marney set up in space borrowed from the Methodist assembly grounds at Lake Junaluska, North Carolina, and welcomed individual visitors and participants in the format Walt Johnson had perfected: group retreats. Marney and England discussed the stress on ministers of being "so far ahead of the congregation" on social issues, of needing to be able to say "what the times demanded," and of wanting a way "to interpret" new ways of seeking to be true to the demands of the gospel. Marney did at Interpreter's House a great deal of the same sort of thing England did traveling around the South and, though they scarcely could have been more different, Marney had a tremendous respect for the integrity and quiet form of service England provided. In 1970, Marney said of England, "His presence is literally the difference between life and premature death for many strugglers. The South has no more vital ministry than his."[55]

Another Southern Baptist with ties to the England-Jordan line of influence was Victor T. Glass, a longtime staff member of the Home Mission Board of the SBC. Glass, who did pioneering cooperative work with the black National Baptists and developed many other programmatic dealings between Southern Baptist agencies and institutions, had known Jordan as a student at Southern Seminary in Louisville. He and his wife lived with Jordan for a time while Glass was doing interracial ministerial work under Jordan's direction.[56]

Other people in the Walt Johnson and Martin England network of influence included three longtime North Carolina pastors, William W. Finlator of the Pullen Memorial Baptist Church in Raleigh, Robert E. Seymour of the Olin T. Binkley Memorial Baptist Church in Chapel Hill, and Robert E. McClernon of the Watts Street Baptist Church in Durham. All three churches became dually aligned with American Baptists and Southern Baptists. All three had various involvements in progressive issues, particularly the civil rights movement. Binkley Baptist Church was named for the progressive Southern Baptist educator and former Walt Johnson associate. Seymour was called as its first pastor in 1958 and served for thirty years, performing many acts of leadership on the state and local scene on behalf of civil rights for African Americans. England had known him when Seymour had served as pastor of the Mars Hill Baptist Church in Mars Hill, North Carolina, where Walt Johnson's sister worked as a librarian at the college and where other people continued to speak of Johnson during Seymour's tenure as pastor. England worked with Seymour, like England a South Carolina native, on a number of civil rights-related initiatives after Seymour became pastor of the Binkley Baptist Church. When Seymour retired as pastor of Binkley Memorial in the 1980s, the church called Bob McClernon, who by then had retired from the pastorate at Watts Street, as interim pastor. The Binkley congregation broke ground again when it named a woman as Seymour's successor.[57]

William Wallace Finlator of Pullen Memorial in Raleigh and Martin England knew each other through direct association with Walt Johnson.

Finlator had been one of Johnson's retreat leaders, as had L.E.M. Freeman. After a pastorate in eastern North Carolina, Finlator became pastor of the Pullen Church in Raleigh, where Freeman was a member of the faculty at Meredith College, a Baptist school for women. Freeman, who is mentioned often in Johnson's articles and notices in *The Next Step in the Churches*, was an ardent supporter of Bill Finlator and his activities. The outspoken Finlator attracted a great deal of attention and controversy for the Pullen Church, one of whose former pastors was Edwin McNeill Poteat Jr., one of Walt Johnson's closest associates. Finlator chose to move away from typical Southern Baptist models and embraced the examples of Poteat; S.L. Morgan, who helped inspire *Christian Frontiers;* and Walt Johnson. One of Finlator's frequent debate opponents in various forums in Raleigh was a right-wing television commentator, a future United States senator, and a fellow Southern Baptist, Jesse Helms.[58] McClernon had come to Watts Street in Durham in 1965 directly from service with Marney as associate pastor at Myers Park Baptist Church. He found ample opportunities to become involved in controversial issues and causes, having inherited a pulpit that was already associated with proclamations critical of the status quo in the South and an expectation that the pastor of Watts Street would play a progressive role in the community. McClernon's direct predecessor, Warren Carr, who had learned about Walt Johnson as a student at Southern Seminary in the 1940s, had been vigorously critical of the power structure in Durham. His activities had generated threats of violence and acts of vandalism against the church building. In one series of incidents in the late 1950s, vandals who did not appreciate Carr's open stands in favor of integration painted on the front door of the church building: "Go to hell you nigger lover." Carr had the church custodian paint over the words. During the night, the incident was repeated, except that Warren Carr's name was added. After that slogan was painted over, the incident was repeated once more, early on a Sunday morning. This time the slogan said, "Go to hell you nigger-loving church." Carr asked the custodian to paint over it, then reconsidered, deciding instead to make the vandalism into an object lesson on the evils of racism. He thought, "You know, that's a real compliment, and I want the church to see how highly people think of them when they come to worship this morning." Not everyone in the church appreciated the gesture, according to Carr, "and they got rid of it pretty quick. But I did want them to understand that . . . to have that symbol painted on your church door was pretty doggone important."[59]

McClernon did not shy away from open expression of his views of what the gospel required of people who lived in the South in the mid-1960s. He built on what he had learned from his years working with Marney and his own relationship with Martin England, and he developed into a biting critic of the southern social and economic status quo. He also worked directly with black leaders in Durham to help the minority community gain political and economic standing in the city and the state. McClernon and another white pastor of a Southern Baptist church, Julius Corpening, worked with a handful of white and black business and civic leaders to provide low-cost housing to black families and to ease tensions during times of riots around the country, especially at the time of the assassination of Martin Luther King Jr. in 1968.[60]

Martin England influenced another pathbreaking Southern Baptist, John Laney, who had pastored small churches in North Carolina mill towns and elsewhere. During the late 1940s, Laney was dismissed from school during his senior year at Carson-Newman College in Jefferson City, Tennessee, Carlyle Marney's undergraduate alma mater, because of his attempts to integrate services of the First Baptist Church in Jefferson City. He had become acquainted with black student leaders of Baptist Student Unions from other colleges and universities at meetings taking place on the grounds of the First Baptist Church. When he invited one of the black students to go to church with him, one of the people who objected was the dean of the college, who did not appreciate Laney's logic that a black student who was permitted to attend a meeting at the church should also be permitted to attend a worship service. The dean advised Laney that it would be better if he found another school to attend. He transferred to Maryville College, a Presbyterian school in Maryville, Tennessee. Laney also went north to seminary, to England's former school, Crozer Theological Seminary in Chester, Pennsylvania. During one of his pastorates in the early 1950s, in the North Carolina mill town of Brookford, he wanted to integrate the church. Knowing the congregation was not ready for such a move, he arranged instead to have a black woman hired as choir director of the small church as a first, and successful, step toward eventual integration of the church. England knew Laney from Walt Johnson meetings and said that he "more closely followed the pattern of church life and ministry that Walt Johnson was trying to promote than anybody else."[61]

Another South Carolinian who made a mark in North Carolina was John McLeod, a longtime faculty member at Mars Hill College whom England called "one of the most faithful supporters of progress, Walt Johnson-style." He "backed Walt Johnson in his integration" and helped bring about the integration of Mars Hill College, the first Baptist school in North Carolina to admit African Americans as undergraduates. A former Johnson associate, Hoyt Blackwell, was president of the college at the time.[62]

Other powerful influences inspired the network of dissidents that grew out of the work of Walt Johnson and his supporters. One was that of Will Campbell, the Southern Baptist minister who became quite well known because of his boldly honest speaking and writing. Campbell's civil rights activism was unusual because he linked the plight of disenfranchised and powerless African Americans in the South to that of their poor white counterparts. Campbell felt that he had to love "rednecks" as well as blacks "because anyone who is not as concerned with the immortal soul of the dispossessor as he is with the suffering of the dispossessed is being something less than Christian." Because of his liberal principles, Campbell had gone through a time of denying his heritage as a white southerner until he came to the realization that poor whites were victims of oppression, and of their own racism, too.[63] Still, Campbell stood out in the 1950s and 1960s because he participated in a number of aspects of the civil rights movement, including direct demonstrations. He served as an escort for black schoolchildren involved in the Little Rock crisis and took part in various activities of the Southern Christian Leadership Conference. Campbell had an acquaintance with and respect and appreciation for Clarence Jordan and Martin England. Campbell's personality and rhetoric held great appeal among the network of Southern Baptist churches that had progressive views on race relations. Although he developed his own style of ministry and traced his "conversion" on the race issue to his reading as a young man of Howard Fast's novel *Freedom Road*,[64] he became something of a combination of Clarence Jordan and Martin England. He had the prophetic speaking and writing gifts and dynamic personality of Jordan, along with the knack England had of showing up when trouble arose. Younger ministers and laypeople in the various churches and agencies around the South that drew on support among Southern Baptists quoted Campbell, as they did Jordan, England, Marney, Finlator, Seymour, and McClernon. From the dually aligned congregations of Virginia and the Carolinas to the camping churches of Texas and neighboring states, Campbell and others like him provided examples of the gospel's power to inspire people to challenge society as they encountered it, in addition to calling on them to worry about the immortal souls of the lost. Campbell, Marney, and the others called on Southern Baptists and others to realize that people's souls were indeed at stake in their need to respond to the societal claims of Jesus' teachings and that those costly claims were not necessarily identical to the institutional values of mainstream Southern Baptists. The dissenters thought that there was more to saving one's soul than professing faith in Jesus and being added to the rolls of a church's membership.

## The Crowded Ways of Life

People who chose the path of dissent in the Baptist South clearly sought sources by which they could legitimate their claims and establish their sense of identity. Many Baptists, no matter how greatly they identified with the traditional southern ways of life, believed quite sincerely that their primary source of understanding who they were and how they should think and live was the gospel of Jesus Christ. They emphasized the spiritual dimensions of the gospel and chose not to take literally the teachings of Jesus that placed his followers on the side of the downtrodden and against the powerful in society. Progressive dissenters, however, believed that the ways they were commanded to think and live came from the same source, the gospel of Jesus. But they took his teachings about social relations literally and chose to deemphasize the spiritual aspects of the gospel or to say that one could not reap the spiritual benefits of having a relationship with Jesus while ignoring his calls for compassion for the afflicted and for solidarity with the power-less. Something happened to each dissenter, one by one, sometimes under the powerful influence of others within the dissident family, that kept them from being able to go along with the South the way it was. Along this path, one of transcending their culture, they had to decide some crucial matters.

For one thing, they had to decide what relationship they would have with the SBC. Many of them embraced the northern branch of Baptist life in the United States, the American Baptist Churches, as a source of nourish-ment and community while remaining affiliated, at least nominally, with Southern Baptists. Some who had nontraditional racial views, such as Victor Glass and Foy Valentine, who could have chosen to depart from the South-ern Baptist mainstream, chose instead to place themselves squarely within the structure itself as denominational employees. Glass earned a reputation for quiet, selfless work trying to build ties with black Baptists, sometimes single-handedly living down the prejudice white Southern Baptists seemed to represent. He did his most noteworthy work as an employee of the SBC's Home Mission Board, which courageously offered places of service from time to time to Southern Baptist pastors who were fired by churches for being involved in or supporting the claims of the civil rights movement.[65]

Compared with that of others who had experienced the influence of people such as Clarence Jordan, Martin England, and Carlyle Marney,

Valentine's work represented quite a different model of working for racial justice. He led the Southern Baptist CLC through its most turbulent times, overseeing the drafting of various statements of principle and encouragement for a more just South that were published by the commission for the consideration of Southern Baptist pastors and laypeople. Battles in the 1960s over the CLC's status within Southern Baptist life took on particular drama at the annual convention meetings, where the commission often prompted progressive resolutions for consideration of the body. In many conventions, proposals to cut the commission's funding or eliminate it altogether were made by enemies of the CLC and considered by the body of convention voters because of the opposition the CLC's stands generated among Southern Baptists. Under Valentine's leadership, the CLC created much inspirational literature, such as that encouraging the observance of Race Relations Sunday. Some ministers used these valuable resources in sermons and other expressions to their congregations and communities.[66]

In the minds of many people, though, the real power for change on race relations came through stories, through the examples of people such as those within the dissident network who lifted people out of the need for civility within the SBC. These were people who saw that the real struggle for the "soul" of Southern Baptists involved issues more important than whether or not Foy Valentine would have a job after the convention's next meeting. Many of them despaired of the possibilities that the SBC could have a significant effect on the reality of race relations in the South, putting their confidence instead in the power of law and government to bring about needed change. Many people in the dissenter network believed that the annual struggles to keep the CLC funded and the self-congratulatory observance of Race Relations Sunday became ends in themselves, substitutes for the real work of racial conciliation that Baptist Christians in the South should be doing. Valentine chose to do what many considered a noble thing by putting his efforts into the CLC approach, going into the heart of the SBC juggernaut. He became very well known, counting such public figures as Bill Moyers and Jimmy Carter among his colleagues, as well as numerous Southern Baptist pastors and officials. He offered pronouncements from within the system, playing the role of semiofficial confessor to the power structure, giving voice to many needed views, but ultimately offering only the criticisms of the "establishment" that a member of it can offer. After his long service as the "conscience" of Southern Baptists in the 1960s, Valentine became in the 1970s and 1980s a symbol of mainstream Southern Baptists, that of a denominational bureaucrat.[67]

Still, Valentine's unique position as someone with ties to the dissident network as well as his standing as a Southern Baptist loyalist gave special meaning to his views on people who challenged the racial status quo among Southern Baptists. His own view was that the people of the CLC were "the heroes" to younger Southern Baptists because "we stood up for trying to do right about race relations, and social action, and these kinds of things." In fact, he believed "there wasn't anybody else in Southern Baptist life that was doing much open talking about this subject of civil rights and race relations" in the mid-1960s.[68] He also believed that the path dissidents chose was one of ineffectiveness, that Will Campbell made "some genuine impact with his writings," but that he had "not been much of an effective voice with Southern Baptists in any organized capacity." Valentine, who maintained lifelong friendships with Jordan and England and considered them to have had great moral courage, also, however, regarded them as idealistic and unrealistic, referring to England, for instance, as a "dreamer." He viewed some of the members of the next generation of dissenters in much the same way, saying that Finlator, Seymour, and Carr, for instance, "followed their bliss," using the expression popularized by Joseph Campbell. To Valentine, their approach was to "spin off in the direction of what they considered to be the Christian ideal, and . . . everybody, for the most part, around them, just sort of took them for granted, and were not all that influenced by them." To Valentine the model of the effective voice was the person who stayed loyal to all Southern Baptist institutions but called the people in them to a higher view of the ethical requirements of the Bible, someone such as T.B. Maston, "who earned that right, and who paid his dues, and went to prayer meeting, and wrote training union lessons, and tithed his money, and . . . used his power, and became immensely influential." The dissenter who chafed at the Southern Baptist models and structures, according to Valentine, was "the outsider, who yaps at the outside, . . . drinking a little whiskey, and privately just doing his own thing. They have some influence, to be sure, but it's really pretty peripheral."[69]

One of the reasons Foy Valentine thought dissenters had limited influence in Southern Baptist life was that "nearly all these people . . . have a bit of a superiority complex from having gone to school in the North and come back and wonder why everybody doesn't give them places of leadership." One of his examples was Marney's friend from his days in Austin, Blake Smith, who "went to Yale and never forgot about it." According to Valentine, "Smith came down and was just everlastingly impressed with the fact that he had been to Yale, and he wondered why everybody from Southwestern [Seminary, where Valentine did his master's and doctoral work] didn't come and bow at his feet."[70]

In fact, however, most of the people in the generation of dissenters that Valentine derided had fairly extensive Southern Baptist pedigrees, even if they had "exiled" themselves temporarily through study in the North, and some of Valentine's own heroes had distinctive northern ties. Johnson, England, Jordan, Marney, Finlator, Carr, and Corpening were educated in Southern Baptist schools. All did seminary study at Southern Baptist Theological Seminary. England transferred to Crozer only when he was told by Southern Baptist officials that he would not be able to fulfill his life's goal of serving as a Southern Baptist foreign missionary. McClernon, a Missourian who did his seminary work at the University of Chicago and never considered himself a Southern Baptist, chose nevertheless to spend his entire ministerial career in the South. Seymour, a South Carolinian, went to Yale Divinity School, but while there he "first understood what it meant to be a southerner" and came "to see myself through the eyes of others where there were all kinds of prejudicial stereotypes about southerners." At Yale, Seymour had black classmates, learned about the social gospel, and wondered if he would be able to survive in Southern Baptist life, but he committed to returning to the South and served his entire career there. Having attended Yale did not make him want to live in the North. In fact, it made him appreciate his southern origins and made him want to help the South by serving churches there. Foy Valentine's role model, T.B. Maston, like Seymour, Blake Smith, and Will Campbell, went to Yale. W.T. Conner, Maston's colleague at Southwestern Seminary who admired the preaching of Otis Strickland's pastor, C.E. Matthews, and one of Valentine's honored professors, had gone to school at Colgate-Rochester, where he knew and came to respect the famous liberal Northern Baptist and social gospel leader Walter Rauschenbusch.[71] Valentine's appraisals notwithstanding, northern study did not seem to suggest an unalterable pattern that determined how people with Southern Baptist roots behaved and thought once they returned to the South.

If the question comes down to their identity as Southern Baptists, the lives of these dissenters present a fairly complex picture. They certainly were Baptists, with traditional Baptist views of the need for regeneration and of the nature of the church, God's appointed instrument to mediate such regeneration by acquainting people with the Christian gospel. Also, one can hardly deny that they were southerners. Martin England's American Baptist ties nourished but did not create him. He accelerated a process of departure from southern norms of church life and of race relations by choosing to study in the North, but the process had clearly begun in his childhood in the South. He went north with his perspectives already altered from those that had been inculcated ordinarily from his culture. His most formative experiences and encounters with people took place in the South. Will Campbell struggled with his southernness and concluded that because "you will never be a whole person until you come to terms with your own history[,] . . . for good or evil, I am of the South." Being from the South became a source of nourishment to Campbell's spirituality at the same time it energized his radicalism and activism. The blending of his identity as a southerner, his faith, and his progressive views made him think that it was extremely important that southern churchpeople lead the struggles to redeem the South from its racist past and troubled present. He also thought that many northern ministers who became involved in the civil rights movement, knowing they would be arrested and quickly released to the acclaim of their admirers, were "hypocrites." To get to the South, where the "action" was, they traveled through areas in their own states with serious problems in race relations. When they got to the South, they often put themselves in danger, no doubt, on behalf of a good cause. But then they went back home, leaving the same southerners there, black and white, to deal with the long-term implications of the tremendous upheavals brought about by the civil rights revolution.[72]

Ironically, England and his colleagues may have been more southern in their ways of dealing with their lives and careers and what they wanted to say and do about conditions in the South than was Foy Valentine. Whereas Valentine and his colleagues issued statements and worked within a large organizational structure increasingly modeled on the large corporations Walt Johnson fretted about, England and the other dissenters used a model of influence that was based on the age-old southern practice of storytelling. England and Jordan used stories to account for the unusual paths their lives followed. Stories of Will Campbell's activities and Carlyle Marney's sermons became legendary. People in the network heard and shared such stories of ministers and laypeople who had placed themselves directly into the fray of the civil rights struggle. Though some dissenters never stopped considering themselves Southern Baptists, many withdrew to greater or lesser degrees from that association, the critical factor that caused Valentine to discount the dissenters. To him, the "dues" one had to pay involved participating in every level of Southern Baptist institutional life. To the dissenters, the Walt Johnson tradition of doubting the legitimacy of that life beyond the congregational level colored their dealings with the denominational establishment. It found its way into their humor. Marney made frequent jokes about the institutional hubris of his fellow Southern Baptists, starting at one SBC meeting the "Humility Club," for ministers "who were humble enough to be proud of it."[73] But Marney was also the person of whom his friend Bob McClernon, at his funeral, said, "There was in him, despite all protestations to the contrary, a great deal of east Tennessee Baptist. Enough to make him haunted by Jesus and possessed by the God whose name he sometimes forgot and at other times believed he did not know."[74] Marney, like most people in the community of dissenters, simply did not believe that the "triumphant" conventions of Southern Baptists, state or national, with all their vast resources and complicated organizational structures and programs, had any real interest in addressing seriously the central issue of southern life in the 1950s and 1960s. The SBC's refusal to do so made it, in the minds of most dissenters, irrelevant.

One can certainly challenge Valentine's view that the CLC stood virtually alone among Southern Baptists sounding the call for racial justice. Were the CLC people the only heroes? England did not consider himself a hero and was described by many people who knew him as a humble, saintly person who avoided the limelight. Was this method of ministry and those of others in the dissident network effective? Within a certain sphere they were, or the genealogy of dissent would not have spawned subsequent generations. Valentine's assessment, that dissenters rendered themselves ineffective within Southern Baptist life by remaining aloof from the common activities of Southern Baptist structures, is correct if one defines effectiveness as recognition by and inclusion within the institutional authority of Southern Baptist leadership.

A different definition of effectiveness begins to emerge if Valentine's vision of an effective voice is compared with that of people who appraised the work of Martin England. England never had a large staff, an impressive budget, or the printing and distribution services available to him that denominational officials such as Valentine had at their disposal. Yet, many people were struck by his unpretentious manner and frugal lifestyle. Sam Proctor linked observations about these aspects of England's life with a judgment about his spiritual quality: "I believe that he is a saint if ever there was one. Every time you would see Martin England, he had on a simple suit, he drove an old Plymouth, and he was always going off to do good in some kind of way."[75] England's meekness, however, did not disguise the fact that he lived a dangerous life in his work in the South in the 1960s. Bob McClernon said, "I've heard of Martin being put in jail, Martin being run out of town, Martin having his life threatened," but he "worked on people," "like water dripping

on a rock. Just always there saying what he wasn't supposed to say . . ."
McClernon told of a man at Myers Park Baptist Church, an ardent segregationist whom England drove to distraction and helped drive to repentance
from his racist attitudes and toward tremendous helpfulness in desegregat-
ing Charlotte, by opposing him with "a persistent sort of gentleness." "[T]hat's
one reason why Martin had so many enemies among segregationists,"
McClernon added. "They weren't accustomed to dealing with that."[76] Furman
University faculty member Albert Blackwell, a longtime associate of England
and one of the people listed in England's journals as someone who might
form the nucleus of a revival of the old Walt Johnson group ideas, delivered
the eulogy at England's funeral. Paraphrasing Mic. 6:6, Blackwell said that
England "did justice, loved mercy, and walked humbly with his God," adding that "Martin is the only person I have known whose friends called him a
saint. Persistently they called him a saint, and Martin hated it." Blackwell
also said that England "is the only person I have known with an appetite for
justice, such as you or I might feel for dinner."[77] Such appraisals and stories
may have had as much power, possibly more, to create change in the lives of
those southerners who knew about Martin England as the pamphlets issued
by the CLC.

Nonetheless, the influence of those in the genealogy of dissent was felt
in ways that did not appear in the institutional data denominational officials
reported in the annual publication of convention statistics. Furthermore, for
every Bill Finlator, there was a Jesse Helms or a Strom Thurmond, usually
more powerful and more popular. For every Brooks Hays, there was an Orval
Faubus. More crucially, for the survival of the denomination Foy Valentine
prized so highly, for every Carlyle Marney, with his few dozen admirers, there
was a W.A. Criswell, with tens of thousands of emulators and hundreds of
thousands of rank-and-file Southern Baptists who thought he was God's own
idea of what a minister should be. Marney said that his old seminary professor W.O. Carver, at the age of eighty-four, sent him a response to a manuscript he had written, "scalded with his own concerns of more than sixty
years, and said it would do. But then he added a line: 'Go on with your work,'
he said, 'in a passionate evangelizing of this meaning of Church, but do not
forget the bent knees and the loyal spirits of those who can never understand.'"[78] If the dissenters erred, they did so not by defying the traditional
civility of life in the SBC on the question of race relations. They played a
role, however, if inadvertently, in the demise of the SBC by becoming tar-
gets for fundamentalist critics of "liberalism" in Southern Baptist life. They
lost touch with those who "can never understand." The story of dissenters on

race relations and of Foy Valentine takes on special significance in connection with the fundamentalist "takeover" of the SBC, with events that showed the ways language and agendas changed, with new holders of power squeezing out both moderates such as Valentine and dissenters such as England, Marney, and McClernon. It was a tide Valentine and others like him were unable to stem, try though they did, and one that dissenters did not feel was worth their resistance.

People on the dissident pathway through the Baptist South crossed a "crowded way of life," indeed, where cries "of race and clan" were heard, entreating them to remain loyal southerners and faithful Baptists. "Above the noise of selfish strife," however, they did not heed the voices of tradition, of civility. They heard instead what they thought was the voice of the "Son of Man," Jesus, the Prince of Peace, a subject to which the story of Southern Baptist dissent now turns.

# An Appetite for Justice

## *Peace, Reconciliation, and Southern Baptist Dissenters*

*Stand Up, stand up for Jesus, Ye soldiers of the cross!*
*Lift high His royal banner, It must not suffer loss:*
*From victory unto victory, His army shall He lead,*
*Till every foe is vanquished And Christ is Lord indeed.*
—George Duffield Jr., *Stand Up, Stand Up for Jesus*

"Southern Baptists" and "peace activism" are expressions that are seldom linked. When the United States has needed military personnel, the South has stood ready to supply more than its share of volunteers and draftees with Baptists representing high percentages of the total. The denomination itself was formed in the crucible of conflict during the events leading up to the Civil War. Southern Baptists are often perceived as more patriotic and more likely to be pro-war than churchpeople in mainstream denominations, contributing to their reputation as archetypal southerners. Southern Baptist hymnody, sermons, literature, and common expressions have attached war imagery to all that is considered good and holy.[1] People whose personal and spiritual identities were formed at least to a significant measure within the genealogy of dissent, however, placed peace activism close to the heart of Southern Baptist life in several ways that broadened and deepened the definition of peace.

Peace activism emerged as a part of the Southern Baptist landscape by means other than the usual organizational involvements that led or nurtured most peace workers in protests against war, militarism, or the amassing of armaments. One of the most important ways Southern Baptists became connected to peacemaking was through a network of activists inspired in large part by their involvement in the civil rights struggles. Many of them saw peace as a part of a larger whole, one pointing toward reconciliation as the chief need toward which people on earth should strive as they sought to create on earth ways of living that would resemble those described by Jesus in the Gospel accounts.

Many of them, in fact, saw the civil rights movement as an expression of this idea of reconciliation, rather than "just" a struggle by African Americans for inclusion in the mainstream of U.S. political and economic life. They saw civil rights more as a need for healing between the races than as a way for disadvantaged people, those who had been systematically excluded from participation in the "American way of life," to gain a foothold in the country's political and economic systems. One might say that this attitude reflected the privileged position of southern white churchpeople, including those sympathetic to the African-American struggle, which afforded them the luxury of seeing civil rights in a larger framework than the basic struggle for decent treatment it represented for African Americans themselves. These white progressive Christians in the South, however, stood in deeper contrast to their southern white conservative coreligionists, who had little appreciation for broad or narrow definitions of the freedom struggles of southern blacks.

This broader view of reconciliation manifested itself within the genealogy of dissent among Southern Baptists in a number of ways besides the quest for racial reconciliation, including activism on behalf of traditional understandings of peace, particularly in avoiding or mediating conflicts between the United States and other nations. Southern Baptist peace activism also took the form of a deep concern for lessening conflict among individuals and groups within American society. This form of peace activism was clearly rooted in civil rights concerns, as evidenced by the fact that it pointed particularly toward abolition of the death penalty, which historically has affected black southerners more than it has whites. Another manifestation of the second form of peace activism grew out of the view held by many progressive Southern Baptists that churchpeople should be involved in alleviating the material causes of social conflict, especially the lack of such necessities as adequate diets. Such concerns led some Southern Baptists to take part in institutionally sponsored campaigns for charitable donations for hunger relief, even though some critics argued that such measures dealt only with the symptoms of the crisis of hunger. Other Southern Baptists were inspired to attack the deeper structures of southern economic relations through labor organizing and other activism. In varying ways, these people had "an appetite for justice," as Albert Blackwell said of Martin England.[2]

## Lifting High the Royal Banner

As in race relations, elements of the SBC provided some support for peace-making, principally in the form of resolutions and other statements of the SBC and state Baptist conventions and agencies. Coming from a body that, historically, had no formal power to make binding pronouncements requiring assent of its members, such statements made for an inconsistent, sometimes confused expression of Baptist thinking on subjects related to peace. Southern Baptists' collective statements on behalf of peace, therefore, varied greatly throughout the twentieth century depending on hostilities the United States happened to be engaged in at the time or the absence of them. They ranged from denunciation of war in general to endorsements of it as the protection of everything that was good and holy, including Baptist principles themselves. Those who had a definition of peacemaking that extended beyond the traditional terms likely found little support for such views among Southern Baptists.[3]

Southern Baptists as a denomination supported World War I, for instance, as an expression of "Christian" values in opposition to German villainy, autocracy, and godlessness.[4] The Baptist Faith and Message statement adopted in 1925, in part as a response to the fundamentalist threat posed by J. Frank Norris and his followers, featured a section on world peace.[5] Although Southern Baptists exhibited a poor regard for outright pacifism, they acknowledged, meeting in convention in 1940, the rights of individuals to declare themselves conscientious objectors. The Social Service Commission in that year registered persons seeking this status, although the convention's executive committee refused to allocate any funds to monitor their treatment.[6]

A noted Southern Baptist minister and champion of the separation of church and state, J.M. Dawson, took an active role in advocating the employment of a moral framework for the post-World War II peace settlement. Dawson made an especially strong presence in the early days of the United Nations, which he saw as a helpful vehicle for promoting the cause of peace around the world. Dawson's involvement in such matters constituted a powerful symbol for Southern Baptists, in light of his strong stance on church-state separation, and provided a model for participation in public affairs that did not compromise traditional Baptist views protecting the free exercise of religion.[7]

Dawson played a supportive role in the life and work of an unlikely activist, Sara Lowrey. A professor of speech and oral interpretation at Baylor University who came from a progressive Southern Baptist background,

Lowrey had had little experience in active politics when she found herself at the center of a hate campaign in Waco, Texas, because of her support of Henry Wallace's presidential bid in 1948. She particularly liked Wallace's stands on race relations and peace and believed that his leadership could have prevented the involvement of the United States in the wars in Korea and Vietnam. Because of her "subversive" leanings at the time, people threw red paint on the door of her house and she was informed by sympathetic students that a key Baylor benefactor had engaged a hostile student to spy on her in class in the hope of catching her saying something politically sensitive that might give the university grounds to dismiss her. Lowrey was in an unusual position as one of the few women on the Baylor faculty and a genteel, Mississippi-born Southern Baptist whom people were calling a communist. She had deep convictions, though, that transcended the day's social strictures of gender, region, and religion. She also had tenure at Baylor and, she thought, a mandate from the president of the university. W.R. White, a traditionalist Baptist minister, had come into office saying that professors should take an active role in politics in order to add a moral dimension to political discourse and events. When Lowrey became the local chair of Wallace's Progressive Party, White found himself in an awkward situation. He wanted to uphold Baylor's tradition of academic freedom, something that had been severely tested during the fundamentalist crusades of the 1920s as J. Frank Norris and others attacked the university for allowing faculty members to refer in class to Darwin's theories on evolution. He also found himself confronted with the problem of having a faculty member who had become a controversial figure in the course of doing something he had urged Baylor professors to do. White refused to fire Lowrey, but tried to persuade her to change her positions. She mused, "He'd made this talk [urging political participation] but he just thought all Baylor teachers would think right!" She spent the summer of 1948 teaching at the University of California at Berkeley and considered staying but had the feeling she "wouldn't have lasted more than a year" because her religious and political orientation was too traditional for Berkeley. Summing up her own views of religion and politics, Lowrey said, "I take Christianity very seriously. And I've always wondered if I'd been there when our Lord was crucified for standing against a political regime, if I would have had both the awareness and the courage to stand by him." She taught one more year at Baylor and then joined the faculty of Furman University, Martin England's alma mater and the school identified with the Poteat family and other progressive Southern Baptists.[8] From the standpoint of peace activists, however, Dawson's and Lowrey's stances were emulated by few Southern Baptists. Their networks of activity and support were based in traditional, not dissenting, views of Baptist life.

As the twentieth century continued, however, quite a different group of persons affiliated with the SBC assumed prominent roles in promoting the idea of a strong, militant nation determined to face challenges from abroad and an equally strong, militant traditional culture determined to turn back threats to time-honored values. They conceived of peace as the period of calm that follows the winning of a military victory, and in the 1970s and 1980s they made up a key segment of the political element called the New Religious Right. James Robison and other prominent Southern Baptist evangelists made names and headlines for themselves serving "as cheerleaders in the arms race" during that period and helped lay the groundwork for the heavy presence of conservative Christians in the political life of the United States in the 1990s.[9]

Southern Baptists similarly felt little inclined toward political solutions to social problems, or even political analyses of those problems, especially if they were characterized as part of a need for the reorientation of society along the lines of any broadscale definitions of such concepts as reconciliation. Southern Baptists could be quite generous to those who were "down on their luck," often viewing charitable acts toward society's less fortunate as being in line with the teachings of Jesus, especially if the bad fortune seemed temporary and not chronic. Offering assistance to the unemployed or to low-paid industrial workers came much more naturally to most Southern Baptists than questioning systems that made such things possible or challenging factory owners and other powerful figures to improve wages and conditions.[10]

On the whole, having an appreciation for the benefits of occasional wars or the fitness of the economic and social order was not just a southern view, it was also a traditional Baptist view. The branch of the Reformation in which they arose inspired occasional civil disobedience, but they moved away from the pacifism held onto, for instance, by cousins in the faith such as the Mennonites. The Christian "royal banner," for many Southern Baptists, could be lifted high for "victory unto victory" by churches over their spiritual foes, but their country could be considered to be on the side of this same Jesus for whom they admonished each other to "stand up." When that country went to war, or when its interests or those of the southern culture came under threat of attack from the advocates of change, the traditional Southern Baptist response was to hold such people to be no less than the same foes against whom the forces of Jesus were to be arrayed.

## A Broader Millennium

Other views of conflict and of peace existed among Southern Baptists, though they were held by smaller numbers of people and were blended with many other impulses and visions. Peace activists seldom committed exclusively to that cause, and they often saw their causes as being so intertwined that the separation of activities from one another for organizational purposes seemed quite artificial. Some of them also had a definition of peace as something more than simply the absence of war. They viewed peace as a broader state called reconciliation, not just between conflicting nations, but between classes and individuals as well. Such was the view of Walter Nathan Johnson, who, earlier in his career, embraced a dramatic view of the value of peace and built it into every aspect of his work. In his mind, he had placed himself squarely in the center of the Christian expectation of the millennium, the thousand years of peace that New Testament prophecy foretold.

Johnson's vision for the program of "church vitalization" operated on a very small scale with handfuls of people meeting in out-of-the-way locations. But he was convinced that such meetings would change the world. In August 1935, four years before the outbreak of World War II, he expressed his hope that churches would "support the peace movement," in opposition to the fact, as he believed, that virtually every government was engaged in the promotion of war as a means of aggrandizing its geopolitical position. He also believed that one of the chief purposes of the "taxing power of our modern states" was the propagation of war." Looking beyond the next war to the crafting of the next "peace," Johnson added: "Oh, that war may be averted ten years more, at least long enough to get our churches awake to their obligations to support peace sufficiently that, after the next war Jesus may have a seat at the conference table to help fix the terms of peace upon an exhausted world. He was utterly shut out at Versailles."[11]

When Walt Johnson held up this view of the role of churches in peacemaking, he did what only a handful of Southern Baptists had done; he departed from a southern tradition of proving oneself through participation in or support for military service as an expression of manly virtue. In 1934, Johnson associate Edwin McNeill Poteat Jr. chaired a committee that presented a statement adopted by the North Carolina State Baptist Convention condemning war in tones directly reminiscent of Walt Johnson. Calling war "irreconcilably opposed" to the teachings of Jesus and prompted by the demands of "competitive" economic systems, the statement called for the conversion of capitalism to the principles of Christ as a step toward the abolition of war.[12]

Koinonia Farm, the interracial experiment in Southwest Georgia whose creation Johnson had helped inspire, also had a strong identification with peacemaking from its beginning. Its very name reflected a view that churchpeople constituted a community, not just the membership roll of an organization. It did not take long for the farm's founders to be subjected to critical examination because of their commitments to peace. During Martin and Mabel England's stay at Koinonia, they were visited by an agent of the Federal Bureau of Investigation (FBI) who wanted them to give information about Burma and the Burma Road that might help the Allies. Martin England refused to cooperate with the questioning, most of which could have been satisfied by consulting a general text on geography, because he was unwilling to give aid that might lead to the death of anyone, regardless of which side of the hostilities they represented. There had been some suspicions about the Englands because of their newness to the community and the fact that they had recently come from Burma and about the Jordans because of Florence Kroeger Jordan's pronounced German heritage. The Englands' son John had a stamp collection with a number of items from the Far East, including Japan; it was confiscated by the principal of his school and formed part of the inspiration for the FBI visit. Mabel England thought her husband's refusal to help the FBI would land them in jail, but the agent judged them not to be security risks or sufficiently disloyal to warrant further investigation. He stayed for lunch and left the Englands to their work.[13]

Martin England believed that Clarence Jordan became a pacifist while a student at the University of Georgia and a member of the Army Reserve Officer Training Corps (ROTC) unit on campus. England's memory was that Jordan went through the entire cadet program but then decided he could not go into military service on the eve of receiving his commission. He chose instead to follow the wishes of his mother, who had long wanted him to become a minister, instead of those of his father, who wanted him to perform a period of military service and then become the manager of the large Jordan family farm in Talbot County, Georgia. Despite the protests of the ROTC commander at the university, Jordan went through with his belatedly developed plan to go to seminary. Jordan "refused to rationalize" World War II by reference to "just war" theory and said the "loving thing to do" if one had been a Christian in Nazi Germany "would have been to put the Star of David on your arm and get in the concentration camp with the Jews." As England put it, Jordan "thought that you couldn't settle a real human issue by killing people, and I believe that too. And we hoped ultimately to make a demonstration of that conviction, among others" in the work at Koinonia Farm. In large part, England traced these feelings he and Jordan shared to the influence of Walt Johnson.[14] Koinonia Farm went on with its peacemaking orientation and adopted a formal position of Christian pacifism in 1950.[15]

Reconciliation was a necessary condition for community, what the Greeks, and Clarence Jordan and Martin England, called Koinonia. The inescapable reality was that reconciliation in the South had to take the dynamics of race relations into account. It was a crucial part, but only a part, of the larger vision of the purpose of the church in their eyes. Its purpose, to them, was not simply the recruitment of people for enrollment in church organizational structures, equating that activity with salvation, and moving on to the next person. It was, instead, the breaking down of barriers of hatred and suspicion between people "here and now," not just in the hereafter.

Martin England, Clarence Jordan, and their associates within the network of dissidents in Southern Baptist life thus posed a direct challenge to southern and Baptist ways of thinking. Their views came directly out of an overall system of analysis and advocacy that was nurtured by the inspiration they drew from one another and practiced in the larger field of church life in the American South. They also drew on the support of non-Southern Baptist groups such as the FOR.[16]

England worked out in great detail the connections between reconciliation and other issues. In his view, the ethnic hostility that in the South lay just below the surface, and sometimes atop it, linked considerations of race to broader forms of social relations. England saw a particularly strong connection between work for civil rights and peace. In fact, he joined the staff of the M&M Benefit Board of American Baptist Churches, which sent him south to work with civil rights activists, largely because he had attracted the attention of M&M board officials through his stands on peace issues. Having been unable to continue as a missionary in Burma because of Mabel England's health, he was given a temporary assignment in the early part of the 1950s to work in the United States on peace concerns for the agency. With additional support from the FOR, England traveled among American Baptists, particularly in the Northeast and Midwest, promoting World Council of Churches stands on peace. He served a term as national treasurer of the FOR and as a member of its governing council. Along with civil rights pioneer Bayard Rustin,[17] he was also an officer of the Peace Action Center in Washington, D.C., in the 1960s. England believed, however, that the authority for and the obligations toward peacemaking came from a source greater than those organizations such as FOR that he and Clarence Jordan supported. In England's mind,

> [I]f Jesus is lord, he must be lord of all life, and every relationship that a Christian has is subject to his lordship and his leading, his commands. . . . And it's that simple that you can't have . . . one standard of values and morals for your relationship with a person of a different race and expect to be a Christian in your relationships with your own kind. But that's why peace and integration and labor relations, economic relations, and relationships between men and women—if you can rationalize that that person is inferior and therefore not eligible to the same treatment, same standards as a person of your own race or class or nation, it lays a burden on you to follow through all these relationships.[18]

England worked out a theology of peacemaking that was particularly related to the work of the Holy Spirit. He said, "We pray for Pent[ecost] power, but shun the Pent[ecost] task," which could eliminate both the fact and the causes of suffering, especially that "caused by war. There is enough Power in God to stop wars, if we Christians would accept it."[19] On the subject of stewardship of resources and its relation to the absence of peace, "Whatever else may need doing, there can be no peace between a world half-starved, half-glutted, between a world that puzzles how to get enough to keep alive and a world in constant danger of suffocation from its surpluses."[20] England's thoughts on the interrelationships of power and aggressiveness were very similar to those of Walt Johnson: "A military state without a dictatorship is impossible. Who the real dictator is, nobody knows. More likely a group of men in the Pentagon." When people turn over responsibility for their public lives to those in positions of worldly power, they do so, he believed, because they feel too insecure and have turned away from faith and trust in the power of the Holy Spirit to reconcile people in conflict.[21]

The urgency of the need for peace and of the continual struggles between divine and earthly authority emerged in a sermon England delivered frequently in the 1950s and 1960s, based on the theme of the choice between serving "Jesus or the Chief." Through his missionary service in Burma, England received confirmation of the understanding he had gained from Walt Johnson of the fateful choice every believer has to make at some point between giving allegiance to the power of the world or to Jesus, who was sent to challenge the ways of the world. He developed an elaborate series of concepts about the meaning of social conflict that he derived from the experiences of people whose new Christian faith came into tension with their obligations as members of tribal communities to obey their chief and go to war on behalf of the tribe.[22]

England also composed a parable based on an incident he had witnessed in Burma. The story illustrated the timeless conflict between the requirements for decent behavior that religious faith places on people and the demands for order on which civil authority places a high value. It also illustrated the enormous waste of resources that accompanies war. He called it "Arithmetic for Christians." In terms strikingly similar to the story of how his grandfather was tended to by a black man who took pity on him, England told of an old woman in Burma who had been hacked with a knife almost to the point of death by her ailing husband. According to England's version of the story, she was carried sixty miles to the nearest hospital over a period of four days. Between her village and the hospital, there were seventy-two other villages. The district police officer had given orders for the leaders of each village to arrange that she be carried only to the next village. England encountered the woman, who "had been sitting by the side of road at Han Te, waiting while the headman and elders argued over who would have to carry her the last stage into town and to the hospital." She had been carried in a canvas camp chair, supporting her weight with poles under her arms. "The old woman beside the road in Han Te village was the most desolate human being I had seen in a long time," England said. "Her wounds now four days old were festering." England and a nurse took her the rest of the way to the hospital in a truck, passing along the way the rusting remains of numerous U.S. tanks and other vehicles abandoned or disabled during the recent war with the Japanese. He was struck by the awesome waste of resources represented by the instruments of war, the value of which could have provided much in the way of medical care in the region, even possibly preventing the episode of abuse against the woman. He was also taken by the efficiency of the police officer, who managed very quickly to have the husband taken away to jail, but took only the barest trouble to get the wife to a hospital.[23]

England linked his theology of peacemaking with similar criticisms of the partnerships between American corporations and the U.S. government and of the complicity that people share in the activities of those entities merely by acting as consumers and taxpayers. His analyses were remarkably similar to those Johnson had offered in many of his writings. "No one can fully escape the guilt of war," England said. "Even though he may refuse to kill, or to pay taxes which provide the bombs and gas other men use, so long as his job, his profits, or any advantage, derives from inequities supported or reinforced by war or other forms of violence, he is guilty."[24] England reaffirmed these sentiments in one of the few pieces of writing he published, a guest editorial in a special peace-related issue of an American Baptist journal of history and theology, saying, "A growing number of people feel that one who pays taxes for war is as guilty of killing as one who pulls the trigger or presses the bomb-release button." In much the same way that England's views of race relations and peace were linked, his answer to the problem of complicity in war that consumers and taxpayers share was linked to another concept that called for radical reorientation of the American way of life. It was not enough to engage in "tax protests," the refusal to pay that proportion of taxes that corresponded to the percentage of the federal budget devoted to military uses. According to England, in reasoning reminiscent both of Walt Johnson and George Stoll, if people spent less money, fewer taxes would be generated. Not only should they borrow and consume less, they should go even further and seek lower incomes so that the income tax receipts available to the federal government would decline.[25]

Citing transitions in neighborhoods and resulting social upheaval in the 1960s that may have had as much to do with economic status as with race, England stated his belief that such economic reorientation would have dramatic effects toward reconciliation between classes. In his journal he described an instance in which a minister had said, "Members of my official board are more agitated when [poor] white children from the neighborhood come to our Sunday School than they are when a black comes." Paraphrasing Jesus, England accounted for the hatred affluent people have toward low-income people, saying, "The poor are always with us. They are always a threat. They are always too many. Their needs are too great and their ability to pay their share of the freight is never enough."[26] England was troubled by an observation by Carlyle Marney "that some of his members [at Myers Park Baptist Church in Charlotte] were more troubled at the occasional 'poor white' who made gestures toward joining the church than at the occasional black person who came."[27]

England's lifestyle received a great deal of comment.[28] What few realized was that his famed frugality flowed from his view of justice, his ever-strengthening commitment to pacifism, and a growing interest late in his life in civil disobedience, especially as the Vietnam War dragged on. Possessions did more than create tax revenues for war-making governments and support for big businesses in league with militarists; they also caused deep spiritual problems for people, because people were meant to hold "the earth in trust," avoiding "the heresy of absolute ownership."[29] Such an ethic could have direct influence on prospects for peace. "If there is such a way [to find peace]," according to England, "one who is prepared to find it must be ready at the least to give up comfort, security, pride, home, food, shelter, life. If there is any truth in [the] words we have professed, we cannot escape a Cross, and must allow for the hope that a sublime Grace will, after it, bring to pass whatever form of Life that may appear."[30]

Thirty years after the founding of Koinonia Farm and his letter to Walt Johnson outlining his vision of a community of reconciliation, England continued to be fascinated by the Koinonia model and Johnson himself. As he worked on plans for such a community into the 1970s, he showed how intertwined his views of racial relations and peace remained. "To be human means caring for the young, the old, the weak," according to England, who felt that true community is built on an old idea familiar to persons of various persuasions: "From each as to his ability/opportunity, to each according to his need."[31] Virtually paraphrasing Johnson, England called for a "planetary network of people who bear good will. . . . We cannot all know each other, but we can begin to know about each other. Through something like a newsletter we can send word about ourselves and our concerns."[32]

As England entered his mid-seventies, therefore, he was increasingly drawn to the ideas of Walt Johnson. In Johnson-like fashion, he considered forming a local group from his circle of acquaintances and drafted a letter calling on some of them to join him in an intensive study of the problems of ownership versus stewardship and citizenship versus discipleship, to build a community that would cut across racial, economic, cultural, political, and educational barriers. He put its possible goals in the form of a series of questions: To "[s]eek release from inner anxiety, fear, guilt, hostility, anger, rage, frustration?. . . To fuse a community of faith, to make a demonstration? To explore, experiment, to study other experiments? To sensitize, awaken, arouse, on a wide scale, people who will risk death, to establish justice, oppose war and oppression, build community across all barriers?" England even revisited one of Johnson's old themes, human sexuality, though his concern centered more on the injustice of forced sterilization as a means to combat overpopulation and scarcity of resources. He believed that less consumption was the answer, not fewer consumers, starting with the people of the United States.[33]

Furman University professor Albert Blackwell viewed England as "a kind of Johnny Appleseed of peacemaking literature" and recalled a time when England's peacemaking instincts helped defuse an unpleasant situation that developed at a meeting, ironically, to consider the threat of nuclear war. The meeting, at England's home church, the First Baptist Church in Greenville,

South Carolina, featured an address by Sanford Gottlieb of the Committee for a SANE Nuclear Policy. "At the conclusion of the formal remarks," Blackwell said, "the first questioner demanded to know whether Dr. Gottlieb was a pre-millennialist or a post-millennialist," referring to the two general positions held mostly by fundamentalist Christians on the question of whether Christ will return to reign on earth before or after the millennium. "Most [people] do not understand what those terms mean," said Blackwell, adding that "Sanford Gottlieb is Jewish, and the look on his face indicated that he had no inkling of what his questioner was asking. But Martin understood," according to Blackwell, "and he knew that for some Christians those . . . are fighting words." He invoked a broader view of the nature and uses of peace when, "After a moment's pause, crackling with tension, Martin spoke up: 'Why don't we just assume that all of us here are *pro*-millennialists!'"[34]

## Into the Third and Fourth Generations

Walt Johnson, Clarence Jordan, and Martin England, representing the first two generations of the genealogy of dissent, broadened their vision of what peacemaking meant and blended it with other manifestations of conflict and suffering in the world. The generations of dissenters who followed them built on this foundation and elaborated its understandings and expressions. The third and fourth generations also fashioned several more formalized networks in connection with the issues of peace and justice than any of the people in the entire genealogy had on race relations. The third and fourth generations made their most distinctive contributions, however, in crafting more highly articulated forms of the vision of reconciliation and criticisms of the unreconciled aspects of society that the first generations of dissenters had formulated.

The cause of peace activism inspired several people in the network to feel more closely drawn to the lives and examples of Johnson, England, and Jordan. Several of these people, such as John Laney, the Walt Johnson associate whom England thought so much of, and Albert Blackwell, the son of Hoyt Blackwell, former president of Mars Hill College and longtime Johnson supporter,[35] developed a strong peace "witness." Johnson associate W.W. Finlator, who served as editor of *Christian Frontiers* for a time, became very active in antiwar and disarmament efforts. He also became aware that the Brethren Service Committee of the Church of the Brethren had given support to Southern Baptist conscientious objectors during World War II. Finlator campaigned for the SBC to reimburse the Brethren Service Committee after the war, but was unsuccessful. Racism and Southern Baptist complicity with it remained Finlator's "most crucial concern," but he took active roles in other areas he saw as being connected to the broader issues of reconciliation, including a heavy involvement in the labor movement.[36]

Carlyle Marney made some of the most powerful contributions to the thinking of the network of dissidents. He knew that reconciliation in the South and in the world derived largely from the righteous definition and use of power. He had known enough politicians, including Lyndon Johnson, from his days in Austin to have formed some strong opinions on the subject, especially related to the differences between moral authority and political expediency. He said that one of the most impressive things about Jimmy Carter was that "I haven't seen Billy Graham's name connected with him in any way, that none of the religious moguls of the South that I can spot have been called to Plains, Georgia."[37] The power that Marney saw as indispensable came from refusing to be "hand-tamed by the gentry." Marney said that a pastor who wants to change the power structure, which may include people in the pastor's own church who have many kinds of interests in maintaining the status quo, has to "use power" against power. This kind of minister makes it clear to the powerful in church and community "that their bounds are not his bounds. They send him a membership in the country club, but he never does open the envelope." Such a pastor, according to Marney, seeks to keep ties open across economic as well as racial lines, because the power structure is built on money as well as skin color: "He will look in on a Chamber of Commerce meeting, but he also goes to a Salvation Army meeting. . . . He begins to notice that sitting in court on Monday mornings seems to make a little difference sometimes. And he gets where he can get into the jail to see people."[38]

Marney's displeasure with Billy Graham reflected the view of many progressives, that Graham's highly publicized associations with U.S. presidents, particularly Richard Nixon, compromised his ability to offer any moral admonitions against government tendencies toward war making and other activities progressives abhorred. When Graham underwent something of a "conversion" on the question of nuclear arms in the early 1980s, endorsing the initiative for a "freeze" on the production and deployment of additional nuclear warheads and missiles and opening communications ties with the leadership of the Soviet Union, conservative evangelicals questioned his wisdom. One, Graham's fellow Southern Baptist and longtime editor of *Christianity Today*, Carl F.H. Henry, criticized Graham for downplaying restrictions on religious freedom in the Soviet Union in his eagerness to gain permission to hold evangelistic "crusades" in the country.[39]

Like Marney, Will Campbell had his own exasperations with Southern Baptists. He gave visible expression to his views of the need for reconciliation in the South through his writing and editing in the journal he cofounded, *Kattalagete*, Greek for "be reconciled." In its pages and elsewhere, he invoked Baptist history and his particular view of the common roots of all Baptists in the radical Anabaptists to explain his sense of his calling and his impatience with the dominant religious force in southern life. The Anabaptists, Campbell said, "believed in the complete separation of church and state. They would not go to war; they were against the death penalty. Southern Baptists have forgotten all that. They spend more time blow-drying their hair than wrestling with their history."[40]

One group of Southern Baptists who wrestled very intentionally with their history and departed from typical ways of conceiving of church and of framing questions having to do with reconciliation developed in and around the Oakhurst Baptist Church of Decatur, Georgia. Oakhurst became known particularly as one of the "alternative" Southern Baptist congregations that embraced nontraditional forms of ministry. Its members operated one of the early shelters for homeless people, took an active part in organizing opposition to the death penalty, and served as the home of several publications that presented a different vision of Southern Baptists and their relations with the world. One of these publications, *Seeds*, dealt first with the Southern Baptist and later with the broader Christian response to the massive problem of world hunger. Its cofounders, Andy Loving and Gary Gunderson, believed a potentially large audience existed among Southern Baptists who were concerned about hunger and "food insecurity." In its pages, authors and editors, usually people with Southern Baptist backgrounds, struggled with their tradition to see what they could embrace from it and what they needed to jettison. Some told stories about their painful realizations regarding the heavy-handed, ill-prepared, and often insincere approach to "missions" in which they had participated and that they had come to view as failed. One recalled a trip his church had organized to enable its young members to spread the gospel to poor Mexican children by the seemingly harmless means of a puppet show.

> I was a teenager in Corpus Christi, Texas. Our church youth group, armed with puppets, headed for the Mexican border in an old yellow bus. When we arrived, we dumped our puppet show (in English) on a small crowd of poor children, and rushed off to the tourists' market to buy straw hats, piñatas and stuffed frogs holding little guitars.
>
> But about one third of the group found its way into a bar where even

teenagers could order beers and margaritas. The trip reached its climax as this delinquent group was running to make the bus before it left. One girl . . . ran into a poor, legless beggar and knocked him off the sidewalk into the street.[41]

Seeds criticized not only traditional, missions-oriented Southern Baptists, but also the many concerned with "social issues" who were "good at putting on tremendous conferences with tremendous speakers, and changing absolutely nothing."[42] It also published articles by familiar dissenters such as Will Campbell, who minced no words in criticizing Southern Baptists. Campbell told of a confrontation he had at a "Baptist party" with a doctor in New Orleans, "a man well-known in local Baptist circles," who suggested that mass starvation might be a convenient solution to the problem of over-population. Campbell told of trying to reason with the doctor about the physical effects of starvation, "leaning slightly toward the histrionic as I tried to imitate the final sounds of an infant sucking from the dry and rigid tit of a mother dead since yesterday." Campbell finally lost his temper when he and the doctor were told by the doctor's wife that they "ought to be ashamed" for creating a disturbance at the party. He burst out, "Ashamed!! Ashamed? Yes. Of a Baptist deacon, trained to relieve human suffering, leader in his church and community, getting filthy rich treating patients in one hospital paid for with the taxes of the state's poor and in another built with the tithes of God's people. Ashamed? You're right I'm ashamed. And sick at my stomach.[43]

By no means, however, did Seeds attack everything or everybody Baptist. It carried articles praising such figures as T.B. Maston, who was lauded for his long advocacy of modest lifestyles for persons wanting to follow the teachings of Jesus, his open assaults on materialism over the course of his long career, and his fervent criticisms of racism. Partly out of traditional evangelistic concerns, Maston worried about the lack of Southern Baptist response to the problems of the poor, "the masses of the world," lest they get to the point "where they'll not listen to us when we preach the gospel."[44] Institutional responses to world hunger by Southern Baptists met with strong approval from Seeds editors, who cited particularly the projects of the Home and Foreign Mission Boards and special offerings among Southern Baptists between 1977 and the summer of 1979; and articles by prominent Southern Baptists appeared in its pages.[45] The intent of the magazine was clear, however, as stated in its masthead. It grew out of a commitment to awaken people to the needs of hungry people around the world, but its focus extended beyond the facts of suffering to its causes. Seeds was "committed to enabling Christians, and especially Southern Baptists, to respond to the poor, not just with charity, but with biblical justice." This kind of response, according to the editors of *Seeds,* "demands a mature understanding of the spiritual, political and economic realities that lie at the root of hunger." One of the two coeditors of the magazine when that statement appeared was someone who wrestled continuously with his history as a Baptist, Ken Sehested.[46]

Sehested became executive director of the Baptist Peace Fellowship shortly after it began in 1984 and editor of *PeaceWork,* published by Oakhurst Baptist Church. In 1989, the Peace Fellowship assumed publication of the *Baptist Peacemaker,* a publication that had begun in December 1980, one month after the election of Ronald Reagan as president. Emerging in response to the arms race that characterized the 1970s and 1980s, it had been sponsored by the Deer Park Baptist Church in Louisville, where it benefited from the presence of such Southern Baptist Theological Seminary faculty members as E. Glenn Hinson and Glen H. Stassen, the son of Harold Stassen, former Minnesota governor and frequent candidate for the Republican nomination for president. Hinson and Stassen, along with Deer Park pastor C. Carman Sharp, worked on the *Peacemaker,* which said that its purpose was "to inform, encourage, and assist Southern Baptists in the mission of peacemaking." It promoted peacemaking within small groups, congregations, community relations, and national and international affairs, based on biblical studies and examinations of "personal and corporate spiritual lives."[47]

In Sehested's thinking, nothing was more central to the Christian, or Baptist, task than peacemaking. He meant by the term something far different from "making nice," as he put it, because he stood squarely in the lineage of the Southern Baptist dissenters. To him, peacemaking was actually making trouble for the established power system, causing disruption in the calm acceptance of injustice and oppressiveness that characterized the way most societies, including the American South, operated. The real and pressing need for reconciliation, according to Sehested, moved followers of Jesus toward breaking down barriers between people. Along the way, however, the path toward reconciliation brought peacemakers to the point where they had to offer prophetic criticisms of their culture, something that the people in that culture seldom welcomed. Sehested embraced a Hasidic saying, "God is not nice. . . . God is an earthquake." Peacemaking requires creating controversy, which a great many Christians, especially southern churchpeople, consider impolite and thus un-Christian. This southern gentility, combined with the boss-dominated local politics he saw as characteristic of much of the South, created a political culture that Southern Baptists emulated as they organized their denominational life. Key pastors and denominational leaders had "ways of doing things" that did not encourage nontraditional methods or organizations that did not appear within the structure of ordinary Southern Baptist life. Because the SBC and its agencies and officials were such integral parts of southern culture, and because they had flourished in that setting, as Sehested saw it, few Southern Baptists with any recognized power were willing to do what was necessary to cause real change, real reconciliation.[48]

Sehested was no foreigner in the South. He grew up in the South of a Southern Baptist family, became a Southern Baptist traveling youth evangelist during his teen years, and went to Baylor University on a football scholarship after graduating from high school in Houma, Louisiana, in 1969. While at Baylor, as other Southern Baptist students had from time to time, he began to question the understandings of his faith that he had embraced as a child, especially as he began to take religion courses and wrestle with the "God question." He entertained little thought of abandoning his Baptist identification, even serving a term as a summer missionary. He felt, however, a growing sense of shame because of the racism and other drawbacks of the South and decided to complete his university education in the North. At New York University (NYU) and then at Union Theological Seminary in New York City, he studied southern history and the history of the Anabaptists and came upon a somewhat startling discovery: that he was a committed Southern Baptist. Like Bob Seymour, who came to appreciate his southernness while studying at Yale, Will Campbell, and others whose northern studies made them want to return to the South, Sehested found that he could not imagine living and working anywhere else. One of the reasons he felt so strongly about returning to the homeland of his Baptist forebears was that he discovered while he was studying in New York the network of Southern Baptist dissenters. One of his professors handed him a magazine article one day and said, "You ought to know about this guy." The "guy" in question was Will Campbell. Another professor told him about Clarence Jordan; another, about Carlyle Marney. Sehested could not figure out why his Baylor religion professors, especially the more progressive ones, had not told him about these people. He also could not figure out how these people could have escaped his attention, when it was so abundantly obvious that they had experienced the same shame about the South that he had felt, that they had embraced the good things about being Baptist that he did not want to abandon, and that they seemed determined to use the strengths they derived from being Baptist to make a difference in the southern homeland. "These people were censored out of my education, informally if not consciously and formally." But, he added, "In my sojourn to 'the far country,' I discovered my own history about my own country." His study of reformist elements in evangelical history and of the history of the Anabaptist movement gave him a sense that his people had not always gone along with and contributed to social injustice and triumphant behavior, that there were deep roots in dissent within his Baptist tradition, his "progenitors," especially among Southern Baptists.[49]

Sehested returned to the South in 1978, along with Nancy Hastings Sehested, another Southern Baptist whom he had briefly known while she was a student at Baylor, before she also transferred to NYU. They became reacquainted in New York, married, and decided to return to the South to serve as copastors of a Southern Baptist church, if possible. They chose to go to Atlanta, found that indeed there were no prospects for a wife-and-husband team to work in a Southern Baptist church, let alone pastor one, but decided to stay anyway. They became involved in Oakhurst Baptist Church, which employed Nancy Sehested after a time as a part-time associate minister, and through its hosting of *Seeds,* indirectly created a job for her husband.[50] Ken Sehested's work with *Seeds* became principally defined by one of the key attributes of the genealogy of dissent: networking. He used the exact methods that Walt Johnson and Martin England had used to build a community among those who were disaffected by the situation in the South but unwilling to give up on it or on the religious identities that had at least the potential of being redeemed and leading people away from what he saw as ungodly about the South. "I consciously refer to myself as an evangelist," Sehested said, having seen "very significant continuity" between his former work as a youth evangelist and the progressive organizing of his adulthood, an association many others might not have made. His understanding, though, was that his purpose was like that of the apostle Paul, to preach grace, by which he meant freedom from fearfulness, a freedom that gives people the ability to help others. He also saw his purpose as being something else Paul did: "raising up communities of resistance, . . . believers who realized they are alien people," those who realized that their vision is deeply "at odds with the way the world is now organized." To engage in the process of alienating themselves from the dominant culture and to survive the process, such people need community with others who share this vision, according to Sehested. Working to build such a sense of community formed the bulk of the activities of the Peace Fellowship, along with training for activism, celebration of the common heritage of those engaged in peacemaking, development of the spiritual lives of the people in this "alien" community, and building an enhanced sense of dissenters' connections to a larger community of protest, to "empower their willingness to speak out" against injustice.[51]

In Sehested's understanding, he was more of a pastor than a prophet, one who tried to encourage the development of prophetic leadership in others and to be a source of comfort to them in times of trial: "I spend a lot of time on the phone, writing short little notes. I have two full Rolodexes, heading for a third." He put people who had similar interests in touch with each other, responded to personal crises, tried to help people find jobs within religious and activist arenas. "I'm a pastor to prophetic people." He thus came to characterize himself precisely the way Martin England had, without knowing of England's self-characterization. Sehested was the same kind of minister to the prophets and troublemakers England had known who held up a different view of the South and of the demands of Jesus on it and called into judgment the forces and people who stood in the way of reconciling the region to the Lord it claimed so steadfastly to honor. His reasons for wanting to build community were similar to those of his predecessors in the genealogy of dissent and sprang from the same perception. The official bodies of Southern Baptist life, they believed, were doing little to advance the causes of real transformation that Jesus embraced. Sehested, then, became the archetypal Southern Baptist dissenter, devoted to the redemption of the South, committed to the original Baptist values of prophetic witness against injustice, disdainful of traditional paths of institutional power and influence in Southern Baptist life, and convinced that networks of individuals in "kindred" congregations would take what Walt Johnson called the "next step in the churches."[52]

Few things were more frustrating to Sehested than the roadblocks put in the way of moving toward that next step by the very group in Southern Baptist life that most people presumed would be sympathetic to the work of peace and justice: the CLC. Southern Baptist churches such as Deer Park in Louisville and Watts Street in Durham sponsored conferences on peacemaking in the early 1980s, focused particularly on the perceived growing threat of nuclear war, both of which included speakers employed by state or Southern Baptist agencies. Speakers at the Deer Park conference in August 1982 included four Southern Baptist heads of agencies, including Foy Valentine of the CLC,[53] but efforts aimed at engaging Southern Baptists in peacemaking that came from entities other than the CLC received remarkably little real support from Valentine, the commission, or other entities within the SBC, a fact that troubled Ken Sehested greatly.[54] The editors of *Seeds*, who had come to a similar conclusion regarding their work on hunger-related issues, realized they seemed to have more support among non-Southern Baptists than among Southern Baptists and began to focus their efforts more ecumenically. As Sehested looked back on his time with *Seeds*, he remembered that "The commission refused to even mention our name, much less promote us, and yet we were winning world-hunger media awards" from secular organizations.[55]

Foy Valentine, in Sehested's appraisal, had many fine qualities and served a terribly important role in raising the consciousness of Southern Baptists to the shame of racism. Valentine and the CLC represented a "lighthouse" for Southern Baptists on the issue of race relations, in Sehested's view, the "apex" of Southern Baptist expression in Christian ethics in connection with racial justice. Valentine's support of Martin Luther King Jr. was often confined to the background. Some of it might be called "backhanded," according to Sehested. But Valentine's overall views and pronouncements in favor of racial justice represented for Southern Baptist people who cared about social ministry a great source of encouragement. The annual convocations that the CLC sponsored functioned like family reunions for these people, in Sehested's view. In this subculture within Southern Baptist life, Valentine played a role similar to that of an office Baptists reject, serving as something of a bishop. He maintained his own network among the "scattered group" of progressive Southern Baptists that had "significant overlap" with the Baptist Peace Fellowship network. CLC-supportive pastors of larger, more influential congregations, however, tended not to support the work of the fellowship. Part of the reason for this lack of support was the impression that the Peace Fellowship, like *Seeds*, was a "rag-tag" outfit—"Who are these guys operating out of a basement in a church in Decatur, Georgia?" In a denominational culture that prized first-class facilities, such a question had great import. Another factor that inhibited support among such people was Valentine's own attitude, one that Sehested believed crippled most Southern Baptist agencies, one that he saw as corresponding to the mentality of the plantation bosses of the Old South.[56]

Heads of agencies in the heyday of the SBC, until the 1980s, operated quite independently. They presided over hierarchies, receiving only advisory counsel from boards of directors over whose selection they had a great degree of power of approval or disapproval. They had tremendous influence in helping secure employment for protégés, including especially a steady supply of young seminary graduates. Such people often spent periods of service in the agencies before going out to serve churches as pastors or Southern Baptist seminaries, colleges, or universities as faculty members or administrators, or agencies themselves, such as CLC, as high-level staff members. Frequently, the level of prestige of such appointments depended on how willing powerful agency heads were to advocate a particular job seeker's position. A high degree of personal loyalty to the agency head often resulted from this system. Job seekers knew that the favor of their denominational patron depended greatly on the willingness they had to support the outlook of the official and refrain from engaging in overt criticism of him or his agency. Furthermore, in the world of Southern Baptist agency heads, as Sehested saw it, protecting the well-being of the institution came ahead of everything else, sometimes even the stated purposes of the agency. The resultant jealousies over "turf" boundaries and overlapping functions created very powerful suspicions and rivalries exactly of the sort found in private business, government, and the military. The irony that such attitudes could exist in organizations inspired by the sacrificial Jesus did nothing to prevent their occurrence. The special irony that such attitudes could exist within the agency charged by the convention with demonstrating the essence of the "Christian life" and in the behavior of the man known as the "conscience of Southern Baptists" likewise failed to keep them out of the CLC and Foy Valentine.[57]

In his work with *Seeds* and with the Baptist Peace Fellowship, Sehested found that the CLC and its director failed to give appreciable support of these efforts to help relieve suffering and to advance the cause of reconciliation—goals Valentine and his agency endorsed. Sehested also became aware that Valentine put out the word within his own circle of influence that those who wanted to be considered loyal to the CLC would take no steps to help *Seeds* or the Baptist Peace Fellowship. Sehested's impression was that Valentine thought the CLC was doing all that needed to be done with Southern Baptists on the issues of hunger and of peacemaking and that the fact that *Seeds* and the Peace Fellowship were targeted specifically at Southern Baptists made them potential threats, instead of welcome allies.[58]

This denominational politicking and intrigue made Sehested and his colleagues in the Baptist Peace Fellowship more determined to form a network of support and encouragement for Baptist activists committed to the reconciliation model that Johnson, Jordan, England, and others had promoted. Sehested was convinced that Andy Loving had been correct that Southern Baptists cared about hunger and that *Seeds* was an effective instrument for awakening and channeling that concern, citing evidence of increased charitable giving to denominational hunger relief efforts during the period between the beginning of publication of *Seeds* in the late 1970s to its abandonment of focus specifically on Southern Baptists in the mid-1980s. To Sehested, the Peace Fellowship spoke to many of the same concerns, attracting the interest of people who shared them. A number of those people had become interested in peace issues as a result of their realizations about the relatedness between militarism and hunger. As Sehested put it, hunger was "the open door into a room in which people could see" the causes of hunger. The Peace Fellowship needed, therefore, to offer ways that Southern Baptists, and other Baptists, could see the connections among many issues related to reconciliation while also providing examples of reconcilers from within Baptists' own history. One of the most important functions of the Baptist Peace Fellowship, therefore, became "recovering and communicating a mostly forgotten history," keeping alive the stories about the "saints" from among Baptist ranks who had worked for "justice and peacemaking, reconciliation work on a wide variety of fronts, from anti-militarism, anti-war work to racial justice work to non-violent resistance to oppression to various kinds of women's issues, prison reform, hunger relief, medical care, a wide range of human-related healing ministries . . ." Sehested believed that these stories had been deemphasized in Baptist life because of the traditional dichotomy between spiritual and material concerns, and the "privatizing of faith," the denial of the communal nature of religious experience. He also blamed the tendency of Baptists to view life as a "test-run for heaven or hell," something that has no purpose or significance other than to determine where one would spend the afterlife, overwhelming the activist impulses he and Andy Loving believed to be present in many Baptists.[59]

Although strengthened by his contacts with people in the network of dissidents, Sehested believed that he had been the recipient of a vision of reconciliation that originated from an earlier source in his own life. He knew about Walt Johnson, the Jordans, the Englands, Finlator, and others. He believed, though, that he had become involved in reconciliation issues in the first place because there were "Baptists around who chose to remain vigilant in this set of institutions called Baptist life in order to find people like me who were growing and maturing and were a fertile field for a different vision of what it means to be a believer." Many of these people had fairly traditional Baptist views of evangelism and missions and the importance of institutional maintenance, but they were also concerned about the failings of Southern Baptist institutions. They "put up with the shame" growing out of public ridicule of Baptists, some of which they recognized as deserved, in order to be present in Baptist life when others such as Sehested came along who were receptive to different ideas about working out the requirements of the gospel. It fell to the network of Southern Baptist dissidents to nourish such impulses in Sehested's life, because the traditionalists in the denomination, including those with strong leanings toward an activist gospel, never could break away from their unwillingness to challenge fundamental aspects of southern, and American, culture.[60]

One of the reasons Southern Baptists could not break their allegiance to the southern status quo had to do with their ambiguity toward their socio-economic origins and the signs they embraced of success in a land that valued success above most other things. To move away from the traditional measures of achievement required an identification with the lowliest members of society, not just a willingness to offer them charity. Increasingly, therefore, many people in the network of Baptist dissidents came to realize that their calling could best be realized in solidarity with the marginalized in society, particularly the poor, the homeless, and the dispossessed, and people who had come to the United States as refugees. No one in the network of dissenters articulated the vision of such a church—a church that was "more than Baptist, more than regional, more than white and male"—more clearly than McClernon did. To him, the key to understanding the appropriate response of churchpeople was in the identity of God and in God's relation to human suffering. God is not the "Bringer of Suffering," according to McClernon, but the Sufferer. As clearly illustrated in the life and death of Jesus, God suffers along with people. God does not tolerate suffering because it is of no consequence and neither should churchpeople. McClernon was not alone in such views. Sehested used an exercise at retreats and similar gatherings in which he asked people to look up the word "poor" in Bible concordances, saying "It's amazing to become acquainted with God's obsession with poor people and the demand that their needs be met." He often pointed out that such biblical texts are so often ignored because "in Southern Baptist spiritual life, the reality of poor people is neither here nor there." Many people disagreed with such thinking, of course. McClernon received an anonymous letter from a critic who admonished him to "get your eyes off of the troubles of the world and get them on Jesus, and tell sinners what will happen to them if they die in sin, because Jesus is coming soon and you all will give an account to him." Despite having received such advice, as he neared his twenty-second anniversary as pastor of Watts Street Baptist Church in Durham, McClernon felt called to a vocational change that would put him in even greater contact with sufferers than he had in his role as the senior minister of a congregation. He left the pastorate at Watts Street to begin a new career as a psychiatric social worker at a state mental hospital in

North Carolina, in his words, "to spend the remainder of my working days with the poor."[61]

Some dissident congregations carried their identification with the powerless to the point of becoming involved in efforts to aid political refugees. The network of dissident churches included Covenant Baptist Church in Houston, a congregation affiliated with American Baptists that had strong ties to Watts Street Baptist in Durham and other "alternative" Southern Baptist congregations. It had connections with and employed as interim pastor Douglass Sullivan-Gonzalez, a former Southern Baptist missionary to Nicaragua who became deeply involved in protesting U.S. military involvements in Central America. He had gone to Southern Baptist-connected Samford University in Alabama, been involved in traditional missionary work of Southern Baptists, done seminary study at Princeton, experienced northern biases against Southern Baptists, and become radicalized through his experiences in Central America. He came to work with Proyecto Adelante, a refugee-assistance group.[62] Proyecto Adelante was one of several organizations that appeared in the early years of the first presidential administration of Ronald Reagan, protesting against and working to circumvent federal policy on Central America and on refugees who fled the region to come to the United States. Several organizations sprang up as part of the overall protest effort, known in some of its manifestations as the Sanctuary Movement, and in some as the Overground Railroad. A handful of Southern Baptists participated actively in these organizations.[63]

One group of Southern Baptists formed a tiny congregation known as the Church of the Prince of Peace in the Baptist stronghold of Waco, Texas. Part of the "New Evangelical" movement that arose in the period from the 1960s to the 1980s, Prince of Peace represented a throwback to the extreme biblicism of the Anabaptist stream of thought during the Protestant Reformation. While theologically orthodox and extremely conservative on most matters of doctrine, members of Prince of Peace followed what one of their number called "the leading of the spirit," something that sometimes led them to engage in acts of civil disobedience. "We respond in obedience to Scripture and the Word of the Lord. If that leads us into a political activity, that's just part of it," said church leader Charles Tindell. In his understanding, the decision to enter an arena traditionally shunned by most Southern Baptists required him and his fellow members to submit their own wills to that of the Holy Spirit in the manner of Pentecostal churchpeople but also informed by the claims of Liberation Theology, to "lay down" their individual social and political views to the point that "what is raised up is only that which the Lord raises up." Prince of Peace members adopted the attitude reflected by one of the European pioneers of Liberation Theology, Jurgen Moltmann, that "Peace with God means conflict with the world." They gave considerable attention to what they viewed as the guidance of the Holy Spirit, which brought them into ways of thinking about and responding to public issues that they considered to be within the direct authority of the teachings of Jesus. In Tindell's mind, they also acted out of the tradition of "Baptist people that I've known all my life—stepping out in faith." Such processes of "discernment" had led the congregation to embark on acts of assistance to Salvadoran refugees that bordered on the illegal and sometimes probably crossed the line into illegality as defined by the Reagan administration. The church modeled itself in part on the Church of the Saviour in Washington, D.C., whose founding pastor, Gordon Cosby, was a progressive former Southern Baptist who corresponded with Martin England. Prince of Peace also developed ties with Koinonia Farm and with another group, the Jubilee Community in Georgia, an offshoot of Koinonia that also counted Southern Baptists in positions of leadership who had been influenced by Clarence Jordan. Jubilee involved itself in assistance to the "eastern stream" of refugees fleeing northward through the United States, seeking safety in more tolerant areas of the United States or in Canada.[64]

As unusual as it was to have a religious community such as Prince of Peace in Waco, Texas, it was not the only concentration of Southern Baptists in that city that departed in dramatic ways from the norms of the denomination's churches. Another congregation, an ecumenical "house church" called Reconcilers Fellowship, had a high percentage of members with Southern Baptist backgrounds and upbringing. Founded in 1978 by Jimmy Dorrell and his wife, Janet Dorrell, as Reconcilers Ministry and organized as a church in 1986, Reconcilers Fellowship carried ideas embodied in its name to logical extremes that defied ordinary conduct of people in the mainstream of Southern Baptist life.[65]

In the first place, Reconcilers chose not to invest in the essential symbol of Southern Baptist institutional development, a church building. They met in the homes of members and thus were part of the house church movement, a phenomenon that arose in the United States in the 1970s. House churches were automatically considered "counter-cultural," in the context of American denominationalism, because they rejected the emphasis on acquisition and maintenance of a "church plant" and on other trappings of ecclesiastical institutions. The bulk of the membership of Reconcilers, which was made up of well-educated whites, went a step further, however, by locating their homes in a racially mixed, high-crime neighborhood in North Waco. They became actively involved in ministry efforts in the neighborhood, including highly traditional evangelistic methods that other people in the dissident network had criticized as being heavy-handed and culturally insensitive. Such efforts reflected the views of the majority of Reconcilers' members, who, like those of the Church of the Prince of Peace, were very conservative theologically while being highly unorthodox, or what some might call progressive, socially and politically. Reconcilers with Southern Baptist backgrounds engaged in tax protests in proportion to the percentage of defense spending in the federal budget and engaged in various efforts to influence city and county service organizations to assist needy persons in the neighborhood. Instead of conceiving of themselves as politically liberal, Reconcilers thought of themselves as heirs to the Anabaptist tradition. Their Statement of Faith and Calling declared that, "The world is idolatrous as it places its trust in money, in tools of destruction, and in its own wisdom rather than in God." Several of the members who came from Southern Baptist upbringings took part in the communal experiment known as the "common purse," a practice whereby two or more families pool financial resources and make expenditures based on needs on which the holders of the joint account have to agree. Like those of Prince of Peace, Reconcilers' members spent a great amount of time seeking to discern what they considered to be the will of the Holy Spirit, in vastly greater detail than did the overwhelming majority of Christians of mainstream denominations, including Southern Baptists. Their principal activity lay in seeking as many ways as possible to break down barriers of race, income level, and education. Their means for achieving their goals included the creation of various kinds of inclusive organizations and activities in the community where they were located, along with an active effort at educating the well-to-do about the needs and perspectives of low-income people.[66]

Jimmy Dorrell, the cofounder of Reconcilers, came from a traditional Southern Baptist upbringing. He said, "I have a seven-year Sunday school attendance pin that I wore for years on my tie so that everybody could know how religious I was." As an undergraduate at Baylor, his "Sunday school faith" was challenged by courses and readings in religion, and he developed what he took to be a deeper level of faith as a result. His continued studies led to a discovery of the Anabaptist tradition and its questioning of "the institutional faith . . . in a corporate community that is very serious about its faith. A primitive New Testament Christianity." He worked with a "renegade Baptist" minister in Houston, Ralph Neighbour, who had traditional attitudes

that equated the principal duty of evangelism with church growth and orthodox theology, but who had extremely nonstandard methods, compared with
most Southern Baptists, for accomplishing these aims. In Dorrell's view,
Neighbour was "beaten up . . . by the denomination" for challenging such
Southern Baptist articles of faith as the primacy of Sunday school as the
vehicle around which church growth is built and what Dorrell called the
"rural" orientation that most Southern Baptist methods seemed to have, principles Neighbour openly disregarded and against which he spoke. His experiences working with Neighbour, along with his reading and other influences,
gave Dorrell a model for building a church community around small group
life with an absence of concern for the interests of larger organizational structures. He and his fellow Reconcilers also drew inspiration and ongoing emotional support from Reba Place Fellowship in Chicago, an ecumenical
intentional community that included a strong representation of people from
the Mennonite and Church of the Brethren traditions, both of which had roots
in the same Radical Reformation heritage that included the Anabaptists. Not
coincidentally, Reba Place Fellowship served as one of the models for the
Church of the Prince of Peace and maintained various kinds of ties with it.[67]

Several Reconcilers expressed their sense of God's passion for peace in
terms that were remarkably similar to those of other dissident Southern Baptists. Nancy Gatlin, who grew up in South America in a family of Southern
Baptist missionaries, and her husband, Joe Gatlin, a Waco native and the son
of a traditional family of Southern Baptists, came to believe "that it wasn't
enough just to say we were pacifists, but our tax dollars were going towards
the nuclear armament buildup. Though we might not be flying the fighter
planes, we were in the same place because we were paying for it." Before the
Gatlins moved to Texas from Chicago, where they had been involved in several inner-city ministries, they went through an audit by the Internal Rev-
enue Service because of the magnitude of their charitable contributions.
Nancy Gatlin declared that, "They didn't feel like we could actually be giving
that much away." She and her husband did defense-related tax protests in
Chicago and in Waco. Joe Gatlin developed his stance on war and peace
during the Vietnam conflict, when he realized that he could not imagine
Jesus' taking the life of another human being. His conclusion was that, if
Jesus' life were "normative" for him, killing "was not a right thing for a Christian to do." Other members stressed the action of the Holy Spirit in making
requirements that caused them to be in similar conflict to the larger culture
in ways other dissidents had described. The connections among such people
reached all through the "Baptist South" and across all sorts of socio-eco-

nomic and cultural lines. Such connections, however, showed the potential strength that could be generated when people with the strong sense of organization and commitment to the advancement of the gospel that Southern Baptists traditionally represented became inculcated with radical convictions of a social and political nature.[68]

## A Genealogy of Reconciliation

Dissenters from the traditional pathways of Southern Baptist life refused to give voice to a theology that viewed the task of Christians as vanquishing foes, moving from victory unto victory, never suffering loss. The Jesus they tried to follow embraced loss as the very ethic on which his teachings centered. To "lift high" his banner meant to sacrifice power, not to amass it; to live in solidarity with the poor, not to shun them; to identify peace as reconciliation of people with God and with each other, not to define it as subduing others. These dissenters lived by a model for practicing their understandings that manifested itself in several key ways that set them at odds with the majority of Southern Baptists who prized the model of triumphalism.

First, they tried to practice what Carlyle Marney called "an ethic of parsimony." In a land devoted to excess, where churches and churchpeople seem to share that particular devotion, followers of Jesus should focus their efforts on sharing the resources of nature and of a market economy as a manifestation of the justice Jesus sought to bring.[69] Once one acknowledged the need of such sharing, the need to address the reasons for unequal or inadequate distribution of resources or the structural elements of society that caused or exacerbated such problems could not be avoided. Then one had to decide how far to go in criticizing such structures, whether one would become involved in supporting labor unions, for instance. Marney extended his influence on such concerns to many of his peers and younger people in the network of dissent in ways that people before him, such as Walt Johnson, could not have done, and in ways more eloquent than those employed by many of the people who came after him. In 1935, when Johnson said, "The man with a job has to take care of the man without a job,"[70] he was doing more than just making a statement about charity during the Great Depression. He was commenting on the historic identification he believed that Jesus, and his followers, should have with the poor. He believed that affluent Christians had a terrific problem in light of Jesus' identification in the Gospels with the poor and vilification of the rich.[71] Marney and others in the genealogy of dissent picked up Johnson's theme and elaborated it in many and diverse ways.

Marney's eloquence, Ken Sehested's organizational skills, or the earnest determination to embrace a sacrificial lifestyle of people in Reconcilers Fellowship and other communities could only accomplish so much in the face of the entrenched alliances between churches and culture in the Baptist South. One of the problems dissenters faced was the socio-economic reality of life for increasing numbers of Southern Baptists. Southern Baptists were upwardly mobile in more than one sense. With regard to their prospects for the afterlife, they had their eyes on heaven. On earth they focused their efforts as a religious body on growth, the institutional form of prosperity. Few ministers or denominational officials became wealthy in Southern Baptist service, although Sehested pointed out that the average salary of pastors at larger Southern Baptist churches probably surpassed the entire budget of the Baptist Peace Fellowship.[72] Few individual Southern Baptists embraced what used to be called the "gospel of wealth." They lived responsible, faithful lives in service to the vision they had been taught by other faithful Southern Baptists, without corrupting their faith into a rage for riches. They were clearly prospering as a group, however, and this upward mobility, along with the preaching they heard week after week to give and work toward the growth of Southern Baptist institutions, placed a wedge between them and the message many people in the dissenter network offered. Few Southern Baptists cared to hearken to a word of caution about the dangers of growth and big budgets, of institutional hubris in a competitive and acquisitive culture. Their appetites were not for the sort of justice the dissenters envisioned.

A sense of irony marked Southern Baptists' attitudes toward poor people and distressed workers, particularly in light of the working-class identities of most members of SBC churches throughout the first century and a quarter of their existence as a denomination. Typically, Southern Baptists stayed out of disputes involving organized labor, siding in most cases, if at all, with owners and management against unionized workers. With few exceptions, principally depression-era statements of support for workers in particular industries,[73] Southern Baptists maintained, individually and institutionally, a conservative stance toward the demands of organized labor. CLC leadership in the Foy Valentine era was more conservative on economic issues than on practically anything else they addressed, offering little other than acceptance of the basic premises of capitalism in the United States.[74] These stances were ironic because many Southern Baptists had modest incomes or had come from humble or even impoverished backgrounds. Perry Perkins, the Mississippi-born son of a Southern Baptist minister who was influenced by Carlyle Marney, was one of the few Southern Baptists who took their work in reconciliation into the realm of labor organizing. The younger Perkins had greatly appreciated the stories he had heard about Marney and the example of Will Campbell, and he participated in a network of influence and encouragement that supported his interests in Christian activism.[75]

In addition to an antitriumphal mentality, people in the dissenter network proposed a view of American and southern culture under the authority of Jesus that called for a conceptualization of peace different from that most southerners, let alone Southern Baptists, were likely to accept. Progressive Southern Baptists worked within and against a resistant culture that viewed peace almost as a negative concept, something suggesting weakness. The dissenters pursued reconciliation, suggesting still another irony. Criticism, and often open hostility, nearly always accompanied their actions. They were forced to learn a lesson formulated by one of their members, that "peace, like war, is waged."[76] It comes, they believed, out of active pursuit of reconciliation, a position that alienates many people whose lives and viewpoints are oriented around the ideas of conflict and oppression. Martin England believed that by attending to the earthly conditions in which people lived, churches could touch their spiritual lives more authentically, saying, "If we worked as hard to get Heaven into people here, as we do to get people into Heaven hereafter, we might do both." Ken Sehested said, "[W]hen you talk about heaven—biblically speaking—you're liable to raise hell."[77] Either way, upsetting messages usually did not elicit grateful responses, whether the message had to do with international affairs or race relations in the South. For some of the dissenters, an intense interest in peace and justice flowed out of their work in civil rights. Their eyes were opened to the broader context of problems in which the drama of race relations was played out. To others, civil rights activism grew out of their work with peace. But like the others, they viewed racial justice as an example, a manifestation of the need for reconciliation, a quest that nearly always brought conflict. Sometimes the conflict appeared within the group seeking to play a reconciling role, particularly in the intentional communities or other intensive small groups that expected personal commitment from their members and that relied on the same few people to do myriad demanding tasks. According to Reconcilers Fellowship member Joe Gatlin, "community is hell"; it does not automatically result in sunshine and happiness. Community requires a vast amount of effort to cultivate and nurture and has to take place alongside the work already under way to fulfill the stated functions of the community. The work of such communities, like that of the broader networks of dissent with which they were affiliated, brought on its own sorts of conflicts with the larger culture.[78]

In another departure from Southern Baptist norms, dissenters demonstrated through their involvement with peace and reconciliation, as they had with race relations, that they had little concern for the traditional institutional goals of the denomination. They also demonstrated that they cared little about trying to change the institutional manifestations of Southern Baptist culture, a position they and others involved in civil rights activism had chosen. Their female colleagues, however, trying to gain a foothold for women in ministry among the vast reaches of Southern Baptist life, had quite a different attitude and experienced quite a different reaction from the mainstream of the denomination. In that part of the story of the genealogy of dissent, the network of women in ministry, one of the key ingredients of cultural change that was missing from the efforts for racial justice and for peace and reconciliation began to emerge, a sense that the network constituted a movement. The reaction it elicited from mainstream Southern Baptist life told volumes about the prospects for survival, let alone success, of a dissident culture among Southern Baptists in the closing years of the twentieth century. It was a reaction that called up forces that went against nearly every goal for which the dissenters yearned in their appetite for justice.

# 5 Community and Faithfulness

## A Genealogy of Dissident Southern Baptist Women

*We've a story to tell to the nations,*
*That shall turn their hearts to the right,*
*A story of truth and mercy,*
*A story of peace and light.*
—H. Ernest Nichol, *We've a Story to Tell*

Most members of the first three generations of the family of progressive Southern Baptist dissidents were males whose networks provided a measure of emotional support in the absence of the relationships that traditional pastors and laypeople received from Southern Baptist institutional life. Their personal ties and their sense of community, if small and far-flung, helped bind them to the causes they embraced, providing encouragement that they were not as alone as they often felt. They and their conservative counterparts knew that the issues they raised and the causes they championed presented threats to traditional southern and Baptist ways of life. As troubling as their activities were to the traditionalists, however, their small numbers and frequent aloofness from denominational institutions and activities made them fairly easy to ignore. A greater threat to the ease Southern Baptists felt in their American Zion came from a source few people anticipated, one within the very backbone of the rank-and-file of their institutional life: women.

Like most Christian bodies throughout church history, Southern Baptist congregations had a clear pattern of division of labor. Women did the majority of the work maintaining the health of the church, while men held most of the leadership positions, especially those of deacons—laypersons set apart from the rest of the membership through ordination—and pastors. New Testament passages refer to deacons as servants within churches, people charged particularly with ministering to the needs of the bereaved and abandoned through acts of comfort and charity, and include women among their number. In Southern Baptist practice, though, deacons functioned most frequently as boards of directors for congregations, conferring with pastors on policy matters such as the willingness of previously segregated churches to admit African Americans as members. While many pastors carried heavy responsibilities for visiting the sick and aggrieved within their churches, women did much more of this sort of ministry than their male counterparts among the laity. Women also did the bulk of the work of religious education for children and young people, countless acts of hospitality and fellowship through the preparation and hosting of meals and other gatherings, a myriad of activities having to do with maintenance of church property, record keeping, and other responsibilities central to institutional well-being. They also assumed most of the responsibility for raising funds for the work of missionaries, one of the most important jobs in Southern Baptist life.[1]

In a denomination that defined itself according to the "Great Commission" found in John 3:16, "going" and "making disciples" throughout the world constituted the highest calling and merited all of the resources churches could put together. Missions often took the form of the local sort of witnessing Otis Strickland and his friend Jess Redford did in Fort Worth, but the more visible and elaborated manifestation of soul winning came through the efforts of full-time missionaries commissioned by the Foreign and Home Mission Boards of the SBC. These missionaries, whose numbers included laywomen as well as laymen and clergymen, were salaried employees of Southern Baptist agencies and were sent by the thousands to many parts of the United States and many foreign countries. Their expenses, and those of maintaining the offices and staffs of the mission boards, required the annual expenditure of millions of dollars. Much of the money necessary to fund Southern Baptist mission work came to the agencies through a disbursement plan called the Cooperative Program, devised in 1925 after the debacle of the Seventy-Five Million Campaign. Southern Baptist congregations sent self-determined amounts of money through central denominational offices, which forwarded designated percentages of receipts to the mission boards. Much additional funding, however, came from two major solicitation campaigns, one for home missions and one for foreign missions. Both campaigns were managed and promoted by the Woman's Missionary Union (WMU), the most powerful group of women in the Southern Baptist organizational system and one of the most significant and remarkable women's groups in the history of American evangelicalism.[2]

Although male ministers did the preaching connected with Southern Baptist mission offerings, exhorting the faithful to give funds necessary to help spread the gospel, the stamp of women was on every other aspect of the efforts. The two offerings were named for Southern Baptist women, the closest the denomination ever came to canonization, Annie Armstrong for home missions at Easter time and Lottie Moon for foreign missions at Christmas. WMU members in local churches and volunteer and paid staff workers on the state and southwide levels organized promotional programs, distributed literature, and personally solicited gifts for the offerings. They gave or arranged for others to give testimonies about the power of changed lives through the experience of Christian conversion, sometimes verging on preaching but always careful not to infringe on pastors' carefully protected roles as the recognized spiritual leaders of congregations and conventions and their various agencies and institutions.[3]

WMU workers toiled throughout the year, not just at Easter and Christmas, particularly in missions-education efforts with their junior counterparts, the Girls' Auxiliary (GA), later called Girls in Action. WMU workers and GAs developed an elaborate system of levels of achievement, similar to those used by women's affiliates of Masonic orders, based on knowledge of Baptist history, missionary endeavors, and the history and culture of foreign countries in which Southern Baptists had missionaries. They met regularly on local, state, and denominational levels for informational and inspirational programs, developing their own subculture within the life of Southern Baptists based on common knowledge, rituals, and especially songs. One of the theme songs of the WMU and GAs was "We've a Story to Tell," which emphasized both the evangelistic nature of their work and their personal involvement in the story that was being told. GA and WMU experiences gave female Southern Baptists a place of dynamic service, leadership training, and recognition for their efforts. They also planted, quite inadvertently, the seeds of dissent among many Southern Baptist women who grew up being told that they should be servants for the work of spreading the love of Jesus to all the world, turning the hearts of the unsaved world "to the right," the kind of relationship with God that the Gospels say Jesus embodied and favored for all people. As long as these women remained content to exercise their inclinations and gifts for leadership within the all-female arenas of WMU and GAs, no one in Southern Baptist life objected to their taking on highly visible roles in the work of the churches and the conventions. Male leaders of churches and denominational structures appreciated the work of the women, both in the WMU and in other areas of church life, but they wanted it to remain clear that what the women did was "women's work." The time came, however, when not all Southern Baptist women were content to allow that understanding of their roles to remain in place.[4]

Southern Baptist women were an unlikely source of agitation for dramatic cultural change within their denomination. Especially through the WMU, they had a distinct voice, if a limited one, within the heart of Southern Baptist life; a great amount of money and other resources under some degree of their control, and a structure that they controlled without direction from any other organizational element in the Southern Baptist system of polity. They flourished under the system as it was and therefore were hardly radicals. They earned, however, a decided reputation as a powerful force, one no pastor or denominational official wanted to alienate or anger. Occasionally over the first 125 years of Southern Baptist history, some women challenged various aspects of the institutional status quo in acts ranging from requesting election as messengers to previously all-male conventions and acceptance as students in similarly all-male seminaries to expressing a desire to preach. One by one, such innovations passed into practice, with the exception of the last. Women won removal of the ban on women messengers and even began addressing conventions in missions-related efforts. They began to take places alongside male seminary students, though it was always assumed that if their intentions were to enter "full-time Christian service" after graduation from seminary, then their work would be as "directors," not "ministers" of education in local churches; as paid WMU staff members; as missionaries in health-related or other nonpastoral positions; or as wives of ministers whom they met during their seminary studies. Until the 1970s, few Southern Baptists, women or men, challenged the accepted wisdom that women were not meant to preach.[5]

When some women in Southern Baptist life began to seek to do that very thing, they drew on a tradition of leadership that had been nurtured within the denomination rather than imported from outside. From their days in the frontier regions of the young United States, Southern Baptists historically depended on women to keep their churches "going," but women only became "strong enough to insist on their right to" an SBC-wide organization of their own in 1888. The courage to make such an insistence came in part from women's determination to live up to the standards and expectations placed before them by their traditional role as the backbone of southern churches. Though their Baptist brethren remained immovable in their opposition to women's rights throughout the nineteenth century and well into the twentieth, they encouraged women nevertheless to continue to take on increasingly important responsibilities on behalf of missionary efforts. The skills women gained in such activities served them well and set them on a course that led to a growing sense of dissatisfaction among ever larger numbers of them.[6]

For women in Southern Baptist life who had a desire or willingness to depart from traditional ways of conceiving and acting out their faith as Christians and their identity as Baptists, one principal issue prevailed: the desire for ministerial positions. More than any other measure of status, progress, or worth, they wanted jobs within convention structures, in congregations and agencies, and in educational, health-care, and similar institutions, and not just in the kinds of roles traditionally seen as women's work. Their desire for such positions came in part from the simple fact that increasing numbers of women entered the workforce in the United States during and after World War II, the period during which small but increasing numbers of Southern Baptist women began to press for positions as ministers and other kinds of paid denominational workers. Like many other women in the United States, they needed work. Other, deeper forces, however, impelled their efforts for change among Southern Baptists, especially the desire for recognition or validation of what they saw as the logical vocational extension of their attempts to follow Jesus, the faithfulness to a vision of the Great Commission that they had cultivated throughout Southern Baptist history. In part, their attitudes reflected the influences of the women's movement in the 1960s and 1970s, but their form of feminism was blended with an ecclesiastical traditionalism that gave it a decidedly Southern Baptist character. They exerted an effort to bring themselves into the mainstream of Southern Baptist employment practices for ministers and similar positions in denominational settings and in the process created the closest thing to an actual movement that Southern Baptist progressive activists ever achieved. Such a program set them apart in several dramatic ways from their mostly sympathetic male colleagues in the network of dissenters among Southern Baptists, particularly regarding their attitudes toward the SBC. Remarkable ironies ensued as women tried to find their way through a rapidly changing Southern Baptist landscape, one that was changing in large part because of the very activities in which they were engaged.[7]

## An Inadvertent Radicalism

Churches and churchpeople, even liberal ones, historically have had ambivalent attitudes toward the idea of women in leadership roles. Walter

Rauschenbusch argued that much of the message of Jesus is directed toward the "release" of people held captive to the oppressive forces of society and that Christian churches often had a liberating effect on women, that people in Christian churches did much to help liberate women from some of the traditional restrictions on their lives, to "elevate" them, in his view. Church contributions to such liberation, however, came about through gradual, often contradictory processes, by "indirect and diffused influences rather than by any direct championship of the organized Church." The great social gospel pioneer believed that, in fact, "most of the great Churches through their teaching and organization have exerted a conservative and retarding influence on the rise of woman to equality with man" and that they often have been "indifferent or hostile to the effects" to which they contributed: "The mother has refused to acknowledge her own children."[8] In this way, except for the well-defined roles traditionally assigned to them, Southern Baptist women lived out the experience of countless churchwomen who had gone before them.

Men in the networks of progressive Southern Baptist dissent were generally sympathetic toward the vocational interests of women in churches, some highly so. Some of them came to their views of the moral authority of women out of personal experience. Martin England believed that Clarence Jordan's mother had been the crucial influence on his rejection of the plans his father had set for him, to gain a university degree in agriculture and military experience and then to return to run the huge family farm. She had wanted him to be a minister all along. England, of course, had been deeply, decisively influenced by a woman, his grandmother, in his vocational direction.[9] England and Jordan had much in common with many of their fellow southern males whose conceptions of the South and of the role of church life in the region were wrapped together with their views of the roles of mothers in society. They embraced a high view of the moral standing and leadership mothers had a right and duty to exert in the Baptist South. England and Jordan, however, and Walt Johnson before them, did not take their appreciation of women's roles in church life to the level many other southern males did. They rejected the repressive web of social relations that required women to stay in their "place." They rejected the social system that meted out harsh punishments to anyone, especially black males who gave the slightest indication, real or imagined, that they dared to flaunt the Maryology of the South, the veneration of white women, especially mothers.[10]

Younger dissidents developed a receptivity to women's calls for inclusiveness as a philosophical outgrowth of their general views of the nature of church life and its place in the larger culture. Some of them saw it as illogical to take stands on behalf of black liberation and refuse to do so on behalf of the freedom of women to choose the ways to direct their service to the same God whose teachings mandated freedom for oppressed blacks. While some dissidents helped create the bases out of which women worked, sexism existed among Southern Baptist "liberals." Many inspirational relationships were formed between dissenters such as Carlyle Marney and women who invoked his honesty and courage as the example that gave them the strength to go against the grain of their religious upbringing. Ultimately, however, the women created their own network to deal in part with the fact that most males in the genealogy of dissent did not, could not, or would not do much to help them. For a variety of reasons, the men failed to do enough to open their part of Southern Baptist life to women who were their natural allies, and to members of various branches of the dissident family tree, by giving them places of service sufficient to keep them connected with the network of dissenters or, in many cases, with Southern Baptist life itself.

An inadvertent form of radicalism arose among Southern Baptist women, derived from several streams of influence, including ties some of them had to the network of reformers that grew out of the influence of Walt Johnson and others. Women moved through the work for civil rights, peace, and abolition of the death penalty at many points and gained organizational and philosophical insights from the efforts of people in the civil rights movement. Some drew strength from the general feminist awakening that took place in the years after World War II and from long experiences in activism by American women, including churchwomen. For women dissidents, however, the strongest inspiration came from possibly the most surprising source in the genealogy of dissent. It came from deep within the heart of Southern Baptist life, the very focus of the denomination: evangelism. Women who had been brought up in Southern Baptist churches from the early part of the twentieth century until well into the 1970s frequently had the experience of training for the support of evangelism and limited participation in evangelism itself. To its planners and supporters, such training and work seemed to have the most traditional and institutionally safe intended results. Furthermore, the work of these women took place in the context of such trusted organizations as the WMU and GA. In many cases, these organizations accomplished their stated goals with remarkable effectiveness. For a sizable number of women, however, the GA and WMU created an unintentional undercurrent of radicalism that caused many women who had grown up Southern Baptist to question the assumptions behind this common experience and sent shock waves through the entire SBC. This radicalism found its most dramatic expression in the quest of growing numbers of women for ordination as ministers.[11]

Some Baptist women in the South who felt called to the ministry did so almost in isolation. Once they made it clear that they could not tolerate fulfilling the traditional roles ascribed to women in Southern Baptist life, they had little in the way of networks of support. They relied instead on their own determination, their sense that God was leading them in the direction of a vocation they could not ignore, and the willingness of a Baptist congregation, and a male pastor, to help them become ordained. One such woman was Addie Davis, the first woman ordained as a minister by a congregation affiliated with the SBC. Once she gained ordination, she went through an experience she described as one of "exile." She had to leave her homeland and seek a place of service in the North to practice the vocation she believed she had been given by God, through the inspiration and nurturing of people in the South. Her experience showed, in some small ways, how people's attitudes are conditioned by what they observe. She once noticed some children of the congregation she was serving in Vermont "playing church." When one of the little boys wanted to take his turn being the preacher, his older sister admonished him, saying, "You can't be the preacher; only women are preachers!" Such was not the attitude of most of the people from the region of her upbringing.[12]

Davis hoped to find a place of service in the South. She went to seminary at Southeastern in Wake Forest, North Carolina, and received ordination from the Watts Street Baptist Church in Durham during the pastorate of Warren Carr. She approached Carr, whom she had known slightly during her years of service on the staff of Meredith College, the Southern Baptist-related women's school in Raleigh. She tried unsuccessfully to interest churches in the Raleigh area to consider her request for ordination, then went to see Carr and told him that she had received from God a "call to be a preaching minister" that was "firm and particular and definite." He was no stranger to hostile reactions to unpopular positions on the questions of the day and agreed to help her achieve her goal. He went to the deacons of the church and told them that Davis had told him "that God will not let her rest until she has answered and is able to fulfill a call to parish and pulpit ministry . . . and I do not intend to . . . hinder that in any way." The deacons also declined to hinder her attempt to do what she considered the faithful thing and recommended that she stand for examination by the associational committee that was used in those days to determine fitness for ordination. In Carr's mind, Davis was helped by the fact that her examination followed a mediocre, yet successful, performance by a young man seeking ordination and the fact that she responded to the questions put to her with obvious orthodoxy and ample eloquence. Those who objected to approving her were in the minority, although the ordination did not pass without adverse publicity for Watts Street, Carr, and Davis. She was quite taken, and a little surprised, by the vitriolic tone of the letters she and he received.[13]

Because she left the South to practice her vocation, and was gone for more than fifteen years of the most turbulent period of women's struggles to win ordination, Addie Davis was virtually unknown, personally, to Southern Baptist women. She served a powerful role, however, as a symbol, a figure of almost legendary quality, not only as a pioneering ordained woman and as someone who had to leave the South to fulfill her calling, but also as a woman who achieved her goal of pastoring a church. Other Southern Baptist women who wanted to be ministers and who were determined to stay in the South and to remain Baptists experienced much turmoil that colored their view of their vocation, the costs of faithfulness, and the need for community.[14]

## An "Incarnational" Ministry

Another woman who walked the lonely path of faithfulness to her sense of vocation was Martha Gilmore, who was ordained to the ministry by Cliff Temple Baptist Church in Dallas in 1977. At the time she was ordained, thirteen years after Addie Davis in North Carolina, Gilmore was one of two women ministers among the two million Southern Baptists in Texas.[15] Her story is an example of what happened to women who tried to break new ground in traditional areas of Southern Baptist life and of the costs of isolation in such ground breaking. By traditional measures, she was no stranger to the denomination, having deep roots in Southern Baptist life, but she was brought up with a fiercely independent way of looking at religious questions that challenged Baptists with their own history as advocates of religious freedom. Part of her own family history had to do with women's fomenting insurrection among Baptists. In 1882, her great-grandmother addressed the Baptist state convention in Alabama agitating for the creation of a women's organization on the model of what later came to be the WMU and creating a controversy among the males in attendance. Gilmore's interpretation of the story was that "the argument really was over money and power," that women might become independent of the convention's control and break out of their traditional roles in handling large amounts of money derived from missions giving. As Gilmore grew up going to church and being involved in children's and youth activities, she developed what she described as an idealistic desire to be of service to God, a sense "of being special and that God would use me in some way," and a strong spirit of competitiveness that made her feel that she had exactly the same resources to offer and right to offer them as anyone, male or female. She also realized that there were limits to how far she would follow the denominational way of doing things. As a member of the church's Sunday school class for sixteen-year-olds, she refused, for instance, to add up the number of people for whom she had prayed during the previous week, one of the items on the checklist of faithful Christian service as understood by Sunday school planners and leaders. To her, "Christian commitment . . . was very incarnational. . . . It has never been for me the adherence to right doctrine. It's just been a loving attitude, loving and caring."[16]

Gilmore's understandings of her place in Christian service underwent some testing and tempering after she left home for school and then marriage. At the insistence of her parents, Gilmore reluctantly enrolled at Baylor University, a place that for women in the 1950s seemed to her in many ways to be "a finishing school." Although she had some challenging professors, including especially an iconoclastic history professor named Ralph Lynn, she became extremely angry during her time in school over the waste of effort required in educating women and then expecting them to do nothing with any other part of their knowledge than that related to homemaking. She left her undergraduate experience with a determination to "take some responsibility for my gifts and graces."[17] An important step in developing that sense of responsibility came during her time in Austin, Texas, where she and her husband, Jerry Gilmore, lived while he was a law student at the University of Texas. They belonged to the First Baptist Church in Austin while Carlyle Marney was pastor, and she came to feel intensely influenced by his commitment to connect the teachings of Jesus with the issues of the day, especially the civil rights struggles to which Marney threw his support and prestige.[18] The turning point for her came in 1973 when she was helping some people put on a seminar for chaplains at Perkins School of Theology on the campus of Southern Methodist University in Dallas, to which she and her husband had moved after his completion of law school. She had done some studies of various kinds of therapy and became involved in helping present some of the material for the seminar through friends who were chaplains, including Ken Pepper and Richard Christian. Near the end of the seminar, Christian "looked at me and he said, 'Martha, have you ever thought about being a chaplain? You'd be a natural.' I don't think it could have been any more powerful had I been Lazurus and the Lord had called me forth. I said, 'Richard, I've been thinking about it for about six months and I haven't even told Jerry.'" She mentioned her idea to a friend who responded, "You've always been a minister," and told her husband, "Don't laugh, but I'm thinking about going to seminary." He did not laugh, and she began to investigate her prospects for theological study, choosing to go to Methodist-related Perkins instead of Southwestern Baptist Theological Seminary in nearby Fort Worth. Southwestern seemed too large, too conservative, and, although she had no intention at that point of seeking ordination to pastoral ministry, somewhat hostile toward the idea of women ministers.[19]

As she went through the process of becoming ordained to the ministry, she believed in the late 1970s that her struggle with the SBC as it was at that time would be difficult enough. Little did she realize that the Southern Baptist environment was on the verge of becoming even more hostile toward women ministers, with the fundamentalist resurgency movement that began with the election of a militant biblical literalist, Adrian Rogers, to the convention presidency in 1979.[20] In fact, she had no intention of being a trailblazer simply for its own sake. Becoming or being one of the few Southern Baptist women ministers in Texas or elsewhere was far less important to her than answering "the call to the gospel." She believed she could remain within the denomination and "represent it well," despite the fact that she had many quarrels with it, including her home church, Cliff Temple, which still had only male deacons when it ordained her as a minister. She wrestled with the question of the appropriateness of women's ordination in the course of her study of historical theology and concluded that the thinking of the early church developed under the influence of primitive understandings of women. Such understandings included outright fear of the reproductive power of women, hence the continuation of limitations that originated among the ancient Hebrews on the activities of women during certain times of the menstrual cycle in various branches of the church.[21] Gilmore likened such practices to ancient views of slavery also reflected in Christian writings but hardly appropriate for or intended to be binding on followers of Jesus for all time. She remembered being told that the pain women experience in childbirth should not be lessened by drugs: "You're supposed to hurt because you're [being] punished because you're evil." Such attitudes, she believed, kept many people, including Southern Baptists, from trusting the role of minister to women. Believing that such views were outmoded and unhealthy did not keep Gilmore from having to struggle to overcome her own hesitancy about going against biblical passages such as Paul's admonitions to women to "keep silent" in church and not to put themselves into positions of authority over men. She began to realize, however, that she was increasingly annoyed over having been made to feel this way, and she began to "claim" or recognize the value of the anger that such a realization aroused in her during her seminary studies. She realized also that she was not alone in feeling such anger, saying, "I can be with a woman student right now for about five minutes and I can tell you how far along in seminary she is. About the second year they're usually romping, stomping mad." To her, the greatest source of anger in her own experience came from realizing that she had "done the whole thing," had had countless responsibilities in connection with her membership in various churches over the years, but had never been allowed to participate in the policy-making, decision-making bodies of the church, because their memberships were restricted to men. For Gilmore, membership in WMU was simply not enough.[22]

In her mind, the worst instance of the harmful effects of traditionalist views of women on the behavior of men in churches came during a meeting of the board of deacons of Cliff Temple Baptist Church, her beloved home congregation, which she and her husband had joined when they returned to Dallas and which she was studying for one of her courses in seminary for a term project on power in churches. The point of the project was to help students become accustomed to the idea that power exists in all institutions, including churches, and that it is not necessarily a bad or "ungodly" thing. She had to reconcile a lot of experience to come to the same conclusion.

> The night I went to deacon's meeting was just awful. It was the first [time] women had been there in years. Things were said like, "Jerry is letting Martha go to school and she's here to tell us what she's doing and ask us something." . . . It was during a recession . . . that the United States was going through at that time, . . . the fall of '74. The chairman of the board of deacons said, "Now our budget's behind, but . . . I see you men buying your women nice rings and dressing them up. . . . I don't think we're going through any recession or that's any excuse." I thought: "I am in a time tunnel and I have suddenly gone back a hundred years." It took me several days to absorb that experience. . . . I came out with a very heavy, oppressed feeling that we're really going to be a long time digging out of this.[23]

Not long after the visit to the deacons at Cliff Temple, Gilmore was asked by a Presbyterian minister friend to preach, her first time to perform that particular pastoral duty. She took a course in preaching at Perkins and found that she felt more comfortable preaching than she would have thought possible in earlier days. At one point a woman told her, "I've never seen a woman minister preach," and she answered her, "I've never seen it either." She was beginning to do something for which she had no model, something she had to make a huge effort to give herself permission to do: "I still have a very awesome feeling about the preached word as being the oldest tradition, that apostolic tradition of how God's Word was transmitted. It's a very powerful responsibility . . . the thought that I can bear the Word for others. It's just such a privilege and such a responsibility."[24]

Gilmore still had to deal with the question of ordination for herself. Despite her studies in a United Methodist seminary and the sense that she was receiving support and nurturing from Methodism, she continued to think of herself "as Baptist by birth. That's my heritage. That's my birthright. That's something that will never be taken away from me." During a term of service as a chaplain-in-training at Dallas's Parkland Hospital, a couple Gilmore had helped asked her if she would marry them. She asked the pastor at Cliff Temple if the church could give her a license to perform weddings. He hesitated at first, saying the county courthouse should be able to take care of her. They referred her back to the church and the pastor somewhat unenthusiastically agreed to make the arrangements. The certificate she received was a form produced by a company that provided office materials for Southern Baptist churches to which the licensing congregation added the name of the person licensed. Hers read "Martha Louise Gilmore has given evidence that God has called him into the gospel ministry." Because licensure did not guarantee ordination in Baptist polity, Gilmore's license to preach did not make her an actual minister but something more akin to an apprentice. After a fairly short time, however, she was ready to ask for ordination, which required a recommendation by the board of deacons of the church, a vote by the members of the congregation, and examination by a council drawn from the membership. Gilmore knew from personal experience serving on ordination councils for men that the process could be considerably streamlined, but the pastor described it to her as a very drawn-out affair with many opportunities to be undone along the way. For Gilmore, the process of receiving validation and authorization from a congregation of which she had been a part for most of her life, a process she had seen take a few days for men, dragged out for two months. She came to realize that the process should always be as carefully crafted as hers was, but she thought it unfair that men's ordinations in Baptist churches seldom seemed to receive such scrutiny.[25]

Some of the resistance to Gilmore's ordination took the form of foot-dragging, some of it coming from the chair of the deacon board and some from the pastor, A. Douglas Watterson. Watterson was generally helpful and publicly supportive. He gave Gilmore the impression that he accepted the validity of ordaining women in principle, and certainly he could have derailed the process completely at various points. He exhibited, however, a lack of enthusiasm for the enterprise that was perhaps understandable in light of the controversy he surely knew would ensue. The fact that Cliff Temple was located in the Oak Cliff section of Dallas and had a less conservative reputation than the city itself did not dilute the fact that the church was embarking on a pathbreaking venture in a city and a denomination that seldom welcomed this sort of innovation. Watterson ultimately did not shy away from the task, though it could have had adverse effects on his career as a Southern Baptist minister. Part of the reason came from the fact that Martha Gilmore was a much-beloved child of the church, a fact that put the issue of women's ordination into a different light in her case. As she put it, if one were to "go up to folk in Cliff Temple and say, 'Do you believe in women ministers?' . . . they would say, 'No.' Then you could say next, 'Do you believe in Martha Gilmore being ordained?' and they'd say, 'Yes.'" She made the issue personal for the people of the church.[26]

In making the issue of women's ordination personal, Gilmore did something many women ministers and other progressive dissenters believe they did in Southern Baptist life. She embodied a principle, doing in a particular instance what Christians believe Jesus did on the universal level, making God's presence visible to people. They embodied, or "incarnated," the love of God on earth in smaller versions of the grand way Jesus did. This sort of "incarnational" theology and practice gave progressive dissenters a mandate for placing themselves among people who needed to hear a prophetic word of reminder of God's expectations of them. They sought to be "present to" people, comforting them at times but challenging them as well when they needed to be challenged. In such ways, they incarnated, on a small scale, the love of God that Jesus embodied on earth and offers perpetually through the Holy Spirit. "Incarnational" understandings permeated the work of Martin England, Ken Sehested, and others who placed themselves among people who needed to be stirred up. It was a model that characterized much of the work of any ministry, including missionary service, that placed the church's representatives in danger of either actual physical harm or social disapproval. The model, however, could be avoided to a great extent by modern institutionalized congregations. Pastors of large urban congregations with multiple staff members to handle the day-to-day contacts with chronic problems such as homelessness and hunger could remain "above" the kinds of situations that required them to do things that could be considered risky. In Gilmore's mind, she was a "godsend" to Doug Watterson because she gave him an opportunity to act on an impulse she thought he had in favor of removing an unjust restriction on women.[27]

Other people in Dallas did not view the matter in the same way. Press reporters began to pick up on the story building at Cliff Temple. Gilmore became the subject of angry callers on radio talk shows: "[T]hese people calling in about this horrible woman that was going to be ordained! It was just a nightmare." On the night the church voted to call the ordination council, one reporter in attendance tried to pit Gilmore against First Baptist Church pastor W.A. Criswell, long noted for his literalist positions on Scripture and opposition to nontraditional roles for women. She answered that there were many different kinds of Baptist views on various subjects, a position she also took during her ordination examination when asked why someone with a Methodist theological education wanted to be ordained as a Baptist minister. She answered that she valued the autonomy of Baptist congregations and their historic advocacy of the idea of the priesthood of the believer. After she passed her examination by the council, another set of objections appeared from outside the congregation. Contrary to the rules governing congregational discussion, the deacon chair, who had strong objections to the ordination of women, allowed students at ultraconservative Dallas Theological Seminary, some of them not members of Cliff Temple, to address the church during the discussion called to consider the recommendation of the ordination council that Gilmore be ordained by the church. Gilmore sat behind the students during the meeting. At one point, one of them turned to her and said, "Now, I do want you to know this is not anything personal." She held her arm out to the student and said, "Touch it. I want you to know it is personal. I am a person who's called to ministry and you're calling it into question. And if you're willing to go forward with that after all we've been through in this church, you take that responsibility." He refused to touch her, "turned around and that was the last eye contact I had with him." The spokesman for the students made a classic blunder by prefacing his remarks with a statement that he and his colleagues had come to the meeting that night to impart the truth to a church that had not been told the truth before. Members of the church, especially older members who had known Gilmore all of her life, began to grumble. When the vote was taken, Gilmore's ordination was overwhelmingly approved, and was opposed principally by the seminary students, several of whom had no right to vote in the first place. Amazingly, to Gilmore, one of them came to her ordination the following Sunday night. She told him that it must have taken courage to come to the service, and he told her that his friends had ostracized him for doing so. She received ordination and began her new life as a minister of the gospel.[28]

Gilmore soon began to realize how alone she was. She was not just a minister; she was a female Southern Baptist minister.[29] The first event she attended as a minister was a lunch meeting of the Oak Cliff Ministerial Alliance. The women serving the food "just could not realize that I was a minister. . . . [T]hey just couldn't absorb it." They seated her at a table by herself. The other ministers could hardly look at her. She also realized that nothing had changed, even at Cliff Temple. Neither she nor any other woman was asked to take major responsibility in the life of the church other than one invitation to Gilmore to "speak," not "preach," at a Wednesday night prayer service, the closest thing to an invitation to preach that she received from any Baptist body. She began to realize that she had entered into a category of experience similar to that of a minister with whom she became acquainted and whose church was kicked out of the Dallas Baptist Association during the time Gilmore was doing her seminary study at Perkins. Howard Conatser led the Beverly Hills Baptist Church in Dallas, which had become heavily involved in the charismatic movement, a neopentecostal renewal effort that cut across denominational lines and alarmed many leaders of traditionalist church bodies that had discouraged such activities as speaking in unknown tongues and faith healing. The Dallas Baptist Association, dominated by the huge First Baptist Church of Dallas, withdrew fellowship from Beverly Hills, whose pastor, according to Gilmore, "was more interested, than any Baptist minister I had met to date had been, in what I was doing in seminary. I felt such a kinship with him. I think it was because we both were questioning authority and structures." Although Gilmore did not consider herself charismatic, she realized that she and Conatser had in common a view "that the Holy Spirit is that which dictates one's own call or one's own direction." Her contacts with him made her aware of how "hungry" she was for fellowship within the denomination of her upbringing. She thought she would find it in the CLC of the Baptist General Convention of Texas, headquartered in Dallas. Several CLC staff members were members of Cliff Temple, friends of hers, and people who were "theoretically, intellectually" in favor of women's ordination, but, she found, "emotionally and attitudinally" resistant to the idea. She recognized some evidence of support for changing roles for women in churches among the Southern Baptist CLC, but found, to her great surprise, that the most dynamic vision for women in ministry came from the WMU.[30]

In 1978, WMU leaders helped organize a conference on the status of women in Southern Baptist life in 1978 that illustrated to Gilmore the division between men and women in the denomination. Various representatives of Southern Baptist agencies and institutions attended the conference, some of whom made presentations, but the highpoint for Gilmore came during comments made from the floor during a time for open discussion. Gladys Lewis, a former foreign missionary,[31] told of returning from missionary service and being proposed as a deacon in her home church in Oklahoma, something that practically split the church. She told of the confusion the experience created in her, knowing, as Gilmore put it, that "she'd served . . . with glory and affirmation as a missionary, but to know this same person could not serve the church as a deacon." Hearing Lewis speak made Gilmore think of her own experience.

> I think she touched my confusion. I've never been the foreign missionary, but I've been . . . the Cliff Temple missionary! I've just done it all. . . . After she spoke, then [Southern Baptist agency head] Jimmy Allen spoke. I appreciated some of what he said very much, yet, . . . I don't see any action that has come from what he said . . . He said for instance, that the churches are responsible for the anger. He hoped that women who are frustrated wouldn't be consumed by anger . . . Yet I am not aware of his calling an ordained woman and asking that woman to preach at his church. He's not called me. Maybe he asked somebody else.

Gilmore's assessment of the attitude of the denominational officials at the conference toward the women in attendance was that the women were like teenagers to whom they had "given everything," yet it was "time to leave home. . . . [Y]ou've given them so much, and you've made it so comfortable, and you just can't figure out why they could be dissatisfied."[32]

The real eye-opening experience at the conference occurred for Gilmore at an informal "caucus" of ordained women in attendance. By the time of the conference about thirty women had been ordained Southern Baptist ministers; Gilmore had met none of them up to that point. Their names were on a list that several of them had compiled. Gilmore felt excited as these women began to spot each other by reading name tags at the conference: "One of them said, 'You're on the list!' and just threw her arms around me." At the caucus, the excitement was tinged with other emotions: "There was pain in that room. Boy! I got in there and thought, 'I haven't had near the struggle that a lot of women have had.'" WMU leader Catherine Allen met with the women and "was appalled at the lack of political sense" and "naive feelings" of many of the women, one of whom, a woman who had not been ordained yet and was having second thoughts about pursuing it, told Gilmore later that she had been "troubled . . . by the anger in the group, and she was scared of becoming angry like that." Gilmore herself was saddened by the disillusionment and disappointment many of the women expressed "at the broken promises and the words that don't have action" to back them up, but was heartened by the fact that one of the women in attendance agreed to edit a newsletter to help the women keep in touch with each other, and others agreed to help organize subsequent meetings. In the late 1970s, however, Gilmore's expectation, based on conversations with Catherine Allen and Southern Baptist WMU executive director Carolyn Weatherford was that the best hope ordained women in Southern Baptist life had to achieve any significant standing was to join forces with the WMU: "Let's face it, ordained women don't have any power anywhere, and WMU's got a lot of power." Gilmore felt hopeful at the time from the fact "that they would be open to us, want to . . . train us, . . ."[33] In the 1980s, Southern Baptist women ministers developed their own organization, with the help of the WMU, but Martha Gilmore was not there to enjoy any possible resulting benefits. Disillusioned by the lack of hospitality by her own denomination, she gave up her Southern Baptist heritage in 1984 and became affiliated with her adopted denominational home, the United Methodist Church.[34]

## A Genealogy of Their Own

Younger women ministers, the second generation in their own genealogy of dissent, had many things in common with Martha Gilmore. The main differences between them and her, and between them and Addie Davis even more acutely, had to do with the availability of a network of support and nurture. Many of them had experience as members of GA and had absorbed as children the Southern Baptist worldview with a great passion and faithfulness.[35] They spoke the same language and knew the same stories. They also knew or found out that incarnation as a model of ministry can be both exhilarating and lonely.

By the early 1980s, several dozen Southern Baptist women had been ordained as ministers.[36] Their numbers had increased remarkably in light of the lack of encouragement they received from the male-dominated denomination and the absence of any formal networks of support for each other. Few of them knew much, if anything, about each other. Those who were aware of other women ministers sometimes had mixed feelings about getting in touch with them, despite the comfort such contact would give, lest they be seen as fomenting a rebellion. Many of them had a lonely existence.

When significant numbers decided that the situation could no longer be tolerated, they began to build in a more formal way what their male counterparts in the family of dissenters had informally, a network of communication and support. Women constructed a separate network and drew examples and some encouragement from other parts of the genealogy, but their tasks, needs, and tactics were different from those of the male dissenters. The ways they understood community also led to different ways of expressing it. Just participating in the (mostly male) networks of civil rights and peace supporters was not sufficient, partly because quite a bit of traditionalism existed even within the ranks of male ministers who held progressive views of race relations and peace. Some of them gave the impression they were threatened by liberated women in general and women ministers in particular. Although some women feared the impression of militancy that any sort of organization might give, more of them felt they needed their own networks of dissent. The result was an organization that devoted itself to helping women fit into traditional forms of Southern Baptist ministry and avoided open criticism of the SBC for the first several years of its existence. Its model, structure, and goals were remarkably, even surprisingly, traditional in light of the fact that its purpose was little short of revolutionary.[37]

In the 1980s, to a large extent, the history of women's involvement in cultural change among Southern Baptists became the history of the organization, Southern Baptist Women in Ministry (SBWIM). SBWIM grew directly out of the need felt by a growing number of women for an information and support network that would help legitimize their claims to standing as ministers and offer their fellow southern Baptists new perspectives on roles of women. Ideas for organization along these lines had existed in the minds of several Southern Baptist women ministers or women who wanted to be ministers for quite some time when Women in Ministry, SBC, formed in 1983. The organization began in direct contact with the SBC, particularly the CLC, and set its first meetings to coincide with meetings of the SBC in the same way other groups such as the (all-male) Pastors' Conference met just before the opening of each year's convention. The women who started SBWIM worked very closely with Southern Baptist officials and drew the plans for the organization with the idea that it would take a place within the institutional life of the convention and then pass out of existence. According to one of its founders, its purpose was to render itself unnecessary by helping women ministers assimilate into the everyday life of Southern Baptist service to the cause of the gospel. Its genesis, however, actually took place at a meeting of dissenters.[38]

In October 1982, a group of disaffected Southern Baptists gathered in Charlotte for a conference that its organizers called Theology Is a Verb. The core group of organizers came from the heart of the network of Southern Baptist dissidents, especially congregations in North Carolina that had historic ties to Walt Johnson. They assembled a mailing list drawn from their contacts in alternative Southern Baptist congregations. Such churches consciously departed from the SBC norm either by having active social ministry programs, dual alignment with the American Baptist Churches, pastors who received theological education at northern seminaries or mainline non-Southern Baptist schools in the South such as Duke or Emory, a history of ordaining women as deacons or ministers, or some combination of these and other nontraditional characteristics. The alternative churches had their own networks of communication and fellowship, such as the camping churches in Texas and neighboring states. People such as Clarence Jordan and Carlyle Marney were key role models for the people in these churches, people who found themselves having less and less to do with the SBC as the 1980s progressed.[39]

Theology Is a Verb revolved around the work of three congregations with strong ties to the genealogy of dissent, Oakhurst Baptist Church in Decatur, Georgia; Deer Park in Louisville; and Binkley Memorial in Chapel Hill. These congregations made presentations that formed the basis of the discussions that occupied the two days of the conference on ministry to impoverished people, peace issues, and women's roles in churches, respectively. Although the stated purpose of the gathering was to give congregations ideas about nontraditional forms of ministry for Southern Baptist churches, one of the key underlying themes of the meeting was the new direction the SBC was taking under its new fundamentalist leadership. Suggestions made during discussion sessions that a new organization of progressive Southern Baptists should emerge from the conference met with little interest, as it seemed too early to tell if the fundamentalist resurgence would be permanent in the SBC or if it would fade away and the moderate leadership return to power. Some of the women in attendance, however, thought otherwise. They devised a plan to form the organization that became SBWIM and turned to Nancy Hastings Sehested to coordinate major aspects of the early planning for the new group. Sehested, who had preached at Theology Is a Verb and who corroborated much of the presentation made by women from Binkley Memorial, was the associate pastor at Oakhurst Baptist and the spouse of hunger and peace activist Ken Sehested.[40]

Its earliest actions revealed two important facts about SBWIM. First, it was made up of women who had no intention whatsoever of keeping their traditional place in Southern Baptist life. They aspired to new roles, new opportunities for leadership, new avenues to use the "gifts" they had cultivated through years of association with Southern Baptist organizations, teachers, literature, aspirations, and energy. Second, however, they also had no intention of bolting the convention. They wanted in, not out. Although the convention's conservative nature did not translate into a particularly welcoming attitude toward change on many issues, especially something as controversial as women in the ministry, they wanted to offer a "prophetic presence" to people in SBC churches, agencies, and institutions in the hope of proving that Southern Baptist women could be both faithful followers of Jesus and authentic ministers. To this end, they turned to the consummate figure who kept one foot in the Southern Baptist world of social ministry and one in that of organizational legitimacy, Foy Valentine. SBWIM organizers approached the CLC for help. Valentine agreed to assign a new female staff member the task of assisting the commission in planning and programming related to women in ministry. An organizational meeting was called for March 1983 to coincide with the CLC annual conference, a plan developed to have a pre-SBC meeting for the nascent women-in-ministry organization. The group remained closely tied to the SBC calendar, kept "SBC" in its name, and otherwise tried to maintain ties to mainstream Southern Baptists for several years. Even after it changed its name to Southern Baptist Women in Ministry, it maintained its pattern of trying to be a "presence" at the SBC, continuing to meet just before the annual convention until the early 1990s.[41]

Despite its attempts to stay in touch with the SBC, SBWIM did not rely on convention agencies for its sustenance. It joined forces with *Folio*, a publication produced by women working out of Crescent Hill Baptist Church in Louisville that had focused on women in ministry among Southern Baptists since 1983. From its first issue, *Folio* described itself as "a communication link with women in ministry in the Southern Baptist Convention." As the 1980s went on and the SBC showed no signs of turning away from its support of the new fundamentalist leadership, *Folio* became more explicit in its condemnation of the restrictions placed on women in Southern Baptist life. SBWIM began making ties with a splinter group of progressive and moderate Southern Baptists, the Southern Baptist Alliance, later called the Alliance of Baptists. Beginning in 1992, the SBWIM annual meeting switched from coinciding with the SBC to doing so with another new organization, one made up of disenfranchised moderate, that is, mainstream but not fundamentalist, Southern Baptists, the Cooperative Baptist Fellowship. SBWIM had solidified its ties with the WMU, but even that move, which would have been seen in the past as a tribute to Southern Baptist traditionalism became a sign of changing times. The WMU was starting to come under criticism by the new fundamentalist leaders of the SBC because of its independence and unwillingness to submit to their discipline. Clearly, women in Southern Baptist life were expected to take a back seat in future activities of the denomination.[42]

Various events in the 1980s, one of which came on the SBC level, underscored this reality. As the fundamentalists solidified their control of the convention, they began using the annual meeting as a forum to advance their political and moral platform. In pursuance of this aim, the 1984 convention, meeting in Kansas City, passed a resolution condemning the idea of women ministers and reaffirming ancient emphases on the responsibility of women, because of the actions of Eve in the Garden of Eden, for the entry of sin into the world. It reaffirmed the ideas that men should be the heads of their households, that women should not take positions of authority over men in churches, that women should continue to serve in church work without seeking ordination, and that such views are biblically mandated by the writings of the apostle Paul and by Hebrew Scriptures, which teach that "the man was first in creation and the woman was first in the Edenic fall."[43] Looking back on the 1984 convention in light of her own experience in seeking a position of ministry among Southern Baptists, Addie Davis recalled the letters she received when she was ordained "suggesting that I was a child of the Devil. . . . Some of them must have attended [the Kansas City] convention!"[44]

Another turn of events, almost as discouraging as the 1984 resolution but not surprising to most Southern Baptist women in ministry, unfolded on the local and associational level with the treatment Nancy Hastings Sehested received when she was called in 1988 to serve as pastor by the Prescott Memorial Baptist Church in Memphis. The local Southern Baptist body of congregations, the Shelby County Baptist Association, withdrew fellowship from Prescott Memorial. Sehested was vilified in numerous publications and other forms of communication by fundamentalist Southern Baptists and other foes of women's participation in ordained ministry. She was described as the very soul of evil by many of the same people who had voted in 1984 for the resolution passed by the SBC essentially blaming women for the presence of sin in the world.[45]

Nancy Hastings Sehested came from a "long, long line" of Baptists. Becoming ordained made her a third-generation Southern Baptist minister. She was very strongly influenced by her father, who had gone to school at

Mars Hill College, Baylor University, and Southern Baptist Theological Seminary. As a member of GA, she became "consumed with what you're supposed to do" to progress through the levels of achievement, "from the Maidens through Queen Regent. I went all the way." In GA she worked hard, but enjoyed learning about the countries where Southern Baptists had missionaries and hearing them give their "deputations," reports of their work that they gave while traveling from church to church during furloughs in the United States. She was particularly taken by the example of Lottie Moon's dedicated service as a missionary to China, where she starved to death during a famine that struck the people among whom she was working. To the young Nancy Hastings, hearing the story of how Lottie Moon progressed as a young Baptist girl to a womanhood of sacrificial service filled her with the desire to be like the great missionary, "wanting to do adventurous things and being willing to give up a lot." To Sehested, her experience as a GA led directly to her becoming a minister: "They were very strong about saying everybody's called. You just need to listen for God's particular call of you. . . . It may be hard and it's going to be rough, but God's going to provide the power and the courage and strength and whatever you need to do it." She described herself as having the same qualities Martha Gilmore remembers developing in her own childhood: an idealistic desire to be of service to God; a sense of being "special" and being convinced that God would find a way to use her in some way; and a strong spirit of competitiveness that made her feel the equal of anyone, male or female. She also formed her sense of ministry out of an "incarnational" understanding, putting herself in positions of identification with the powerless in society as she believed one should do in seeking to follow the example of Jesus. Ordained to the ministry in 1981 by Oakhurst Baptist in Decatur, Sehested believed she could never abstract her situation as a woman minister because of the "incarnational" model: "If what I'm doing in naming injustice for women in ministry in the SBC does not have any connection to the woman down the street who cannot read and write and who is struggling to support her three children, then I want no part of it." The treatment she received for taking a pastorate, in her mind, was no worse than that experienced by other women in the day-to-day circumstances of living in their own forms of oppression.[46]

In the minds of some Southern Baptist women ministers, the movement toward ordination for women and the actions of SBWIM had erred in focusing to such a great extent on securing employment for women in traditional ministerial roles. Longtime member and former SBWIM president Libby Bellinger offered a criticism of the organization in her brief history of it, saying it "has not modeled new forms of leadership for the church but conformed to the white-male system of control and structure." To Bellinger, SBWIM did perform the valuable service, however, of helping create a sense of community among the women who had challenged the Southern Baptist status quo. It encouraged women "to fuller ministries in the church and . . . provided an avenue for the sharing of the joys and struggles of women in ministry." It also did something that the women knew would happen when they began the organization, "frightening" many Southern Baptists in the process of broadening the opportunities for service available to women.[47]

Indeed, persons in Southern Baptist life who desired no end to traditional roles for women had reason to be frightened, especially if they were paying attention to events on the campuses of their educational institutions. Southern Baptist seminaries had begun centers for the study of women in ministry, offered prestigious lectureships to female scholars, admitted unprecedented numbers of women to degree programs, and taken steps to remove sexually exclusive language from their publications.[48] Furthermore, although the Baptist Press reported in 1984 that only one woman served at the level of division director in any of the thirty-seven state convention hierarchies of Southern Baptists, that woman, Sara Ann Hobbs of North Carolina, said, "It is likely that the single most important issue among Southern Baptists today is women in ministry." Her position, director of mission, had once been Walt Johnson's job, and to her, jobs were the crucial question. While she acknowledged the presence of other concerns women had, such as sexist language, in her mind, "The opportunity of serving God is the critical issue," and the way she defined "serving God" in this instance was employment in churches and denominational agencies and institutions. The numbers of women in ministerial positions represented small percentages of conventionwide totals, but they were growing and their growth had become the subject of much debate in Southern Baptist life.[49]

In the spring of 1984 the possibility still existed, in the minds of those who favored women's ordination, that Southern Baptists' devotion to their traditional piety, their historic trusting of the Holy Spirit to lead each individual congregation in all sorts of decisions including whom to endow with special leadership, would overcome the fearful views that women's new roles would weaken churches and, thus, the faith of the people. One of these observers, Baptist historian Bill J. Leonard, described an ordination service for Cindy Harp Johnson in a small-town congregation in Wolf Creek, Kentucky, an event that symbolized to one of the deacons that the church was not "ordaining a woman. We're just ordaining a minister."

[I]t was the laying on of hands that convinced me that Southern Baptist piety is stronger than dogmatism. Cindy knelt and the ordained preachers and deacons initiated the rite of the laying on of hands. Then, since the congregation authorizes ordination, all the members were invited to participate in that powerful symbol of "setting aside." They came, young and old, men and women. The formal laying on of hands turned into emotional embraces. Tears flowed freely. Then I caught sight of an old woman hobbling her way to the front, bracing herself on first one pew, then the next. It was Miss Ethel, the matriarch of the congregation and the personification of Baptist feminine piety. She reached out for Cindy, hugged her close and said, "I love you, honey, and I'll support you, whatever you do." There was not a dry eye left in the place.

If they want to stop women from seeking ordination, Southern Baptists must give up much of their devotion. If they do, they may give up something of the Spirit as well.[50]

## A Story of Peace and Light

Fundamentalists did not share Leonard's interpretation of Southern Baptist piety or his view that it could be seen at its best in the unfolding of a drama of insurrection, the setting aside of a woman for standing in pastoral leadership. Some women found staff positions with moderate and progressive congregations and in hospital chaplaincy programs, though few served as pastors. The summer after Bill Leonard witnessed the ordination of Cindy Harp Johnson, however, hostility within the SBC toward women in ministry turned more explicit. The 1984 resolution upholding traditional views of the place of women in church life in particular and in the overall framework of God's relationships with humankind suggested to many observers that women in ministry had become the "focus of fundamentalist furor."[51] Partly because of the symbolism of the resolution as a seeming turning point, some women gave up on Southern Baptists. Others did so because of the general growing hostility toward their efforts to achieve vocational freedom. One, Jennie Batson Mobley, viewed the resolution as a "catalyst," something that helped her stop feeling guilty about having taken a ministry position with a United Methodist church in Louisville. To her, "The question . . . is not 'Why did I leave the Baptist church?' but rather 'Why did Southern Baptists leave me?'"[52] Others, such as longtime *Folio* coeditor and codirector of the Center for Women in Ministry Reba Sloan Cobb, left work connected with the ministry. Upon leaving to take a position in government with the State of Kentucky, she said that her work with the center and with *Folio* helped her "channel" her anger about the "oppression of women in the Southern Baptist Convention." Other women quietly despaired of finding a place of service. One who had been a pastor's wife for twenty-five years, gone to seminary, and become ordained wrote of her experience.

> The church is my life. I have been a part of the SBC since birth. I have served in most every capacity. . . . I have never been inactive, rather I have performed all the functions expected of the "pastor's wife." I feel that I am now a pastor myself, and I would like very much to find a place where I could serve in an equal capacity. My husband is in entire agreement. . . .
>
> I am experiencing one of the more difficult stages of my life now—having just been graduated with the "pastor's degree" [Master of Divinity] and finding that no one wants/needs me in that role. It is the first time in my life that I have experienced difficulty in getting a "job." It bothers me a great deal. I guess I was naive enough to think that a women had a chance if she graduated college . . . and . . . seminary with a 95 average that surely someone would see her as capable of doing a good job. This is becoming a very depressing time professionally. . . . All seems very hazy.[53]

Signs began to appear that the old ways by which the various doctrinal parties in Southern Baptist life related to one another were passing into memory. One was the formation of the Southern Baptist Alliance (SBA), which SBWIM board member Libby Bellinger hailed in 1987 as the possible beginnings of a new "reformation" among Baptists. In 1988, the SBA began partial funding of SBWIM activities, including a five-thousand-dollar gift for *Folio*. Another sign was the continuing deterioration of relations between women in ministry and the SBC. In 1990, Cindy Harp Johnson told of the euphemisms she sometimes used to describe herself as an unemployed minister. Other congregations ran afoul of Baptist associations and conventions.[54]

The attitude of many Southern Baptist women in ministry was best summarized, perhaps, in the expression that began to appear on lapel buttons and other paraphernalia at SBWIM meetings in the mid-1980s: "Ordain women or stop baptizing them." Few Southern Baptists recognized, however, that ordination was the logical extension of Christian commitment. Because of that, in 1988, Libby Bellinger called for Southern Baptist women in ministry to think very carefully about getting out, to deny the claims to power that women had allowed the fundamentalists now in charge of the SBC to make, to recognize the possibility that "God's presence can be experienced in other conventions and other denominations. . . . [T]he Southern

Baptist Convention . . . is being swallowed up in chunks by ugly, dark nothingness."[55] In 1990, the board of SBWIM began to consider "meeting at a time and a place separate from" the SBC. In 1995, SBWIM began considering dropping the word "Southern" from their name.[56]

Most progressive and a few moderate men helped form a base of acceptance for women in ministry in Southern Baptist life. Some of these men openly supported the movement of women for ordination. They were regarded by the women as allies in their struggle. However, what these male allies did or could do for the women was limited. They had the power to change some minds within their circles of influence, but not institutions, and whether they could have or not, they did not create significant numbers of places of service for women ministers. Not having enough power to create such places for themselves, women created the next best thing, networks of support for each other. They had to decide if they could tolerate being part of a denomination that increasingly told them that their efforts were not appreciated, that they were in fact sinful. Those who stayed Southern Baptist soon realized that they had failed to achieve many permanent places of leadership within the convention and its affiliated agencies and congregations and that they had contributed to the strengthening of a new denominational leadership quite determined to stop, and reverse if possible, the progress of social change among Southern Baptists.[57]

Women had a different story from that of their male counterparts in the subculture of Southern Baptist dissent. For one thing, most of the men already had jobs and support networks. The women had to create their form of community to sustain their drive toward remaining faithful to their call to ministry, their "incarnational" vision that led them into a form of inadvertent radicalism. They wanted validation of their identities as Christians, the culmination of which was a professional setting in which to live out their vocations. They were the most Southern Baptist of dissenters, the most loyal to denominational structures, especially in relation to missions. They were the most shut out of denominational life because of what might have seemed an accident of history. Their rise coincided with the rise of the fundamentalists, the least hospitable of Southern Baptists toward the aspirations of the women, to unprecedented power in the SBC. Those events were not accidental. The movement of women toward ordination may have been the single most important factor in bringing about the fundamentalist resurgence in the SBC.

Women, the most loyal of progressives among Southern Baptists, became the most vilified, and their efforts actually contributed to the downfall of the moderate consensus more decidedly than those of any other progressive element because they threatened the last major area in which Southern Baptist ultraconservatives thought they still had some control: gender relations. Racism had become such a thing to be avoided that nobody dared express racist sentiments openly. But as fully as public racism came to be shunned in the South, even among the most fundamentalist Christians, restrictive views of women's roles in society became one of the cornerstones of the traditionalist structure that fundamentalists planned to "restore" to Southern Baptist life. The efforts of the fundamentalists and the understandings that underlay them must be explored to complete any examination of the effects of dissenters in the denomination.

# The "Return" of Southern Baptist Fundamentalists

6 →

## The Other Dissenters

*Rise up, O men of God!*
*The church for you doth wait,*
*Her strength unequal to the task;*
*Rise up, and make her great!*
—William P. Merrill, *Rise Up, O Men of God*

Martha Gilmore and other progressive Southern Baptists were not alone in paying attention to the unorthodox stands of Blake Smith and Carlyle Marney in Austin in the 1950s. A fellow student and good friend of her husband Jerry at the University of Texas school, Paul Pressler, also paid careful attention to Smith and Marney. Unlike Martha Gilmore, however, Pressler did not like what he heard. Smith's and Marney's progressive theology and liberal political stands offended the young Pressler, who had experienced more than he wanted of such thinking during his undergraduate studies at Princeton University. He determined at an early age to use his training to do something to change the course of Southern Baptist life. In the late 1970s, he and a collection of allies began a move to take control of the key leadership positions of the SBC that not only succeeded in achieving that goal, but also did much to influence the general direction of American evangelicalism in the 1980s and 1990s. They wrote a new chapter in the history of fundamentalism and brought dramatic changes to the landscape in which all Southern Baptists, including progressive dissidents, sought to give shape to their vision of faith.[1]

In the early days of the twentieth century, Southern Baptist fundamentalists had contemplated various approaches to their denomination that mostly involved separating congregations or splitting significant portions of church members away from it, seldom contemplating the possibility that they might be able to assume control of it from within. In 1925, fiery preacher and evangelist Thomas T. Martin called for the SBC to split along literalist/modernist lines. He was upset about a statement by an association of Southern Baptist educators that the Bible should not be "taken literally," something it "never was meant to be." Martin proposed that the convention "divide peaceably" according to agreement or disagreement with the Southern Baptist Education Association statement, most likely knowing full well that the majority of Southern Baptists agreed with him, not the educators. But convention leaders, including some who agreed with the educators, issued mollifying statements, and in 1926, a resolution affirming the Genesis account of creation passed by the convention meeting encouraged fundamentalists sufficiently to avoid the split Martin proposed. In 1925, Martin had predicted that "fearful division and strife" would result if the problem were not addressed head-on.[2] Southern Baptist diplomats kept the split from occurring on the basis of the old devotion to denominational civility and unity, but they could not postpone indefinitely the onset of fearful division and strife.

Southern Baptist fundamentalists became a powerful force after World War II in large part because they blended their religious views with the growing activity of American conservatives in secular politics. Furthermore, much of the fundamentalist energy directed toward politics, especially the crusade against communism and other perceived threats to conservative Christian views of society, transformed many apparently secular issues into religious ones. Southern Baptist fundamentalists were inspired particularly by the example of one of the principal heroes of anticommunism, John Birch, who had been a student for a time before World War II in the Fundamental Baptist Bible Institute in Arlington, Texas, later renamed Bible Baptist Seminary, one of whose chief patrons was J. Frank Norris. Birch's death at the hands of Chinese communists paralleled for many Southern Baptists the sacrificial life and anguished death by starvation of Lottie Moon, the sainted Southern Baptist missionary to China.[3] Many Southern Baptist fundamentalists blamed communism for such progressive initiatives as desegregation and the movement for civil rights for African Americans. Through much of the 1950s, archconservative Southern Baptists supported white supremacists' efforts to resist racial integration and attacked such pro-integration figures as T.B. Maston, the Christian ethics professor at Southwestern Baptist Theological Seminary in Fort Worth.[4] Fundamentalists' energies, however, were seldom directed toward intradenominational goals from the 1920s until the late 1970s.

When the change in goals and strategy for fundamentalists came, it did so largely because of the vision of W.A. Criswell, longtime pastor of the gigantic First Baptist Church of Dallas, who burst onto the national scene as a result of highly publicized remarks critical of racial desegregation. Militant fundamentalist Texas Baptists, as well as others throughout the SBC, looked to Criswell for leadership and inspiration beginning in the 1950s. Unlike Norris, Criswell never removed himself or his church from Southern Baptist affiliation, but his antimodernist biblical literalism made him and his church the focal points from which a growing movement emerged that challenged the entire structure of Southern Baptist work in the 1970s. First Baptist Church, Dallas, furthermore, sponsored its own separatist system of private schools, fostered a close relationship with Dallas Baptist University, and in 1971 created a seminary, the Criswell Center for Biblical Studies. In these schools, the children of church members and like-minded people could move from kindergarten through graduate study in school environments that were theologically safe, unlike those found in the public schools and universities and in denominationally affiliated schools such as Baylor that were "wayward." Such actions by Criswell and his staff set themselves and historic First Baptist, Dallas, at odds with its earlier role as a bastion of loyalist Southern Baptist sentiment and defense against the charges of fundamentalism.[5] Criswell became the godfather of the fundamentalist resurgence, serving as mentor to a generation of younger ultraconservatives and openly campaigning for the election of militant biblical literalists to the SBC presidency. Criswell's immediate predecessor as pastor at First Baptist, George W. Truett, had borne the wrath of Criswell's fundamentalist forerunner, J. Frank Norris. The church had stood in Truett's day for everything good and true to the SBC and its agencies, its mission, and its worldview. It had also stood at the head of a group of strong loyalist churches holding the line against the fundamentalist onslaughts, including the church of Martha Gilmore's upbringing, Cliff Temple Baptist. Simply being associated with First Baptist meant that Cliff Temple was a target of the invective of J. Frank Norris. Now, in the 1970s and 1980s, the First Baptist Church and its pastor were embarked on a program of creating rival institutions and agencies and encouraging like-minded Southern Baptists to do the same in other cities. Southern Baptist allies of Criswell in the Dallas-Fort Worth area, including James Robison and Jimmy Draper, helped promote an atmosphere of discontent with what they saw as the moral drift of modern society and of the SBC. They called for Southern Baptist pastors to take stands opposing changing roles of women, the abolition of mandated prayers in public schools, and, with increasing importance, abortion. Criswell and his colleagues also promoted a sense of discontent with their denomination for failing to prevent, and in some cases for helping inspire, moral relativism. They did these things, using an authoritarian approach to pastoral leadership that seemed to contradict the historic Baptist practice of congregational polity, with Criswell's saying, "The pastor is the ruler of the church. There is no other thing than that in the Bible." They also did these things with frequent reference to people in the dissident network whose views of progressive reform, and biblical interpretation Criswell found repugnant. First Baptist, Dallas, had changed quite dramatically, and its leadership planned to help bring those changes into the broader reaches of Southern Baptist life.[6] It became in many respects the staging ground for the return to prominence of fundamentalists in Southern Baptist life.

Modern Southern Baptist fundamentalism was energized further by a controversy involving a scholarly work by a Southern Baptist professor, Ralph Elliott. A member of the faculty at the denomination's Midwestern Baptist Theological Seminary in Kansas City, Elliott wrote a commentary on the Book of Genesis that acknowledged and analyzed the mythological character of some of the biblical narratives. Biblical literalists responded by forming the Baptist Faith and Message Fellowship in the early 1970s, which gave literalists a forum in which to complain of the "liberal drift" in Southern Baptist scholarship, and by calling for the removal of Elliott from the Midwestern faculty. They protested hiring practices at the seminaries that seemed to favor employing professors with modernist views. While they rarely advocated the outright firing of a faculty member as they did in the Elliott case, they found little receptivity among seminary administrators to their suggestions that a balance or "parity" be sought in filling faculty positions. They proposed that the fair thing to do would be to hire at least some, if not equal numbers of, biblical literalists to balance out the numbers of modernists already on seminary faculties. By the late 1970s, fundamentalists had become visible enough in the affairs of the SBC that they were seen by some moderates as "a new Frank Norris movement" of "schismatics."[7]

During the last quarter of the twentieth century, the SBC became the key arena in which fundamentalists perfected a new strategy for acting on their theological and cultural concerns, conquest from within. Their target was not the network of progressive dissenters about whom they complained, but the moderate leadership of the SBC whose biblical views progressives largely agreed with but whose activist commitments progressives had often doubted. Two Southern Baptists from Texas, Criswell Center for Biblical Studies president Paige Patterson and Judge Paul Pressler of Houston, the old friend of Martha and Jerry Gilmore, orchestrated a long-range strategy for gaining control of the SBC built around winning its presidency, a largely ceremonial office but one with the enormous power of appointment of trustees of Southern Baptist agencies and seminaries. On the strength of their claim to speak for the majority of Southern Baptists and of their superb organizational abilities, the Pressler-Patterson faction won the first of a remarkable string of victories at the 1979 convention in Houston and appeared to have assured control of the denomination by the 1985 meeting in Dallas. By the mid-1990s, the militant fundamentalist wing of Southern Baptists controlled nearly every aspect of institutional life in the SBC. In 1994, fundamentalist trustees of Southwestern Seminary, for instance, consummated their control of the Fort Worth school when they fired its moderate president, Russell Dilday.[8]

For many Southern Baptists in the 1980s and 1990s, there was no enemy on the right. Generally, such an attitude had characterized most grassroots Southern Baptists throughout their history. Before the fundamentalist resurgence, though, convention messengers tended to be better educated, more affluent, and somewhat more progressive than typical Southern Baptists, as was the SBC bureaucracy: "The old guard was never truly 'liberal' by any national standard," according to one observer, "despite fundamentalists' claims. Just the same, the leadership was much friendlier to the academic notions of historical criticism of scriptural texts and the theory of evolution than were most of their constituents." They and their better-educated leaders, however, had managed to maintain the consensus that held the SBC together and kept its missions and related work going for the first 135 years of its history. With occasional exceptions such as J. Frank Norris, before the late 1970s, enough Southern Baptists had embraced the idea that productivity in soul winning was more important than doctrinal uniformity that the convention never faced a serious threat of splitting. The fundamentalist resurgence in the SBC coincided with and contributed to the rise of an alliance between arch conservative religious leaders and right-wing political figures. This alliance sought to stamp out "liberalism" in the denomination and make church structures available for mobilization on behalf of conservative political causes.[9]

In the minds of many moderate Southern Baptists and some progressives, the fundamentalists' goal of stamping out liberalism was only an excuse to put the convention in a position to achieve the second one, a broader goal set by a few powerful Southern Baptists with a national political agenda. Moderates, even many actual progressives, contended that there were no "liberals" in the SBC. The specter of liberalism, to them, was a ruse fundamentalists used to steal control of the convention and its agencies and institutions from the coalition of theologically tolerant and institutionally focused moderates who had led the SBC for most of its existence. Southern Baptist moderates saw abundant parallels between the fundamentalist "takeover" of the SBC and the methods and goals of McCarthyism. They also agonized over the prospects of having to turn over control of institutions and agencies that fundamentalists had openly shunned for years in favor of their own schools and organizations.[10]

Fundamentalists, however, made a convincing case to convention messengers year after year that they were the true Southern Baptist conservatives who could return the SBC to its historic qualities and purposes. They pointed out that the pronouncements of progressives on the need for radical changes in social and gender relations and criticism of such things as U.S. national defense policy proved that the SBC needed help. They also pointed out that if the moderate leadership of the convention did not actually agree with progressives politically, then they might as well agree with them theologically because they had "silenced" the voices of "true biblical conservativism" in the SBC so effectively. Despite the fact that an occasional representative of their viewpoint held elective positions in the convention, including the presidencies of W.A. Criswell and K.O. White, and various agency trustee appointments from time to time, they made plausible claims to have been excluded from SBC leadership positions. They cast their struggle as one of faithful populists versus wayward elites, of those in touch with the grassroots battling those who had lost touch.[11] They felt free, however, to depart from one form of Southern Baptist traditionalism. They exhibited little intention to employ the niceties Southern Baptists had traditionally used in discourse with each other in transacting convention business. Fundamentalist takeover architect Paul Pressler accused Baylor University professors of teaching "garbage."[12] In 1979, in a speech to the SBC Pastors' Conference in Houston, on the eve of the election of the first fundamentalist SBC president, James Robison compared moderate Southern Baptists to "rattlesnakes" and "termites" and said that some moderate denominational figures were "little devils." In 1988, in a sermon before the same group, W.A. Criswell denied the moderate label to fundamentalists' foes in the SBC. Using a word that was essentially a curse word among the New Right and among most Southern Baptists, Criswell said that so-called moderates in Southern Baptist life were actually "liberals," though they tried to avoid being branded as such, and that "a skunk by any other name still stinks."[13]

Fundamentalists said to everyone who would listen that they were alarmed by the rise of "liberalism" in the institutional life of Southern Baptists. Their primary rallying cry was what they perceived to be the diminished respect accorded the Bible, which to them was the "Sword of the Lord," especially by professors at seminaries affiliated with the SBC and at colleges and universities affiliated with the state conventions. To fundamentalists, however, no evidence of that decline was stronger than the rising popularity of a handful of positions advocated by progressive Southern Baptist dissenters. The checklists that emerged in fundamentalist circles to determine the fitness of persons for Southern Baptist leadership were usually headed by changing roles of women in society, particularly their ordination to the ministry; capital punishment; abortion; pacifism; public assistance for persons with low incomes, which represented to progressives a veiled hostility toward blacks; and even the sanctuary movement.[14]

For the new fundamentalist leaders of the convention, their ways of believing depicted a strict view and strident manner of presentation of the gospel, the prospects ministers and churches had of spreading it, and the battle between good and evil that the gospel represented. They had a strict view of what Scripture said about these matters, and about the range of scriptural interpretations that they deemed proper. They had a strident manner of presenting their views on these subjects, a militant way of acting and talking. They believed they were the "Christian men" to whom God had given the "Words by which all men can live." They had been given "a sword to fight the wrong," and the wrongs they fought were not just spiritual ones, but actual, verifiable wrongs perpetrated by liberals in Southern Baptist agencies and institutions. They were also convinced that their values, their definitions of what was right and true, were the only proper ones for leaders of the SBC and for any employees of their agencies, institutions, and congregations. Such views gave them no reason to act or speak in moderation and left little room for progressive dissenters to negotiate, whether their passions moved toward racial reform in the South, peace activism, or ordination for women. The fundamentalists' message and methods also obscured the real differences that existed between genuine progressives in the SBC and the moderates who controlled most of its institutions and agencies. Whatever possibilities might have existed, therefore, for the spread of influence of people within the genealogy of dissent were fading away with each electoral triumph of the fundamentalist party. This fact, frankly, offered most progressives little grief because they had little expectation that the masses of Southern Baptists would rally to their causes. The fundamentalist resurgence only confirmed for many of them their low opinion of much that went on in Southern Baptist life. For the women who sought ordination by and places of service among Southern Baptists, however, the timing of the fundamentalist takeover seemed disastrous. They were swept aside by a wave of intolerance for their viewpoint, for the very fact of their presence in the denomination, that was awe-inspiring in its efficiency and no less frustrating because of its perfect legality.[15]

Fundamentalists who took control of the SBC did so in exact accordance with the rules and procedures established to govern the conduct of the annual meeting. Moderate critics saw themselves being squeezed out of positions of influence, both elected and salaried, in convention life and complained bitterly about the tactics of the fundamentalists. They especially objected to the "busing in" of profundamentalist messengers who stayed just long enough to elect the fundamentalist slate of officers and then left. Moderates cited such behavior to reinforce their claim that they were the true Southern Baptist conservatives. The new people had little knowledge of traditional convention behavior, according to the moderate convention veterans, and had to rely on floor captains to make sure they did what they were supposed to do. In a special affront to moderates, the fundamentalist-bloc voters departed en masse each year before the traditional high point of the convention, the Home and Foreign Mission Board annual reports. These increasingly elaborate multimedia celebrations of the year's accomplishments had always been used as motivational devices to send people home filled with enthusiasm for the time-honored institutional goals of Southern Baptists. Fundamentalists countered by saying that their supporters were simple Southern Baptists who could not afford to stay in expensive hotels in such places as Houston, Atlanta, and Las Vegas until the last sessions of the convention. They used the moderates' complaints as further evidence that they had gotten out of touch with grassroots Southern Baptists, a claim that seemed increasingly to have some basis in fact. Thomas T. Martin's prediction of a split in the convention, if an informal one, finally came true sixty years after he made it, but by then, fundamentalists were no longer content to part company with their moderate opponents, taking with them their share of the membership of SBC churches. By 1985, they knew they stood a good chance of winning the whole prize, the largest Protestant denomination in the United States.[16]

## The Transformation of the CLC

By the end of the 1980s, fundamentalists shifted their focus from the calls for "parity" of earlier days to actually discharging agency and seminary officials who disagreed with them. After the seminaries, their favorite target among Southern Baptist agencies was the CLC.[17] The CLC had long been a source of annoyance to the more stridently conservative Southern Baptists. SBC fundamentalist leaders held a longstanding animosity as well toward the Baptist Joint Committee on Public Affairs (BJCPA), a citizenship education and lobbying agency that Southern Baptists helped fund. Fundamentalists sought to direct the SBC away from "liberal" positions the CLC and BJCPA had taken on separation of church and state and ethics in public life, positions the agencies' leaders believed reflected traditional Baptist beliefs.[18] It was obvious, though, that the CLC was intended to serve as a focal point for the fundamentalists' attempts to reverse the tendencies of moderate Southern Baptist leadership, especially in the areas of modest social change the commission had advocated over the years. After the fundamentalists had gained a majority of positions on the actual commission that oversees the work of the agency staff, they forced out the transitional director who had taken the place of Foy Valentine, who retired in 1987. Once the beacon of Southern Baptist racial consciousness, the CLC was placed in the position of having to distance itself from the remarks of one of its commission members who had referred to Martin Luther King Jr. as a "fraud," which earned him the charge of racism. Its new director was much more sophisticated than the racist demagogues who sometimes appeared on the stages of Southern Baptist life. He was determined not to make such a mistake. Many fundamentalists opposed the "social liberalism" inherent in CLC positions on civil rights and "equated a positive response to civil rights with encouragement to civil disobedience, left-wing politics, and theological liberalism attributed to Martin Luther King, Jr., the National Council of Churches, and other advocates of racial reform."[19]

In 1988, though, the commission hired a director who could lead the agency in directions that would gratify the ultraconservative elements in the denomination and avoid most of the bad publicity that might accompany such changes. The new director, Richard Land, a fundamentalist protégé of W.A. Criswell and Paige Patterson, came to the agency from the Criswell Center for Biblical Studies in Dallas. In keeping with the academic origins of fundamentalism in the late nineteenth century, Land was a highly educated and articulate advocate of the inerrancy position in all its ramifications for social relations. He held a doctorate from Oxford University and brought a scholar's mind to the process of reversing many of the positions for which the CLC had become known. He also set about the task of convincing Southern Baptist ultraconservatives that the commission could become something other than the "liberal" mouthpiece that had plagued them for so many years.[20]

While pledging not to abandon the commission's opposition to racial discrimination, a decision that would have attracted more unwelcome charges of racism, Richard Land made it clear that the CLC would take positions that seemed increasingly identical to those of the "family values" stance of conservative politicians. The commission canceled publications on women in ministry and began a fervent antiabortion emphasis.[21] Land also reflected fundamentalist views in favor of capital punishment, saying that "Southern Baptists overwhelmingly support capital punishment." He thus reversed a position that Southern Baptist progressives had considered a cornerstone of both racial justice and peace and reconciliation. Under his direction, the CLC withdrew a pamphlet that had been in circulation for several years opposing capital punishment on the grounds that it was "contrary to the spirit and teachings of Christ." Land also wrote letters to the Baptist Peace Fellowship asking that his name be removed from its list of advisers, a position he inherited from his predecessors.[22] On the issue of women's roles in society, particularly with regard to church leadership, Land took the old route of invoking the injunctions of the apostle Paul. Land quoted Eph. 5:22-24, for instance, to bolster his opinions that women should not be in positions of authority over men. Land was in direct line with the will of the convention as expressed in resolutions passed in convention session, especially the 1984 SBC resolution condemning the ordination of women on the basis of scriptural teaching, principally Pauline epistles, and on the basis of the fact that Eve had ushered in the fatal fall from grace in the Garden of Eden.[23] By cleaning house administratively, securing the appointment of sympathetic commission members and firing or otherwise removing staff people left over from the days of Foy Valentine, the CLC became a model of fundamentalist rectitude and utility.

Ironically, the CLC, the agency that was intended to be the repository of moral courage and inspiration for Southern Baptists, actually presided over the events that led to the firing of the first person whose job was lost during the fundamentalist resurgence. The CLC provided the setting for a drama that unfolded several years before Richard Land came on the scene, even before it was apparent to anyone that the fundamentalist takeover of the SBC would be successful. The events took place in connection with the annual CLC seminar on putting theological beliefs into action. The theme of the conference for 1981 was the authority of the Bible, the single most important watchword for people in the fundamentalist movement, who had built the concept of biblical "inerrancy" into the key theological litmus test for Southern Baptist fellowship. Those who acknowledged the Bible as inerrant with regard to any category of fact, including scientific, set themselves apart from their moderate counterparts. Many moderates viewed the Bible as authoritative but grounded in the times in which it was written. It contained material that should not and was not intended to prevent people from using modern knowledge to supplement what it said on various subjects. Moderates said that one could view stories such as Joshua's making the "sun stand still" as stories the ancient Israelites told to remind them of their beliefs in the absolute power of God and of God's high expectations of them. To many moderates, one could view the Joshua story, for instance, as mythical without having to abandon its power to purvey biblical "truth," that God is sovereign and that those who would seek to have a relationship with God must keep that fact in mind. To the fundamentalists, if one questioned any part of the Scriptures, "Old" or "New," one might as well throw out the whole thing, including the saving work of Jesus.[24]

In the spring of 1981, after only two successive SBC presidential victories by the fundamentalist party, the CLC explored the volatile issue of views on the Scriptures. A raging controversy grew up around a presentation by Robert G. Bratcher, a translator employed not by Southern Baptists but by the American Bible Society (ABS). Bratcher had grown up on the mission field in Brazil. Like most Southern Baptist "missionary kids," he came to the United States to a Southern Baptist-related college. He then went on to graduate school and made a promising start in the field of biblical studies. He had a particular felicity for the study of languages and mastered the Hebrew and Greek necessary for biblical study, in addition to modern scholarly languages and his native English and Portuguese. He also had a high awareness of the historic Baptist principles of religious freedom and of their scholarly equivalent of academic freedom. He returned to Brazil in the early 1950s to teach in a Southern Baptist seminary there and ran afoul of the institutional priorities of the Foreign Mission Board when he began researching and writing about an age-old debate in Christian and Baptist circles, the ideas of perseverance and apostasy. His conclusion was that there were indeed scriptural bases for the beloved Calvinist and Baptist notion of "once saved, always saved," but that there were also passages in Scripture that point to the possibility that one could lose one's salvation. In the minds of most Baptists, such a thing was nothing but heresy and was declared to be so by one of Bratcher's colleagues, a senior professor in the seminary where Bratcher taught. W.C. Taylor threatened to publish reports of Bratcher's findings in Southern Baptist publications in the United States exposing the fact that a Southern Baptist missionary professor had the views of a heretic. Well aware of the potential risks of such a public relations disaster, the director of the Foreign Mission Board, Baker James Cauthen, called Bratcher in and told him, "Bratcher, if Dr. Taylor gets this published, it will cost the Foreign Mission Board a million dollars." He declared that Bratcher was free to return as a field missionary in Brazil but would be forbidden to teach. The seminary faculty, its board of trustees in Brazil, and the Brazilian Baptist Convention all went on record supporting Bratcher and attesting to his orthodoxy, but the Foreign Mission Board refused to allow him to return to his position in the seminary.[25]

No stranger to controversy, but also someone who felt great freedom to depict the understandings he believed he had developed through careful and honest study of Scripture in both manuscript and translation, Bratcher accepted the invitation of Foy Valentine to address the CLC seminary on biblical authority. Bratcher understood that his invitation was to bring "anything [I wanted] to develop along the line of the authority of the Bible." As requested, he submitted a copy of the paper to the commission office in advance and understood that Valentine had reviewed what Bratcher planned to say, which was critical of the idea of inerrancy and of the "intellectual dishonesty" of people who made inerrancy a test of fellowship. The paper also said that inerrancy can lead people to make an "idol" of the Bible, worshiping it instead of the God to whom it points people. Reporters, including Kenneth Briggs of the *New York Times*, picked up on Bratcher's presentation and reported on it in the context of the larger questions on biblical interpretation being debated in connection with the fundamentalist resurgence in the SBC. Briggs and other prominent reporters were present, in large part, because of the controversy caused by the fundamentalist SBC president, Bailey Smith, who had created an earlier uproar when he said, "God almighty does not hear the prayer of a Jew." The resulting publicity from Bratcher's comments caused problems for the ABS, which received substantial funding for its work from the SBC, and Bratcher was forced to resign his position before the upcoming SBC meeting in June.[26]

Bratcher felt betrayed by both the ABS and by the Southern Baptist CLC. The ABS could have disclaimed his remarks as being those of a Southern Baptist addressing a meeting of Southern Baptists, he believed, instead of allowing itself to be bullied into acquiescence by the threat of controversy and the possible loss of money. Valentine's position also disappointed Bratcher.

In the Texas Baptist weekly *Baptist Standard*, Valentine was quoted as saying, "I had asked Dr. Bratcher to speak with regard to the Bible and the prophetic tradition. . . . The choice of his specific topic and the decision to include the remarks in question were his, not mine." Valentine went on, "I had no prior knowledge of what he intended to say." He was careful to point out that no Southern Baptist funds had been used to bring the speakers to the seminar, but that "still, the meeting was under our sponsorship; and we are deeply concerned that Southern Baptists understand that it was planned to help God's people. . . ." Bratcher's own response was to apologize for using "intemperate" language that "cast aspersions on those who do not agree with my position." He affirmed the Bible as "true and indispensable" and emphasized that his remarks did not represent the position of the ABS or the CLC, although he did not back down from his statements about the inadequacies of the concept of inerrancy.[27] Bratcher could not understand the response of Foy Valentine to the controversy over his presentation at the seminar, which was, after all, on the authority of the Bible. "The one bad thing I feel about Foy Valentine is that he issued a statement saying that he did not know what I was going to say, but if that is actually true, literally true, it is true because he didn't read my paper. I had sent the paper with all the material in it, so he had not read it. . . . I'm not saying Foy told a lie; he didn't read my paper, so he didn't know. But it was not because he couldn't know if he'd been curious about it."[28]

In fact, Valentine said,

> If he had talked with me about it, I would have said, "This is a good thing. It ought to be said, and don't say it at an ethics seminar . . . [D]on't put it in the arena of the inerrancy fight that the fundamentalists have foisted off on an otherwise unsuspecting bunch of Southern Baptist people. Do it somewhere else, and you talk to us about something related to Christian ethics." That's what I would have done and said if I had had the foggiest notion what he was going to do. . . . I had not seen the manuscript. If he had sent it, I had not read it.[29]

Valentine's account of the events presents in microcosm the differences between the institutional orientation of the moderate Southern Baptists and the more independent outlook of people influenced by the genealogy of dissent. Bratcher had many ties to the dissenter groups in the SBC, having studied the work of Clarence Jordan and that of Carlyle Marney. At the time of the CLC controversy and thereafter, Bratcher was a member of the Binkley Memorial Baptist Church in Chapel Hill and deeply supportive of its work in racial justice, peace activism, and women's liberation.[30] His and Valentine's careers unfolded as opposites of each other. Bratcher began as a denominational employee, was forced out of missions work because of his beliefs, and became a member of one of the most liberal of Southern Baptist churches. Valentine, who embraced many of the ideals of Jordan and other progressive Southern Baptist dissenters early in his life and ministry, moved beyond the "idealistic" perspective that had first attracted him to Koinonia Farm and made his career as a consummate denominational insider. Valentine's assessment of Bratcher's speech to the CLC seminar was that "I asked him to come and speak to us on some such subject as 'the Bible and life.' And he chose, to my absolute amazement and consternation, to use that occasion to change the subject and to speak on inerrancy." To Valentine, "It was a strong excellent speech on the subject. Didn't have much to do with ethics, and that's what we did try to focus our seminars on . . . But at any rate, the fire storm came immediately, because he had done the buzz word of inerrancy." Bratcher "was shattering that idol," the "shibboleth" of fundamentalists, which made Valentine think that Bratcher "was shooting himself in the temple . . ." According to Valentine, after the controversy began, he told Bratcher that he would not distribute copies of the speech or publish it in the conference proceedings "because his [Bratcher's] job was at stake. . . . And so to protect him, we did not publish the manuscript." Although he agreed that Bratcher did what "needed to be done," Valentine believed that Bratcher's actions suggested he "could have a death wish for employment," or that Bratcher might have reasoned that "he had the truth and was going to say it, and that this was the only opportunity that had presented itself for a pretty good public hearing."[31]

Disagreements between Bratcher's and Valentine's accounts of the events leading up to Bratcher's speech and the controversy surrounding it point to a deeper significance than their value to recreate the facts of a series of events. Their accounts have particular meaning for the different interpretations they place on the possible role of the core of Christian ethicists in Southern Baptist life in the greater controversy then in its early phases in the SBC. In Valentine's view, fighting the fundamentalists, people he called "Criswellites and Presslerites and Pattersonites and Adrian Rogersites," referring to the godfather, the two chief architects, and the first president in the new fundamentalist movement for control of the convention, was a "battle [that] needed to be fought." However, in Valentine's mind, "We were not the ones in the social concerns agency to provide the platform for that fight." He thought that "since the absolute first day of that fundamentalist effort to take over the machinery of the Southern Baptist Convention, it was appropriate for me to oppose them and everything they were trying to do, and I have done that without any equivocation and without any compromise." He did not feel, however, that he should use the CLC or its events, publications, and allotted time for reports to the SBC as forums to criticize the fundamentalist takeover group: "It's not because I'm a coward about it. It's just not appropriate . . . It's just not the thing for me to do." Valentine not only thought that he should not use the CLC seminar as a forum for criticizing the fundamentalists, however. He believed that Bratcher should not have done it either: "[H]is judgment was not a good judgment about it, and I never told him that, and don't want to fuss at him. I just asked him to do something else, and he didn't do what I asked him to do."[32] Most people in the family of Southern Baptist progressive dissent probably thought that protesting the fundamentalist viewpoint and its service in the SBC takeover effort had a definite connection with the work that Valentine and his own network of supporters did on other issues. The irony was that Valentine and his supporters had a great deal more to lose in the takeover than the progressive dissenters did. They were unwilling to speak against the fundamentalists, even though they were the recognized representatives of the "social concerns" agency and its various viewpoints supporting the right and responsibility of Baptists to put their faith in action on behalf of social justice. Robert Bratcher thought he knew the reason.

Bratcher saw the controversy over his remarks partly as the same sort of ultraconservative criticism that caused the controversy over Ralph Elliott's commentary on the Book of Genesis, suppression of which Bratcher had protested at the time, and partly as an expression of institutional protectiveness. Scholars, denominational agencies, or organizations such as the ABS "can do or say anything that could offend the liberals, for the liberals don't protest, and the liberals don't make a point. So, if I go out to some church and say, 'I believe the King James Bible is inspired from cover to cover by God Almighty,' there would be no offense given or taken." Bratcher acknowledged that administrators such as Foy Valentine and the leaders of the ABS have to keep the survival of their institutions in mind and have to take criticism seriously, have to address it, and sometimes have to apologize for the words or deeds that prompted the criticism. In the case of the CLC, most of the criticism over the years had come from the right wing of Southern Baptist life, and the fundamentalist resurgence certainly represented an escalation of such criticism. In Bratcher's mind, however, Baptist administrators also had the obligation to be true to their heritage, including a historic commitment to freedom of interpretation of Scripture and expression of one's sense of what Scripture had to offer the day: "[E]ven they had a responsibility, when it comes right down to it, as Baptists."[33]

If Robert Bratcher can be seen as the first casualty of the fundamentalist "holy war" for Southern Baptist conquest, others followed, including people with whom Bratcher was linked. The summer after the CLC seminar, Bratcher was scheduled to teach a class at Southeastern Baptist Theological Seminary. The president, Randall Lolley, was willing to honor the commitment to Bratcher to work that summer, although they agreed to postpone Bratcher's appearance in order to let the controversy die down. When they agreed to try again, in the summer of 1984, reports circulated among fundamentalists that Bratcher would be teaching at Southeastern. He offered to back out, although Lolley had demonstrated the seriousness of his commitment to Bratcher by paying him for the course in the summer of 1981, but Lolley said, according to Bratcher, "You've got to stand up to these people sometime." By then, however, the fundamentalists were strengthening their hold on the SBC. In 1989, they forced Lolley out of the presidency at Southeastern. As in the case of the CLC and Richard Land's directorship, after a transitional term in office by a weak successor to Lolley, the Southeastern presidency was given to an associate of W.A. Criswell's, the coprincipal architect of the fundamentalist SBC resurgence, Paige Patterson.[34]

## Farewell to the SBC

As the struggle over control of the SBC subsided, it became obvious even to most die-hard convention loyalists that the fundamentalists had won not just a succession of battles but the war itself. Positions that Southern Baptist progressives and some moderates had advocated were repudiated with remarkable vigor. The mood also turned ugly in various quarters of Southern Baptist life. Molly Marshall Green was told during the summer of 1994 by the new fundamentalist president of Southern Baptist Theological Seminary, Albert Mohler, that she would have to resign her tenured appointment as an associate professor of theology "or face heresy proceedings." Exact charges against her were not revealed. She chose to resign her position. The female dean of the Carver School of Social Work at Southern Seminary was fired because of public criticisms she had made of the seminary's new hiring practices restricting employment to inerrantists. Southern Seminary trustees issued a statement supporting her dismissal that referred to the "convictional consensus of the churches of the SBC" opposing women's serving as pastors, citing the 1984 resolution on women's roles in churches and in society. Similar events took place in various SBC agencies, especially the Home Mission Board, which took steps to remove support from ordained women missionaries. One of the casualties of Home Mission Board actions was the dismissal from the board of chair Jerry Gilmore, husband of Martha Gilmore, because of the disapproval of fundamentalists over the actions of his ordained wife.[35] Furthermore, terminations and dismissals on the denominational level were paralleled on the congregational level. A survey in the late 1980s showed a dramatic increase in forced terminations of pastors of local churches.[36]

Tinged with anger, some sadness, some resignation, progressives' responses to the changes in Southern Baptist life varied, though most had in common the realization that they were departing their traditional church home. When the Home Mission Board withdrew sponsorship from the National Workshop on Christian-Jewish Relations because Southern Baptist speakers on the program, particularly Nancy Hastings Sehested, were not "'representative of the denomination,'" she offered a bitter rejoinder. "I was told," she said, "that the Home Mission Board could not support a program in which I was a speaker because I was 'the center of a raging controversy within the Southern Baptist Convention.'" She found a grave irony in the depiction of her as not representative of Southern Baptist women who had grown up being told they should serve Jesus as fully as they felt led, adding, "It must be exhausting for you to keep your guns loaded and pointed at your imagined enemy, women ministers of the Gospel."[37] Other progressives elaborated on the themes of loss that saying goodbye to the SBC prompted.

Sehested's husband, Baptist Peace Fellowship director Ken Sehested, took a view that mixed regret with relief. He saw the two competing sides in the fundamentalist-moderate struggles for control of the SBC as having essentially the same views, especially as he compared the moderates' "heavy-handed boss" approach to leadership with that of the new dominant force. Though Sehested believed that moderates did not exhibit the level of "meanness" of the fundamentalists, the political system and methods of operation of the "current owners and the former owners" were no different from each other. He believed the inerrantists' claims, however, that they had been excluded from convention leadership, partly because of his knowledge and opinion of Southern Baptist moderate leadership. He believed that the same people who tried to suppress the founding of SBWM and who did almost nothing to help *Seeds* were quite capable of excluding fundamentalists, whose education and social graces moderates enjoyed ridiculing.[38]

Other Southern Baptist progressives simply departed by a route lined with ironies and awareness of lost opportunities. Martha Gilmore left, followed by her husband, after he was removed from membership on the Home Mission Board. Glenda Fontenot, president of the Baptist Peace Fellowship, and who had been ordained a minister by a Southern Baptist church, put it simply: "I no longer consider myself a Southern Baptist."[39] Robert Bratcher was left to contemplate the irony that Foy Valentine agreed with his observations on the nature of inerrancy belief and the dangers of making the Bible into an idol, as Valentine himself admitted: "I found his speech very erudite and very Baptistic and very defensible and very excellent and I, personally, agreed with all of it, as I remember now." In all probability, most of the registrants at the 1981 CLC seminar and the commission staff agreed with Bratcher, too.[40] One of the greatest ironies came in 1995, the SBC's sesquicentennial. In observance of the fact that the convention had been founded for the purpose of protecting the claims of Baptists in the South to the right to own slaves, messengers assembled 150 years later passed a resolution seeking forgiveness. The 1995 resolution apologized for the role their forebears had played in perpetuating and profiting from the institution of slavery. It showed how acceptable open espousal of the claims and results of the civil rights movement were, even among the people who had criticized progressive dissenters for their activities on that very issue.[41]

Progressives realized fairly quickly that the days when they might have had any voice in the SBC were over, although some thought that the changes presented an opportunity to create a new form of intercongregational cooperation that could make some good things possible, yet avoid some of the heavy-handed approaches of denominational institutionalism. They particularly hoped something would emerge from the breakdown of Southern Baptist comity that would emphasize the traditional Baptist passion for freedom. Progressives had hoped the Alliance of Baptists would become such an "alternative" structure, and its leaders acted in some ways that reflected the suspicions members of the genealogy of dissent had often held toward institutionalism. They chose very consciously not to assume the trappings of denominationalism and opted for a cautious relationship with the newer Cooperative Baptist Fellowship (CBF), a move that annoyed some progressives because of the relatively conservative nature of the CBF. Progressive organizations such as the Baptist Peace Fellowship got modest amounts of funding from the CBF and received permission to place literature tables in meeting facilities, something they and *Seeds* were never permitted to do at SBC meetings. CBF meetings featured much more openness to the presence and participation of ordained women and minority members than the SBC had, before or after the rise of fundamentalist leadership. Various progressives, however, began in the early 1990s to sense that the CBF was working diligently to recreate the SBC. Its statements of priorities, including its attention to the old Southern Baptist measures of success, seemed unpleasantly familiar. So many of the old "warhorses" of the SBC found their way into the CBF, including into positions of leadership, that some progressives began to call it "SBC Junior."[42]

Probably the greatest irony produced by the fundamentalist takeover of leadership of the SBC was overlooked by progressives and moderates alike, the fact that the fundamentalists viewed themselves as dissenters, as indeed they were.[43] The fundamentalist dissenters departed from the norms of Southern Baptist belief and behavior, just as the progressive dissenters did. They differed from their counterparts on the other end of the theological and political spectrum in more than one respect, however. For one thing, the culture of protest they created was much stronger than that of the progressives. It was formed into a movement, something done among progressives only by the women in ministry. This happened partly because the fundamentalists cared more about the institutional life of the SBC than did any progressives except the women. Also unlike the progressives, however, the fundamentalists built on the traditionalist foundation of Southern Baptists in clear rhetorical, organizational, and tactical ways. Progressives were legitimate Baptists, they said, because they harked back to the days of the martyrs of the faith. They appealed to the examples of the past as sanction for changes rank-and-file Southern Baptists saw as radical. Fundamentalists outsmarted them and the moderates in control of the convention by cloaking their appeals for their own forms of radical change in a combination of traditional and modern language. Their form of radicalism would turn the SBC on its head by centralizing power; replacing congregational governance with one openly dominated by a small number of powerful pastors; and putting the convention apparatus and its considerable resources at the disposal of secular political causes, compromising Baptists' historic commitment to the separation of church and state.[44] Fundamentalists attracted support for such radical changes by appealing to the past in the context of their claims to be able to take the SBC back to its roots.

Fundamentalists broke new ground, however, and employed modern images in their rhetoric by linking their goals to the broader goals of the rising tide of a new form of political conservatism in the South. They caught that tide just as it was beginning its sea change in southern politics, and the moderates were powerless against it. The fundamentalist offensive overwhelmed the defensive strategies of the moderates, who persisted in playing this new game by the old rules of engagement. For their part, the progressives were rendered irrelevant by the repudiation of most of their goals by convention resolutions or statements by the new wave of SBC officeholders and by the dramatic changes in the institutions from which they had tried to remain aloof traditionally. As long as the seminaries and missions organizations were simply traditional Southern Baptist institutions, the progressives could chide them for narrowness and call on them to join a different kind of effort on behalf of a gospel of reconciliation, an "incarnational" counterweight to triumphalism. Once the fundamentalists had control of the convention, progressive claims sounded vaguely hollow, as if they were being deflected off a giant shield. The "men of God" had risen indeed and supplanted the people who they believed had kept the SBC "unequal to the task." Fundamentalists had taken advantage of an opportunity for which they had been prepared by their own genealogy of dissent.

# Conclusion

## *The Ways of Being Baptist*

*Would you be free from the burden of sin?*
*There's pow'r in the blood, pow'r in the blood.*
*Would you o'er evil a victory win?*
*There's wonderful pow'r in the blood.*
*Would you be free from your passion and pride?*
*Come for a cleansing to Calvary's tide;*
*Would you do service for Jesus your King?*
*Would you live daily His praises to sing?*
*There's wonderful pow'r in the blood.*
*There is pow'r, pow'r,*
*Wonder-working pow'r in the precious blood of the Lamb.*
—Lewis E. Jones, *There Is Power in the Blood*

Progressive Southern Baptists had always prompted a range of responses among their more traditional brothers and sisters. Some moderate Southern Baptists absolutely hated what the progressives said and did, while others, for a variety of reasons, actually admired them but chose not to emulate them. To some conservatives, both the more moderate Southern Baptists and those with fundamentalist leanings, the progressives were like carriers of a disease. That disease, liberalism, threatened everything dear to the common believers of the gospel who came up through the ranks of Baptist churches in the South and occupied the pews and voted for the leaders who made the statements that embraced "the old, old story," not just of Jesus and his love but of the fitness of Southern Baptists to proclaim it. When fundamentalists declared open war on liberalism, the moderates were quick to disavow the label, knowing that the only people in Southern Baptist life who came close to being actual "liberals" were the people in the networks of progressive dissent. These moderates did not appreciate being tarred with a brush that they had used periodically to separate themselves from those progressives. To think that the persistent, if marginal, presence of progressives in Southern Baptist affairs could help cost them control of the convention filled moderates with some sense of irony, but greater amounts of anger. Many of them discounted the claims of the fundamentalists to be genuinely concerned about the liberal tendencies of the SBC, saying the fight was all about power. Whatever the various motives of the fundamentalists, they expressed a plausible concern based in part on a verifiable experience of exclusion from convention leadership and were supported by a remarkable series of majority votes at annual meetings of grassroots Southern Baptists from 1979 onward. If the actions of fundamentalists were indeed "all about" power, those actions were more likely and more welcome because of the perceived threat to Southern Baptist life represented by progressive dissidents.

If the progressives had not existed, one could almost imagine that the fundamentalists would have needed to invent them. The progressive dissenters' refusal to play active roles in the affairs of the denomination, to do what was necessary to gain appointment to convention boards and other positions, annoyed such moderates as Foy Valentine. But their relative invisibility in convention affairs probably prolonged the survival of moderate control over the SBC. It annoyed moderates to be accused by fundamentalists of believing and doing things that the progressives, not the moderates, believed and did, but the progressives were kept out of leadership positions by the moderates almost as successfully as were the fundamentalists. If the progressives, the only virtual or actual liberals in Southern Baptist life, had held visible positions of leadership or even fairly recognizable forms of presentation, the fundamentalists would have had a much stronger case for a takeover bid at an earlier date.

For their part, the progressives reacted to the fundamentalist resurgence in the SBC in a variety of ways. Once the fundamentalist party accomplished its goal of assuming leadership of the SBC, the choice many progressives made was simply to leave. Though few people in the SBC were sad to see them go, the progressives varied in their reactions to leaving their denominational home. Some did so with sadness. Many Southern Baptists in the networks of progressive dissent began to identify with American Baptists, following the example of Martin England, or to affiliate with the Alliance of Baptists. Some left Baptist life altogether and became involved with other church bodies. The progressive dissenters who stopped being Southern Baptists, for example, included labor and community organizer Perry Perkins, who became a Lutheran for a time; peace activist Ken Sehested, who remained a committed Baptist but no longer identified himself with the SBC, saying, "My mission money goes to the Alliance of Baptists"; and Martha Gilmore, who become a Methodist to fulfill her dream of serving a congregation as an ordained minister. Peace Fellowship president Glenda Fontenot maintained her membership in a church affiliated with the SBC but said, "I no longer consider myself a Southern Baptist." A second-generation Baptist minister, Fontenot left fulltime Christian service to become a communications consultant, leading seminars on business and technical writing. Other women left church work or transferred their energies to hospital chaplaincies, a career option long exercised by women who wanted to serve in some form of ministry when they found it impossible to gain positions with congregations. Will Campbell made it well known that he considered himself "a Baptist minister in the South" but not a Southern Baptist minister.[1]

Many progressives gave up their ties to Southern Baptists after the fundamentalist victory was assured, but their discouragement with Southern Baptist life was already well in place before the fundamentalist resurgence. Such alienation was provoked by the attitudes of moderates, not those of fundamentalists. The CBF, which made genuine efforts to be inclusive of women and minorities, appeared in some ways to be trying to hold ground until moderates could make a comeback in the SBC as a group or recreate in the CBF the same old structures that led them to their triumphant position in southern and Baptist life. Many progressives wanted little part in either plan. In several ways, the progressives had more in common with the fundamentalists than they did with the moderates. Fundamentalists were willing to sacrifice denominational harmony for the sake of their convictions, something moderates were not willing to do. Moderates' convictions were essentially identical with the institutional health of the convention and its agencies and programs, factors that all depended on denominational harmony. Progressives were somewhat more willing to upset the comity of the convention, but when the fundamentalists brought open disunion to the convention, many progressives knew there was little point in remaining. They had long since worn out their welcome.[2] The progressive dissidents ended up with a far greater possibility of having a voice in denominational affairs by virtue of their new involvements in the Alliance of Baptists and possibly, though to a lesser extent, the CBF.

Differences among the three principal groups of Southern Baptists reflected their activist sensibilities, their theology, and their views of the nature and purposes of institutions. Moderates placed their faith in the goodness and wisdom of their peers to operate in the best interests of Southern Baptist institutions and for the perpetuation of goodwill within the Southern Baptist consensus, viewing organizational ineffectiveness as one of the greatest sins. Fundamentalists trusted in the purity of traditional doctrine and authoritarian leadership styles, in opposition to the notion that institutions should be maintained by means of doctrinal flexibility and accommodation, and worked to remove those institutions from the control of compromising moderates. Doctrinal impurity, to the fundamentalists, was one of the greatest sins. Progressive dissidents put their faith in small-scale means of living out their beliefs, particularly local congregations and informal networks of like-minded believers instead of in large-scale denominational institutions. For them, one of the greatest sins was "hyperspirituality" of religion. They wanted to make use of their prophetic gifts to bring about changes in the political and economic behavior of the world, something about which the moderates cared less but the fundamentalists cared a great deal. In this way also, the progressive dissidents had more in common with their fundamentalist counterparts than they did with moderate Southern Baptists.

One of the most important lessons to come out of the dramatic changes in the SBC was a reminder that there were many ways to be Baptist. Moderate Southern Baptists thought that the fundamentalists who took control of the convention away from them did so in a spirit of meanness. Fundamentalists thought moderates had acted in ungracious ways toward them for years, even generations. Moderates belittled fundamentalists, making fun of their supposedly inferior educational attainments and backward notions long after their leaders had educations just as impressive as those of the moderates' leaders and theological positions just as carefully worked out. Then, the new breed of fundamentalists arose, organized and determined to avoid the old mistakes that had forced them outside the boundaries of traditional denominations, and focused on remaking the SBC from within. Unlike their progressive counterparts, they were not content to remain simply an irritant force or a group of gadflies. Like the fundamentalists, the progressives were dedicated to a vision of Southern Baptist life different from that of the moderates. But unlike the fundamentalists, progressives could not or would not do what was necessary to avoid being, within the context of the denomination, irrelevant.

There were decided similarities, then, between the progressives and the fundamentalists. In a strange way, progressives and fundamentalists found themselves arrayed, if not allied, against a common enemy: the moderate elite who had carved out a territory within Southern Baptist life in which they were free to do as they pleased administratively, this having grown out of an increasing sense of theological untouchability with little real accountability to the larger body. For moderates, the beauty of the Southern Baptist system was that through its agencies and educational institutions it centralized a great deal of power without subjecting them to the kind of internal discipline exercised by other centralized denominations. Thus, they thought and believed in ways that set them apart from the fundamentalists and their latent majority constituency. The moderates did not carry through with the social and cultural extensions of their theology, however, choosing not to translate their views into the kinds of reforms that progressive dissidents advocated. The progressives kept lines of communication open to the moderates. Moderates maintained a spoken high regard for the integrity of progressives, commonly saying that progressives were doing things that they would do if they could get away with it. But they also put up roadblocks to keep progressives from accomplishing what they wanted to do, saying, "Our people just aren't ready for this." While many progressives refused to consider moderates their enemies in the SBC, fundamentalists very clearly considered moderates theirs. Fundamentalists did their most effective work at that task, however, by accusing the moderates of being progressives. The moderates were simply more conservative politically and socially than they admitted, or probably even believed, and much more so than the fundamentalists were willing to admit.

Finally, however, it must be acknowledged that Foy Valentine was correct in one sense when he derided the progressives for what he saw as their ineffectiveness. Their influence, by traditional Southern Baptist standards of success, was small indeed. Progressives, for example, made the mistake of losing touch with the plain Southern Baptists whose populist tendencies could have been a source of power for some of the changes they sought. They forgot the lesson of Carlyle Marney's professor, not to forget "the bent knees" of the people who could never understand the high-class theological expressions that often accompanied reformist sentiments. The earnest piety and modest socio-economic status of many Southern Baptist laypeople could have been combined with the revolutionary reconciliation theology of Jesus to create a force for reform at least on economic issues that progressive Southern Baptists advocated. Progressives may not have been able to claim the "high moral ground" on every issue that concerned rank-and-file Southern Baptists, but they might have enlisted greater numbers in their efforts against the more overt expressions of injustice, such as racial discrimination. They might have been able to communicate a message put forth by a Southern

Baptist historian that dissent "is not a social disease," that it is "essential to ongoing life even if we do not always know precisely how, when, or where" it performs its tasks.[3] Unfortunately for the progressive agendas of Southern Baptist reformers, the political conservatism of most southerners outweighed the appeal of the revolutionary aspects of Jesus' message, a fact the fundamentalists understood very clearly.

Ironically, progressives and moderates made the same crucial mistake that they criticized the fundamentalists for making: assuming that their interpretation of the gospel was the only commendable one. They forgot or ignored the fact that in the Gospel accounts of the life of Jesus, the Prince of Peace sometimes does strike a militant note, and he does indeed separate himself from others with different beliefs and different values. These accounts present a mixed picture that affirms, on the one hand, liberation for the downcast and little but contempt for the rich and powerful. On the other hand, however, Jesus takes positions that clearly point toward a belief in the prospects for heavenly reward for those who embrace his message. The progressives concentrated so diligently on affirming the revolutionary aspects of that message that they neglected its otherworldly qualities, qualities the moderates institutionalized by means of Southern Baptist agencies, boards, and schools. Although overspiritualizing the message of Jesus provided many people with an excuse to ignore human suffering on earth, it did not take away the other fact that Jesus himself called his followers to seek the bliss of everlasting life in heaven.

Nonetheless, the history of Southern Baptist progressives is not one that disappears into irrelevance. They made their mark in ways that reaffirm their roles as classic examples of Baptists. They did not seek national or even "Southwide" influence because their measure of success was different from that of their triumphalist counterparts. Their principal interest lay in changing things where they were, by which most of them meant social and political changes in localities. They could be faulted for not having had a larger view, but only if one concludes that not having had ambitions for broadscale influence disqualified them from being considered "real" Southern Baptists. Some of them were indeed interested in exerting such influence. Clarence Jordan became quite widely known, far beyond the range of Southern Baptist life. But he and others in the genealogy who sought to make a broad impact on Southern Baptists were not interested in capturing the hierarchy of the SBC to make their views more widely known and accepted. The cost of that goal was too high for them because it was a goal to which they felt no attraction. These dissidents were too diverse, which is to say too Baptist, and not single-minded enough to seek hierarchical control. In an ironic twist on the typical assessment by Southern Baptist conservatives that progressives were not spiritual enough, one might say that the progressive dissidents were not worldly enough to undertake a task as bloody as taking over the convention. The option simply never occurred to them. They were much more fulfilled, even satisfied, by their roles as gadflies. They did not reject everything southern or Baptist. They tried to live out what they saw as the best, to embody it, not following the institutional line, but by being more authentic Baptists than they thought the moderates and fundamentalists were.

How southern the progressive dissenters were was a different matter. They certainly did not want to be archetypal southerners in the sense of the racist, militarist, sexist images of the people of their region. They had seen enough behavior among some of their counterparts in the Southern Baptist mainstream to inspire them to want to depart from its worst traditions. But they were southerners, nonetheless. They hurt for the South, even when many of its people behaved hatefully, the ways ministers hurt for wayward souls. They were unwilling to play denominational politics in the manner in which Foy Valentine and his peers were so skilled. The progressives were unwilling to "play" much of anything denominational, but they still cared about Southern Baptists. They rose above denominationalism, even while trying to speak prophetically to their fellow Southern Baptists. Every member of the genealogy knew that other denominations, or other regions, might be more attuned to them philosophically. When they tried to make a difference in the lives and beliefs of people in the SBC, what stopped the dissidents from switching denominations was their identity as *Southern* Baptists.

That identity carried them through many stormy dealings with others in the denomination, but it never translated into denominationalism. Even if they had wanted to do so, the progressives would have had a difficult time mounting anything like the effort the fundamentalists exerted to take control of leadership of the SBC. It is extremely unlikely that they could have rallied behind one leader, or a handful of them, including one like Jordan or Marney, if someone could have been persuaded to take on the job. Progressives never had a central leading figure because they were more interested in freedom than in control. If they lacked the discipline as a group to accomplish what their counterparts on the right did in taking over the leadership of the SBC, that lack of discipline resulted in part from their refusal to impose their will on other Baptists. Further, other than the women who pursued ordination and employment as ministers, progressives lacked what historian Lawrence Goodwyn called a "movement culture."[4] There was no group discipline because there was no organized group, not at least until the fight was essentially over in the mid-1980s, and at that point the group was not made up of former dissidents but of elements from the deposed moderate leadership. No movement culture arose among progressives because, except for the women who did so much to inspire the fundamentalists' rise to power, there was no movement. People on various branches of the dissident family tree that had its loose beginnings with Walt Johnson's departure from the mainstream of Southern Baptist life in 1920 moved in and out of issues and concerns, and they developed ideas and strategies for addressing them as the times befitted and as they were inspired by one another and by myriad other influences. Fundamentalists, conversely, cut across all sorts of issues and never got sidetracked by internecine warfare on anything, including the various interpretations of the concept of inerrancy.

All three groups believed they were the true representatives of historic Baptist beliefs. This fact alone illustrates how very diverse Baptists were in the twentieth century, a diversity welcomed by progressives and most moderates. At issue was the question of how to act out being Baptist. It was a point of view that had implications for ecclesiastical behavior but set no single standard for it, leaving the definitions of techniques for living in the faith to believers and what they made of God's expectations. Fundamentalists defined authority as the central element needed to maintain the faithfulness of Baptists to God, the authority of Scripture, and their supposedly unique ability to interpret it properly. Moderates developed a system of expediency to achieve their vision of faithfulness, to do whatever was necessary to keep the institutions they believed were God's true instruments of grace alive and effective. Progressive dissenters had the strongest trust in the traditional Baptist value of freedom, believing for the most part that they needed neither to coerce certain forms of doctrinal assent among church members nor to assert their primacy among their fellow seekers after the way of Jesus. Their historic Baptist identity showed through also in their preference for congregations over conventions and convention agencies and in their shunning of success as the measure of faithfulness.

With their roots in radicalism and rejection by the established elements of society, Baptists had a message of simple redemption to share with the world. When they attracted converts who admired their courage and simplicity, their numbers obviously grew. When growth became an end in itself, however, and the methods and measures of attainment of growth an indication that Baptists had embraced an ethic of success, their identities as the children of martyred forebears became dramatically confused. Progressive dissenters, though, were less confused than their counterparts in either of the other two groups of Southern Baptists. They were more willing to embrace the view of the gospel that Jesus seemed to present, that his followers live by dying, gain by giving up, and are exalted by being humbled. Whether they were right or wrong, faithful or foolish, is a matter of opinion. That they lived out their faith the best way they knew how, just as the people in the other two groups did, is easily demonstrable. But few people in any of the three groups believed that many of the people in the other two groups were doing their best to live in faithfulness to their callings. This turn of events demonstrated one simple fact that few of the anguished observers of the fundamentalist resurgence in the SBC wanted to admit: that the convention had outlived its days as a pluralistic body. Being Baptist never required the kinds of unanimity of belief that fundamentalists demanded or the silent assent to the wisdom of one clique of leaders that moderates craved. Either a split or some other form of dramatic reminder of what it meant to be Baptist was long overdue in Southern Baptist life.

To the extent that progressive belief and behavior, especially that of women, energized fundamentalists to begin their conquest of the convention, the progressive dissidents actually did the convention and all Baptists a favor. All three groups had their share of "passion and pride," and all three thought they could serve Jesus the King, but they had all lost track of the lesson that the power "in the blood" was not something over which any one group could claim a monopoly. Fundamentalists faced the most difficult task of the three groups in remaining true to Baptist traditions, having invested so much power in a new governing elite, but they were the closest of the three groups theologically and culturally to the Southern Baptist majority. If control of the convention could be achieved as easily as the fundamentalists achieved it, it seems likely that they had more support going for them than their critics aknowledged. Many Baptists, therefore, must have desired the kinds of change that fundamentalists offered the SBC. By creating an unintended and unacknowledged common cause with fundamentalists against the moderate status quo, progressives helped bring about the long overdue division of the SBC into three groups. Once that was accomplished, all three groups were free to get back to being what they should have been in the first place: Baptists.

# Notes

## Preface

1. Hughes, "The Baptist-Baptists of Pampa," *Texas Observer*, 21 October 1988, 23.

2. The expression "Southern Baptist life" is commonly used in scholarly and denominational literature to denote the broader community of Southern Baptists. Because of their congregational polity, Southern Baptists do not refer to themselves as the "Southern Baptist Church." Such an expression would be used only in reference to one congregation and then only with a lowercase *c* in the word "church." Likewise, one also does not refer to Southern Baptists as the *"Southern Baptist Convention,"* which, as congregational purists like to point out, technically exists for only three days a year, when it meets in session each June. One may use "Southern Baptist Convention" to refer to the body of Southern Baptist churches, but it would be correct to do so only when referring to traits or practices common to Southern Baptist churches, not implying any absolute denominational authority over individual congregations.

3. Gardner, *"Ain't That Weird?"* Dave Gardner, unfortunately, was also a thoroughgoing racist. He had a panoply of radical views on the nature of society and government that could best be described as paranoid. see King, "Whatever Happened to Brother Dave?" 54-84.

4. Matt. 6:3.

5. For decades, Southern Baptists have conducted extensive missionary efforts in the North, resulting in the creation of Southern Baptist congregations and even conventions in northern states. The concept of "Southern" Baptists in Minnesota and New York bothered few Southern Baptists, either those in the southern homeland or those in northern mission fields, but it was clear to everyone within Southern Baptist life that the denomination's heartland would always be the South. American

Baptists in the South are found mostly in black churches, many of which are dually aligned with the American Baptist Churches and the predominantly black National Baptists. American Baptist congregations in the South that are predominantly white, most of which are dually aligned with Southern Baptists, number fewer than twenty.

6. Robinson and Sullivan, *New Directions in Civil Rights Studies*, 10, 13.

7. Degler, *Place over Time*, 22–23; Hill, et al., *Religion and the Solid South*, 49. See also Hill, *The South and the North in American Religion*, 124–35.

8. See especially Flynt, "Feeding the Hungry and Ministering to the Broken Hearted"; McDowell, *Social Gospel in the South;* Storey, *Texas Baptist Leadership and Social Christianity;* and, to a certain extent, Rosenberg, *Southern Baptists.* Storey said that some reform-minded Texas Baptists in 1915 thought of Jesus as "the great sociologist." See Storey, "Battling Evil," 382. Paul Harvey pointed to connections between Southern Baptist progressivism in the period between 1895 and 1925 and the popularity of the notion of "scientific management," *Redeeming the South,* 197. Two older works that point toward the presence of a southern social gospel movement, "though . . .slower and more cautious" than its northern counterpart, according to Robert T. Handy are his *Social Gospel in America,* 12; and Bailey, *Southern White Protestantism,* 42–43. Keith Harper, *Quality of Mercy,* i–ii, ix, saw connections between Southern Baptists and the social gospel movement and describes treatments of the north-south dichotomy as false, 113.

9. Boles, *South through Time,* 403, 404. See also Bailey, *Southern White Protestantism,* 42-43.

## Introduction

1. Marsden, *Fundamentalism and American Culture,* v.

2. Ibid., 3, 164 ff.; Ammerman, "North American Protestant Fundamentalism," 4ff.; Wilcox, *God's Warriors,* 2, 6, 7, 8; Ammerman, "New South and the New Baptists," 487.

3. As R. Scott Appleby pointed out, one should be careful not to ignore the prominence of some theological doctrines among Southern Baptists. He overstepped, however, in declaring "the strict inerrancy of the Bible" to be the prime doctrine of Southern Baptists. It is indeed the "litmus test" for resurgent fundamentalists in the SBC, as the cardinal tenet of all fundamentalists, but Appleby erred in assuming that all Southern Baptists are fundamentalists, or inerrantists, for that matter. Appleby, review of *Southern Baptist Politics,* 835–36.

4. Leonard, "When the Denominational Center Doesn't Hold," 909; Leonard, *God's Last and Only Hope,* 119–120.

5. Flynt, *Dixie's Forgotten People,* 147; Wyatt-Brown, *Honor and Violence in the Old South,* 26–27.

6. Wilson, *Baptized in Blood,* 7, 8-9, 36, 41, 68, 79; Ahlstrom, *Religious History of the American People,* 426-28; Lasch, *True and Only Heaven,* 47-48; Queen, *In the South the Baptists Are the Center of Gravity,* 15-16.

7. Vigorous theological controversies have broken out in Southern baptist life over the years, but they have usually taken place among college, university, and seminary professors, and administrators and officials of the denominational agencies charged with funding and oversight of educational institutions. Until the 1980s, most rank-and-file Southern Baptists dismissed such controversies as squabbles among preachers that had little bearing on their day-to-day lives in the faith. See *s.v.* "Graves-Howell Controversy"; *s.v.* "Toy, Crawford Howell"; *s.v.* "Whitsitt, William Heth" in *Encyclopedia of Southern Baptists* for descriptions of early-day controversies in Southern Baptist life, Bill J. Leonard related the struggles over the control of the SBC to other Southern Baptist controversies and to habits and methods of dealing with disunity within the convention in *God's Last and Only Hope*

8. Ginger, *Six Days or Forever?* 4-5; Marsden, *Fundamentalism and American Culture,* 184-89; Russell, *Voices of Fundamentalism,* 184-86; Farnsley, *Southern Baptist Politics,* 8-10, 18-19; Marsden, *Understanding Fundamentalism and Evangelicalism,* 66ff.; Martin, *With God on Our Side,* 16-18.

9. Ahlstrom, *Religious History of the American People,* 932; Bedell, Sandon, and Wellborn, *Religion in America,* 260ff.; Russell, *Voices of Fundamentalism,* 43-44, 214, 218; Wuthnow, *Restructuring of American Religion,* 60-61; Farnsley, *Southern Baptist Politics,* 21-25; Hill, "Story before the Story,"43-45.

10. Ahlstrom, *Religious History of the American People,* 934-35, 938-43, 947-48. Boles pointed out that southern Protestants who embraced the idea of the social gospel in the early part of the twentieth century remained silent on the subject of the injustice of race relations, as their northern counterparts had. Boles, *South through Time,* 403-4.

11. Paul Harvey illuminated these interrelationships in *Redeeming the South,* 3-4 wherein he argued for a more reciprocal notion than that usually presented by the "cultural captivity thesis." Instead of seeing the churches of the South only as captives of southern culture, Harvey said, they should be seen as well as formers of the culture(s) of the south.

## 1. Religion and Culture in the Baptist South

"On Jordan's Stormy Banks," words by Samuel Stennet, 1787, in McKinney, ed., *The Broadman Hymnal,* 249. Broadman Press was one of the principal publishers for Southern Baptist educational and worship materials.

1. Shurden, "Rebellion," 29, 30, 31; Isaacs, *Transformation of Virginia,* 161-63. Isaacs, 163-66, described the role Baptists played in creating a "counterculture" in colonial Virginia in the 1760s and 1770s, the beginnings of a social rebellion against the Anglican gentry and a contributor to the revolution against English rule itself.

2. Isaacs, *Transformation of Virginia,* 164.

3. Leonard, *God's Last and Only Hope,* 40-41, 81; Ahlstrom, *Religious History of the American People,* 317-18, 663-65; Sweet, *Story of Religion in America,* 246.

4. Leonard, *God's Last and Only Hope,* 32-34, 85-86; Ahlstrom, *Religious History of the American People,* 320-23; Isaacs, *Transformation of Virginia,* 163; Boles, *Great Revival,* 76-77, 87-88.

5. Leonard, *God's Last and Only Hope,* 114, 115, 119-20; Isaacs, *Transformation of Virginia,* 163-65.

6. Spain, *At Ease in Zion,* 43, 56, 67, 127-29, 144-45, 149, 165-67, 198, 209, 210-11, 213-14; Isaacs, *Transformation of Virginia,* 164. See also Wilson, *Baptized in Blood,* 8-9; and Queen, *In the South the Baptists Are the Center of Gravity,* 10-11. Queen's title is adapted from a quote by Victor I. Masters in the July 1920 *Review and Expositor,* the theological journal published by Southern Baptist Theological Seminary. Masters said of the centrality of Southern Baptists' importance in world evangelization, "As goes America, so goes the world. Largely as goes the South, so goes America. And in the South is the Baptist center of gravity of the world." Queen, *In the South the Baptists Are the Center of Gravity,* 16.

7. Charles Reagan Wilson, quoted by Anne Lowrey Bailey, "Encyclopedia of the South Links Legend and Reality," *Chronicle of Higher Education,* 3 August 1988, A-6.

8. Rosenberg, "Southern Baptist Response," 148.

9. Martin, "Hearts and Minds," 160.

10. Carlyle Marney, "Preaching the Gospel, South of God: An Interview with Carlyle Marney," interview by Bill Finger, *The Christian Century,* 4 October 1978, 920.

11. Martin, "God's Angry Man," 154.

12. McClendon, *Biography as Theology,* 19-20, 112-15, 126-28, 138-39; Bronner, *s.v.* "Storytelling," *Encyclopedia of Southern Culture.*

13. The expression "conviction" is used by evangelicals to describe the sense a prospective convert to Christianity has to feel to be able to "receive" Christ, to embrace the belief that Christ's sacrificial death and resurrection has "saved" the convert's soul from the threat of eternal damnation in hell and made it fit to spend eternity in paradise with God. To "accept" Christ as "personal Lord and Savior," according to this view, one must first acknowledge the sinfulness of one's previous life, that is, be "convicted" of one's sins. By "witness," evangelicals mean the verbal "sharing" of a believer's faith experience in the hope of converting a nonbeliever. In its more rehearsed, somewhat more formal state, such as an expression is referred to as "testimony," usually meaning a brief talk given before a group. The use of legal terms such as "conviction," "witness," and "testimony" is no accident, for evangelicals usually see salvation as a matter of the gravest consequence, tried before a heavenly judge. God is prepared to forgive those who sincerely ask for forgiveness, make a "profession" of faith in Jesus, and seek a new life in relationship with Christ. God can even forgive the same person repeatedly for occasional lapses into sinful behavior or thought. But God, in standard evangelical view, is also prepared to condemn the unrepentant to an everlasting punishment. See Balmer, *Mine Eyes Have Seen the Glory,* 4, 239, 240-41; Harvey, *s.v.* "Atonement," *A Handbook of Theological Terms,*

33; Hunt, *s.v.* "Atonement," and Trentham, *s.v.* "Guilt," Encyclopedia of Southern Baptists; and Johnson, "Lawyer and Preacher," 1. Hunt called the "satisfaction" or "substitutionary" ("sometimes 'penal'") theory of atonement "the most prominent" in "orthodox circles." This view of atonement explains Christ's sacrifice as a means of satisfying God's wrath. Christ took the place of, or "substituted" for, sinners by taking their sins upon himself and suffering crucifixion. Thus, instead of condemning all humanity, God made it possible for repentant sinners to escape their just punishment by sending Christ to suffer, die, and be raised from the dead, so that believers could have eternal life through belief in his redeeming love. Trentham said that "Man's guilt means that he deserves the condemnation of God." Otis Strickland, interview by Glenn O. Hilburn, 21 August 1972, Interview 1, transcript, The Texas Collection, 4-7. Conversion stories abound among Southern Baptists. Another account of an emotionally powerful conversion experience is found in Bailis William Orrick, interview by Rufus B. Spain, 11 July 1975, Interview 1, transcript, The Texas Collection, 17-18. Orrick said that when he "went forward and made my profession, was received for baptism,... I wept and wept. I couldn't answer a question they'd ask me."

14. Strickland, Interview 1, 6-7.

15. Ibid., 7-8.

16. Ibid., 17-18, 19, 26. Matthews was not the only minister to receive this sort of harassment from Norris. He sent similar messages to his bitter rival George W. Truett, W.A. Criswell's predecessor as pastor of the First Baptist Church of Dallas. Rosenberg, *Southern Baptists*, 15; Fletcher, *Southern Baptist Convention*, 140; Hankins, *God's Rascal*, 186, n.87.

17. Strickland, Interview, 26.

18. Norris was acquitted of the charge of murder. He pleaded self-defense. Hankins, *God's Rascal*, 24, 118-120; Marsden, *Fundamentalism and American Culture*, 190; Taylor, s.v. "Norris, John Franklyn," *Encyclopedia of Southern Baptists.* Norris was such an antagonistic presence in Southern Baptist life that he attracted the disciplinary attention of every level of denominational organization. The local association of congregations withdrew fellowship from First Baptist Church, Fort Worth, in 1922. The statewide Baptist General Convention of Texas censured Norris personally the same year, refused to seat him during its 1923 meeting, and permanently excluded him in 1924. So determined were Texas Baptist leaders not to readmit him, says Wilburn Taylor, that "The convention and the association amended their constitutions to prevent readmission, except by majority vote." With consequences reaching into the end of the twentieth century, the furor caused by Norris and like-minded fundamentalists caused the SBC to revise and enlarge its statement of faith, resulting in the issuance of "The Baptist Faith and Message" in 1925. This statement became one of the focal points of battles between Southern Baptist moderates and fundamentalists in the 1980s and 1990s. Fletcher, *Southern Baptist Convention*, 140.

19. Strickland, Interview 1, 24-25.

20. Ibid., 19-20.

21. Ibid., 25-26. Hilburn referred to Matthews as "Dr. Matthews," because he received an honorary doctorate from Baylor University in 1947. Wilbanks, *s.v.* "Matthews, Charles Everett," *Encyclopedia of Southern Baptists;* Strickland, Interview 1, 20-21.

22. One writer recalled the burial of his great-grandfather, a Civil War veteran and Southern Baptist, and the epitaph written for him by another former Confederate: "An unreconstructed Johnnie, who never repented, who fought for what he knew to be right from '61 to '65 and received one Mexican dollar for two years' service. Belonged to the Ku Klux Klan, a deacon in the Baptist church and master Mason for forty years." Flynn, "Genesis, Jeremiah, and Gospels," 190.

23. Maston, Interview 1. Maston became well known for his remarkable attempts to raise Southern Baptists' awareness of the ethical dimensions of Christianity, particularly concerning race relations. While he never would have excused Ku Klux Klan membership, he emphasized the Klan's fervent Protestant sympathies and accounted for what he understood to be his colleagues' associations with it by virtue of their deeply held suspicions of the Roman Catholic Church.

24. It could be, of course, that Otis Strickland was mistaken about what he took to be Matthews's membership in the Klan. Biographical information about C.E. Matthews is not plentiful, but what exists does not mention any Klan involvement, although C.E. Wilbanks's article in the *Encyclopedia of Southern Baptists* confirms most of the other details of Matthews's life as Strickland outlined them. An archival search in material related to Matthews at Southwestern Seminary revealed nothing on the subject.

25. Strickland, on the prompting of a brother who was an undertaker, believed that one could tell whether someone had been a Christian by the look on the face of a dead body. "He said you die like you live....he says, 'I can tell the difference between a Christian man and a lost man in their countenance'" Strickland, Interview 1, 36.

## *2. Fellowship of Kindred Minds*

"Blest Be the Tie," words by John Fawcett, 1782, in *The Broadman Hymnal,* 239. Hymnals are good indicators of the theological and social concerns of Southern Baptists at various points in the twentieth century. The Broadman Hymnal of 1940 includes a heading for "Social Service" in its topical index, among the more traditional headings such as "Assurance," "Cross," "Resurrection," and "Soul Winning." Twenty titles appear under "Social Service." Only one, however, seems to call for attention to the needs of people in the "here and now." It is Charles Wesley's "A Charge to Keep," which includes the line, "to serve the present age, my calling to fulfill," and does not spiritualize, at least openly, the meaning of the expression "present age." All the rest, such as Isaac Watts's "Am I a Soldier of the Cross?" have little to say about service to others apart from the duty to impart to "lost" persons teachings about the gospel of Jesus. Howard Arnold Walter's "I Would Be True" says, "I would be friend of all—the foe, the friendless." But it, like Fanny J. Crosby's "To the Work," which says, "let the hungry be fed," obviously intends that such images of earthly concern serve as metaphors for the meeting of spiritual needs. See 64, 157, 176, 368. Washington Gladden, the northern social gospel leader, wrote "O Master, Let Me Walk with Thee" in part as an expression of his devotion to the cause of organized labor. Most Southern Baptists who sang it likely failed to note the effect of Gladden's sympathies on his writing of hymn texts and embraced the song because of its strong evocation of the spiritual dimension of human struggles. White and Hopkins, 6.

1. Bailey, *Southern White Protestantism,* 42-43.

2. Handy, *Social Gospel in America,* 29. Rauschenbusch acknowledged the relative absence of "social propaganda" in the preaching and writing of the leaders of the early Christian church. He accounted for their failure to oppose first-century slavery as an example of the kinds of issues they had to postpone addressing in favor of the urgent necessity of establishing the institution Christ had commissioned for the spreading of his message. Rauschenbusch accepted the need to avoid causing the church to die at birth by antagonizing the political power structure before it had the strength to do so, and pointed out its eventual contributions to several kinds of social change. Rauschenbusch's only comment on slavery in the United States was to propose that "If the convictions of William Lloyd Garrison had burned in Paul, we should probably not know that Paul had ever existed." Rauschenbusch, *Christianity and the Social Crisis,* 153. See also 150, 152.

3. Fletcher, *Southern Baptist Convention,* 133; Eighmy, *Churches in Cultural Captivity,* 96-98. Miller, *s.v.* "Christian Life Commission," *Encyclopedia of Southern Baptists,* which outlines the history of the Social Service Commission and its successor, the Christian Life Commission, as it became known in 1953. Samuel S. Hill Jr. said that southern Protestants' obsession with the evils of liquor provided their version of the social gospel and caused them to abandon their traditional avoidance of political involvement. Baptists, he said, "who adhered to separation of church and state principles, threw theory to the wind in this case, so definitely did they identify liquor as the prime moral evil." *South and the North in American Religion,* 132-33.

4. Miller, "Christian Life Commission"; Bailey, *Southern White Protestantism,* 46, 47; Grantham, *Southern Progressivism,* 19.

5. Hays and Steely, *Baptist Way of Life,* 47-49. See chapter 3 for comments on the role of Brooks Hays in Baptist life and in changing race relations in the South.

6. Routh, *s.v.* "District Association," and Sauls, *s.v.* "Associational Missions," *Encyclopedia of Southern Baptists.* See "No Women Clergy," 1104; and "Church Expelled for Ordaining Gay Man," 983, for examples of associational discipline toward "erring" Southern Baptist congregations.

7. Miller, "Christian Life Commision"; Bailey, *Southern White Protestantism,* 42-43. Matthews, *s.v.* "History of Preaching," *Encyclopedia of Southern Baptists,* contended that Southern Baptist ministers generally stayed with uncontroversial, "safe" themes in their sermons or "lost their pulpits and thus their audiences." Cotes,

*s.v.* "Southern Baptist Preaching," in the same volume of the *Encyclopedia of Southern Baptists,* proposed that Southern Baptist ministers have preached more on social issues than usually believed, saying, "Baptist preaching is attuned to the times." Three Th.D. theses written at Southwestern Baptist Theological Seminary bear out the general impression of the lack of social gospel or activist preaching among Southern Baptist ministers during most of the period of the Social Service Commission's existence: Lacy, "History of Representative Southern Baptist Preaching"; Brown, "History of Representative Southern Baptist Preaching"; Fasol, "History of Representative Southern Baptist Preaching."

8. Fletcher, *Southern Baptist Convention,* 230-33; Warren T. Carr, interview by the author, 18 April 1985, Texas Collection; Martin England, interview by the author, 27 July 1984, Interview 2, Texas Collection.

9. Miller, "Christian Life Commission"; Strickland, *s.v.* "Christian Life Commission, Texas," *Encyclopedia of Southern Baptists;* Miller, "Texas," 331.

10. Moore, *s.v.* "Stewardship," *Encyclopedia of Southern Baptists;* Moore, *s.v.* "Stewardship Commission of the Southern Baptist Convention," *Encyclopedia of Southern Baptists.* Cullom, *s.v.* "Walter Nathan Johnson," Encyclopedia of Southern Baptists. Two unpublished sources on Johnson are a thesis written by his nephew, Daniel Calhoun Johnson, "Walter N. Johnson"; and Melvin, "Life and Thought of Walter Nathan Johnson." Some of the research for the present study was conducted in materials that were not available at the time Dr. Melvin did his work on Walt Johnson. Southern Baptists considered stewardship so important to the SBC that the convention made it the focus of one of its permanent commissions in 1960. Moore, "Stewardship Commission."

11. Cullom, "Walter Nathan Johnson"; Burkhalter, *s.v.* "Seventy Five Million Campaign," *Encyclopedia of Southern Baptists;* St. Amant, *Short History of Louisiana Baptists,* 101-2.

12. Walt N. Johnson, "An Adolescent Problem Child," *LCV Quarterly Communication,* July 1949, 1-2. The North Carolina Baptist Historical Collection in the Z. Smith Reynolds Library of Wake Forest University in Winston-Salem has a full run of Johnson's newsletters, as well as Johnson's personal papers. All materials cited herein, including *The Next Step in the Churches* articles, that were generated by or correspondence received by Johnson can be found in the Baptist Collection. In a way, Johnson and J. Frank Norris were in accord on one issue. Norris, too, was suspicious of the SBC's emerging role as a system of centralized funding of ministry efforts, though for very different reasons from Johnson's. Rosenberg, *Southern Baptists,* 15; Lippy, *Bibliography of Religion,* 242.

13. Burkhalter, "Seventy-Five Million Campaign"; Baker, *Southern Baptist Convention and Its People,* 393-94, 402-3; Walt N. Johnson, "Another Mass Million Movement?" *The Next Step in the Churches,* October 1944, 1; Walt N. Johnson, "Correcting a Blunder," *The Next Step in the Churches,* February 1937, 2. Calhoun Johnson downplayed his uncle's most strenuous objections to the campaign, citing his effectiveness in organizing the pledges of North Carolina Baptists, his pleasure

with the success of the pledge phase of the project, and the good terms on which he left the employ of the SBC. "Walter N. Johnson," 41-43, 47-49. For his description of Johnson's objections to the campaign, see p. 86. Apparently, Walt Johnson kept his reservations about the program to himself until he was quite well removed from his former position, at least the mid-1930s.

14. Walt N. Johnson, "Aggression and Restraint," *The Next Step in the Churches,* May 1939, 1; Johnson, "Another Mass Million Movement?" 1-2; Walt N. Johnson, "The Release of Power," *The Next Step in the Churches,* October 1945, 1-4; Walt N. Johnson, "A Two-Weeks Adventure in Worship Experience," *The Next Step in the Churches,* November 1945, 1-4.

15. Walt N. Johnson, "Church Integration or Church Divisions—Which Is It to Be?" *The Next Step in the Churches,* October 1942, 2.

16. Melvin, "Life and Thought of Walter Nathan Johnson," 1, 8, 35, 53, 54, 61-63, 100, 101. Melvin taught at Mars Hill College, with which Johnson had a long relationship and to which his library was donated after his death. Illuminating the powerful influence on Johnson of mysticism, as well as the social gospel, Melvin quoted Johnson's article in *The Next Step,* June 1931, "Which Way Religion," 2, in which Johnson said, "Stanley Jones and Harry Ward are our two greatest living prophets," 101. See the introduction in Handy, *Social Gospel in America,* 13. Jones was quite well known for his propagation of ideas and techniques of Indian spirituality in the United States. Johnson often used Jones's understanding of the Indian concept of the ashram as a model for his own retreats. L.L Carpenter was one of Johnson's close associates who was asked to contribute to a file of tributes to Johnson assembled in 1964 and placed in the library of Southeastern Seminary. See his piece, "Dr. Walt N. Johnson," 1964, Special Collections, Denny Library, 2. One of the tributes in the same collection was written by M.A. Huggins, who was a student at Wake Forest College when Johnson was pastor of Wake Baptist Church between 1909 and 1912 and said, "I heard him preach...every Sunday for three years, save one Sunday when I was afflicted with boils." Christian, Seer, Pioneer," 1.

17. Melvin, "Life and Thought of Walter Nathan Johnson," 53-54. Melvin's analysis of Johnson's theology, especially his thinking on stewardship and ecclesiology, led him to believe that Johnson had more in common with the social gospel movement during its earlier years than in its full flowering. In fact, he said, "One is perhaps justified in viewing Johnson's concept of stewardship as evidence that there was a substantial time lag in the movement of social Christianity from the northern churches to those in the South," 95.

18. Walt N. Johnson, "The Plainest and Most Personal Letter that I Have Ever Written," *LCV Quarterly Communication,* January 1949, 3; see also *The Next Step in the Churches,* August 1944 and August 1946. Johnson had a highly distinctive writing style that featured frequent use of capitalization. All quotes from Johnson's writing are presented as they appear in their original settings. No emphasis is added in any case. Penrose C. St. Amant said of Johnson's manner of expression during his days as a Baptist leader in Louisiana, "Secretary Johnson's somewhat effusive elo-

quence was often penetrating but sometimes his figures of speech were spectacularly grotesque," *Short History of Louisiana Baptists,* 102.

19. Gilmore, "Schools of Applied Stewardship," 4. The *Biblical Recorder* is the weekly newsmagazine of the Baptist State Convention of North Carolina. See Melvin's discussion of the stewardship schools in "Life and Thought of Walter Nathan Johnson," 26-30.

20. Walt N. Johnson, "Jesus—Stalin or Ghandi?" *The Next Step in the Churches,* October, 1.

21. Walt N. Johnson, "Nearing a Turn in the Road," *The Next Step in the Churches,* October 1936, 1.

22. Walt N. Johnson, "Rival Movements," *The Next Step in the Churches,* January 1933, 3.

23. Walt N. Johnson, "Don't Get Excited," *The Next Step in the Churches,* March 1933, 2.

24. Walt N. Johnson, "Cast Out Materialism," *The Next Step in the Churches,* November 1931, 3; Walt N. Johnson, "Our Seminaries and Stewardship," *The Next Step in the Churches,* August 1927, 3. Johnson persisted, however, in saying that his efforts were aimed at revitalizing Southern Baptist churches, not withdrawing them. See, e.g., "Aggression and Restraint," 1, in which he said, "Our approach is not *inter*denominational, but *intra*-denominational."

25. Walt N. Johnson, "Pagans, Tithers, or Stewards–Which?" *The Next Step in the Churches,* February 1936, 1.

26. Walt N. Johnson, "Worship and Interracial Discipline," *The Next Step in the Churches,* October 1946, 3.

27. Walt N. Johnson, "What Is 'the Next Step' in Our Churches?" *The Next Step in the Churches,* October 1946, 3.

28. In most Christian doctrine, the Holy Spirit serves as a source of comfort and inspiration, especially sought after by those believers who are engaged in demanding or dangerous activities on behalf of the church. Johnson had a particularly active view of the work of the Holy Spirit and a critical appraisal of the understanding of it held by many of his contemporary Christians. He said that those who talked about the Holy Spirit but separated understandings of it from daily life were uttering "pious moonshine." Such people, said Johnson, were waiting "with longing hearts and open hands for a celestial something to swoop down on us out of the sky." "Take Dynamite," *The Next Step in the Churches,* December 1931, 1. W.R. Grigg referred to Johnson's many references to "the continuous presence of God in the person of the Holy Spirit in the 'here and now,' (a phrase that he often used)." "Concerning My Recollection of Walt N. Johnson," 1964, Special Collections, Denny Library, 1.

29. Walt N. Johnson, "A Dialogue," *The Next Step in the Churches,* May 1935, 3. See also Walt N. Johnson, "What Is to Be Demonstrated before Our Churches Will Ever Fully Cooperate in a World Program Radically Christian?" *The Next Step in the Churches,* November 1934, 1.

30. Walt N. Johnson, "World Response to Live Churches," *The Next Step in the Churches,* August 1945, 3.

31. Walt N. Johnson, *The Next Step in the Churches,* May 1946, 4.

32. Walt N. Johnson, "Greater Things Gathering among Us," *The Next Step in the Churches,* June 1938, 5. Conner's apparent interest in Johnson supports the notion held by T.B. Maston that Conner's ties to the Ku Klux Klan, if Maston was correct that Connor had such ties, resulted from concerns other than overt racism. One could hardly have reconciled pronounced racism with support for Walt Johnson.

33. See *The Next Step in the Churches,* May 1939, e.g. He even served a term on the executive committee of the SBC from 1927 to 1931. Walt N. Johnson, "Why I Retire," *The Next Step in the Churches,* July 1931, 2.

34. Walt N. Johnson, Raleigh, to W.P. Biggerstaff, High Point, 1 May 1952; Johnson, Raleigh, to O.L. Sherrill, Wilmington, 27 April 1952; Johnson, Raleigh, to W.C. Laney, Brookford, 8 May 1952; all Walter Nathan Johnson papers, North Carolina Baptist Historical Collection.

35. Walt N. Johnson, "Wake Forest College Dramatizes Our Current Situation," *The Next Step in the Churches,* June 1946, 1.

36. State Baptist Convention of North Carolina, *North Carolina Baptist Annual* (Raleigh: State Baptist Convention, 1952).

37. E. McNeill Poteat Jr., "Passing of a Modern Saint," 5.

38. Walt N. Johnson, "Stewardship and Evangelism," *The Next Step in the Churches,* October 1927, 1; Johnson, "Cast Out Materialism," 3, written in 1931; Walt N. Johnson, "Getting Ready for Real Evangelism and Re-Education in Our Churches," *The Next Step in the Churches,* August 1938, 1-2; Walt N. Johnson, "Are Our Modern Churches Gone Futile?" *The Next Step in the Churches,* August 1947, 4.

39. Melvin's doctor of divinity thesis, which is a critical study, is silent on the subject, as is the master of theology thesis written by Johnson's nephew Daniel Calhoun Johnson at Southeastern Baptist Theological Seminary. The 1964 tributes to Johnson in the files of Southeastern Seminary do not mention the story that follows. Some of the inattention to this part of Johnson's life probably owes to the unavailability of the documentary material in which I later was privileged to work.

40. Walt N. Johnson, "Worship and Social Action," *The Next Step in the Churches,* January 1940, 4. Johnson had made somewhat unusual use of sexual imagery in his writing for some time. For example, see "The Gospel Mutilated," *The Next Step in the Churches,* March 1926, 2, which refers to "sterilization" and "castration" of the gospel message.

41. Questionnaire headed "Sterilization and Metasexual Impregnation," n.d., Walter Nathan Johnson Papers, North Carolina Baptist Historical Collection. Sealed final drafts of Johnson's novel, "The Lighted Couch," and a companion volume, "Letters from the Lighted Couch," are in his papers. I had an opportunity to read earlier, unsealed drafts of these manuscripts. He said late in 1949 that the "Lighted Couch" manuscript had been ready to go to the printer for three years, but that he had held

it back because "neither our churches nor our ministers were ready for it. It pounds our closed interpretations of the New Testament with so many cracking questions, we had delayed publishing it." He added as well, "We knew it would likely be ignored. Or worse, it might raise so much...controversy on side issues as to miss the central point in it." Walt N. Johnson, "Inspired or Insane?" *LCV Quarterly Communication,* October 1949, 1.

42. Mary Lou Duckett, Duke University, to Walt N. Johnson, Raleigh, 1 June 1950; Walt N. Johnson, Raleigh, to Claude F. Gatty, Raleigh, 13 May 1952; Falk Johnson, Evanston, Ill., to Walt N. Johnson, 25 February 1951; Wayne E. Oates, Louisville, to Walt N. Johnson, Raleigh, 12 February 1951; W.R. Cullom, Wake Forest College, to Walt N. Johnson, Raleigh, 5 October 1951; all Walter Nathan Papers, North Carolina Baptist Historical Collection. W.R. Cullom was the same person who wrote Johnson's biographical entry in the *Encyclopedia of Southern Baptists.* He and Johnson worked together on the Seventy-Five Million Campaign and maintained a relationship throughout Johnson's life. See particularly "Walter N. Johnson," 31-32, 40.

43. Johnson, "Inspired or Insane?" 1. I raised the possibility of mental instability, in light of Johnson's many comments on his health and the stress he experienced over most of his career, with one of his closest associates from the period of the 1940s, who firmly stated his opinion that Johnson's ideas were not the result of poor mental health. Garland A. Hendricks, interview by the author, 12 March 1987, Interview 1, Texas Collection. Calhoun Johnson gave detailed accounts of Walt Johnson's health problems over the years and describes his last years as a time of fulfillment and optimism. "Walter N. Johnson," 29, 128-29.

44. Melvin, "Life and Thought of Walter Nathan Johnson," 13.

45. Walt N. Johnson, "A Frank Word and a Friendly Answer," *The Next Step in the Churches,* August 1940, 1.

46. Walt N. Johnson, "The Plainest and Most Personal Letter that I Have Ever Written," *LCV Quarterly Communication,* January 1949, 1.

47. Walt N. Johnson, "'Bro Walt' in Intimate Mood," *The Next Step in the Churches,* August 1946, 2.

48. J. Martin England, *The Next Step in the Churches,* July 1941, 1-2; Martin England, Interview 2; Mabel C. England, interview by the author, 26 July 1984, Interview 1, Texas Collection; Chancey, "Demonstration Plot for the Kingdom of God," 321. See Chancey's dissertation at the University of Florida, "Race, Reform, and Religion: Koinonia's Challenge to Southern Society, 1942-1992." See also K'Meyer, "What Koinonia Was All About," 1-22.

49. Chancey, "Demonstration Plot for the Kingdom of God," 351-53; Robert E. McClernon, interview by the author, 17 April 1985, Interview 1, Texas Collection; Foy D. Valentine, interview by Thomas L. Charlton and Daniel B. McGee, 8 March 1980, Interview 6, Texas Collection; Martin England Testimonial, taperecording.

50. Valentine, Interview 6; Fletcher, *Southern Baptist Convention,* 313-14; Carter, *Turning Point,* 16-17, 21.

51. McClernon, Interview 1; Oscar Blake Smith, interview by Thomas L.

Charlton, 27 October 1972, Interview 4, Texas Collection. McClernon said Marney once told him, "Every now and then, when I travel around Texas, I find myself on the trail of Walter Rauschenbusch."

52. Martin England, interview by the author, 25 September 1984, Interview 4, Texas Collection; McClernon, Interview 1; Wilson, s.v. "Moyers, Bill," *Encyclopedia of Southern Culture.*

53. Martha Gilmore, interview by the author, 8 July 1978, Interview 4, Texas Collection.

54. The name "camping churches" came from the principal activity of the network, the sponsorship of weeklong summer camps for teenage members of the churches, to which the churches agreed to send delegations every year, including the pastors. The camps became settings for numerous formal and informal meetings that spread the progressive ideas of the congregations. For years, Marney himself participated in the camps, then was referred to in vast numbers of connections as the patron and inspiration of the plan and its theological and moral exemplar. Roger A. Paynter, interview by the author, 1 July 1995, in possession of the author.

55. McClernon, Interview 1; William W. Finlator, interview by the author, 12 September 1984, Texas Collection.

56. Chancey, "Koinonia in the '90s," 892-93; Valentine, Interview 6; Fuller, *No More Shacks!* 20, 25-29.

57. Charles Morris Tindell Jr., interview by the author and Jaclyn Jeffrey, 9 April 1986, Interview 1, Texas Collection.

58. Ken Sehested, interview by the author, 1 December 1995, taperecording, in possession of the author.

59. Connelly, s.v. "Campbell, Will," *Encyclopedia of Southern Culture;* Will Campbell, "Jesus in the Brush Arbor," 229-30.

60. Perry Perkins, interview by the author, 1 July 1995, taperecording, in possession of the author.

61. Perkins, interview.

62. Ibid.; Joe W. Gatlin, interview by the author, 16 November 1988, Interview 1; Nancy Gatlin, interview by the author, 22 December 1988, Interview 1; Jimmy Dorrell, interview by the author, 1 August 1990, Interview 3; all in Texas Collection; Tindell, interview.

63. Perkins, interview.

64. Olin T. Binkley, "Dr. Walter N. Johnson," 1964, Special Collections, Denny Library; Wayne E. Oates, Louisville, to Walt N. Johnson, Raleigh, 12 February 1951, Walter Nathan Johnson Papers; Snider, *"Cotton-Patch" Gospel,* 13. Snider made no mention of Johnson, but see Lee, *Cotton Patch Evidence,* 27, who mentioned Johnson's influence on Jordan.

65. Robert E. Seymour, interview by the author, 13 March 1986, Texas Collection; Carr, interview. McClernon served Binkley as interim pastor after Seymour's retirement.

66. Johnson, "Walter N. Johnson," 80; Doctor of Divinity Citation for J. Martin

England, Furman University, Greenville, SC, 15 May 1988, Office of the Chaplain, Furman University; Linder, *William Louis Poteat,* 76.

67. The school and the church do not have a formal relationship, but there are numerous strong ties between  the two institutions, including their common rootedness in the town of Wake Forest. Carr, interview. See Bryan, *Dissenter in the Baptist Southland.*

68. Eighmy, *Churches in Cultural Captivity,* 155-57. Eighmy said that Barnett and his associates represented "the only group specifically organized to promote liberal social and theological ideas within the denomination." Their failure, according to Eighmy, left "the molding of the social conscience of Southern Baptists" with the seminary faculties and the Social Service Commission and the Baptist Joint Committee on Public Affairs, Ibid; see *Christian Frontiers,* February 1946, March 1946, April 1946, December 1946, March 1947, February 1948, *Christian Frontiers* files, Southern Baptist Historical Library and Archives. These files contain a considerable amount of correspondence detailing Barnett's and his associates' views, controversies they were involved in, and the remarkable role in the life of *Christian Frontiers* played by Southern Seminary's W.O. Carver, who put his considerable prestige on the line at several points to try to defend Barnett particularly from charges of liberalism and outright heresy.

## 3. "Who Is Their God? Where Were Their Voices?"

"Where Cross the Crowded Ways of Life," words by Frank Mason North, 1903, *The Broadman Hymnal,* 405.

1. Oates, *Let the Trumpet Sound,* 222-23, 230.

2. Valentine, *Historical Study of Southern Baptists and Race Relations,* 21-22; Manis, *Southern Civil Religions in Conflict,* 25-27; Knight, "Race Relations," 165-67.

3. Leonard, *God's Last and Only Hope,* 21-22; Manis, *Southern Civil Religions in Conflict,* 114, n. 16.

4. Southern Baptist Convention, *Annual* (Nashville: Southern Baptist Convention, 1906), 33; Dewey Grantham said that in the period during and after World War I, Southern Baptists began to make some limited efforts at addressing the social needs of the South. *Southern Progressivism,* 239.

5. Southern Baptist Convention, *Southern Baptist Annual* (Nashville: Southern Baptist Convention, 1947), 47, 342-43; Hays and Steely, *Baptist Way of Life,* 96-98; Bailey, *Southern White Protestantism,* 141.

6. Bailey, *Southern White Protestantism,* 137.

7. Southern Baptist Convention, *Southern Baptist Annual* (Nashville: Southern Baptist Convention, 1954), 87; Hays and Steely, *Baptist Way of Life,* 96-98; Bailey, *Southern White Protestantism,* 142-43; Eighmy, *Churches in Cultural Captivity,* 192-93.

8. Hill, "Southern Baptist Thought and Action in Race Relations," 200; Leonard, *God's Last and Only Hope,* 160; Bailey, *Southern White Protestantism,* 141-42.

9. Eighmy, *Churches in Cultural Captivity,* 106; Bailey, *Southern White Protestantism,* 153. Presumably, most of those with open membership for African Americans would have responded to the Baptist General Convention of Texas survey. Of the 4,000 contacted, 1,259 responded. Congregations that went to the trouble to change their membership policies would have been interested in encouraging others to do the same. Making their policies known through an anonymous survey conducted by a denominational office would have been such a way to let other congregations know of the rising presence of open membership policies and would not have attracted any more publicity than they wanted to generate themselves.

10. Dehoney, "To Tell It like It Is!" 5-6.

11. Criswell "Church of the Open Door," 81.

12. Monroe, "Southerner's Dilemma," 23, 24-25.

13. Sherman, "Way Things Are," 48, 50, 51.

14. Wayne Dehoney, introduction to Brooks Ramsay, "Partial Christians and an Impartial God," 84-85; Paul Turner, "A Quality Life," Mid-South [*Commercial Appeal,* Memphis, Tenn.], 1 February 1987, 7. For a sermon from one who later became known for his service to churches within the dissident network, see Claypool, "If I Go Down into Hell," 95-105.

15. "Threatening Picture," 105; see correspondence and news releases in files on Race Relations and Southern Baptists, Southern Baptist Historical Library and Archives, especially "Negro Baptist Board Deplores SBC Withdrawal of Race Material," November 1971, and Jim Newton to Hal Wingo of *Life* magazine, 17 November 1971, in which Newton called the Sunday School Board decision "unfortunate and downright incredible," adding that the SBC was "being clobbered" because of the bad publicity.

16. Dean Wright, telephone interview by the author, New York, 16 November 1994, author's files; Martin England, Interview 3.

17. Martin England, interview by the author, Interview 1, 27 July 1984, Texas Collection. Many historical details of England's, or his grandmother's, account of Jasper Wilson's experience are questionable. Among other things, conscription for service in Confederate armies was not authorized until April 1862. Also, Confederate money was not printed before May 1861, while the battle for Fort Sumpter took place in April, a battle, incidentally, that resulted in very few casualties. According to some scholars, England's story illustrates the difference between "narrative truth" and "historical truth." See Donald P. Spence, *Narrative Truth and Historical Truth,* 31-33. What he and his grandmother believed to have been the "truth" of his grandfather's story outweighed the historical accuracy of its details.

18. Martin England, Interview 1.

19. Ibid.

20. Martin England, Interview 2; Mabel England, Interview 1. Mabel England

attributed her husband's decision to transfer out of Southern Seminary to the fact that it was "too conservative" for his taste, but agreed that his decision not to seek appointment as a Southern Baptist missionary stemmed from the scandal at the SBC Foreign Mission Board.

21. Martin England, Interview 1 and Interview 2; J. Martin England, Louisville, to Walt N. Johnson, Mars Hill, N.C., reprinted in *The Next Step in the Churches,* July 1941.

22. George Stoll, Louisville, to J. Martin England, 30 September 1932, copy provided to the author, original in University of Georgia archives; Martin England, Interview 1 and Interview 2.

23. In a move intended to avoid conflict with each other but also reminiscent of the Catholic Church's assistance in the division of the western hemisphere between the Spanish and the Portuguese, finalized by treaty in 1494, Northern and Southern Baptists agreed not to compete with one another in their overseas mission work. Burma was one of the fields traditionally allotted to the Northern Baptists. Some interesting geographical quirks developed out of this plan. For instance, northern China was the territory of Southern Baptist missionaries while southern China was that of Northern Baptists. Not surprisingly, such distinctions were usually lost on the indigenous persons who were the intended beneficiaries of missionary activity. Martin England, Interview 1 and Interview 2; C.K. Zhang, interview by the author and Gerald Fielder, 2 February 1989, Interview 14, Texas Collection; Barnes, *Southern Baptist Convention,* 264-66; cf. Baker, *Relations between Northern and Southern Baptists,* 183-86.

24. Martin England, Interview 1 and Interview 2.

25. Martin England, Interview 1; Calhoun Jackson, "Walter N. Johnson," 79.

26. Martin England, Interview 2.

27. Ibid.

28. Ibid.

29. McClendon, *Biography as Theology,* 114-16.

30. "Embattled Fellowship Farm," 79.

31. Martin England, Interview 2.

32. Ibid.; Mabel England, Interview 1 and Interview 2.

33. Martin England, Interview 2. England stayed in touch with Johnson until the end of Johnson's life. See J. Martin England, Brooklyn, to Walt N. Johnson, Raleigh, 17 May 1952, North Carolina Baptist Historical Collection.

34. Mabel England, Interview 1; "Friends and Enemies of Koinonia Farm," 2-3, 3-4; "Koinonia Farm," 3.

35. Ibid., 3-4; Lee, *Cotton Patch Evidence,* 105-6; Owen, "Friends and Enemies of Koinonia Farm," 5-7, 13-14; McClendon, *Biography as Theology,* 120-21, which is part of a chapter on the life of Clarence Jordan; Carter, *Turning Point,* 16, 21.

36. Mabel England, Interview 2; Martin England, Interview 3 and Interview 4; Wright, interview.

37. Martin England, Interview 1, Interview 2, and Interview 4; Wright, interview.

38. Martin England, Interview 4.

39. Martin England, Interview 1, Interview 2, and Interview 4.

40. Martin England, Interview 3.

41. Ibid.; Wright, interview; J. Bruce Evans, Baton Rouge, La., to the author, Batesville, Ark., 18 September 1995, author's files.

42. Martin England, draft letter, 2 February 1954, which says, "When I asked Wayne Oates if he would give a week or two a year to a group in such a center, he said, 'You couldn't keep me away.'"; (American Friends Service Committee members) Wilmer and Mildred Young, Abbeville, S.C., to Martin England, 19 February 1954, (Quaker community member) Courtney Siceloff, Penn Community Services, St. Helena Island, Frogmore, S.C., to Martin England, Somerville, N.J., 11 January 1995; Gordan Crosby, The Church of the Saviour, Washington, D.C., to Martin England, Somerville, N.J., 22 August 1955; all Martin England's personal files, in possession of the family of Martin and Mabel England. Penn Community Services was a remnant of an old abolitionist organization.

43. Martin England, Interview 3; Wright, interview. Many sources hold that King's letter was published only after a fairly lengthy delay, remarkable in light of the eloquence and subsequent fame of the document. Peter B. Levy, *Documentary History of the Modern Civil Rights Movement*, e.g., said "Ironically, King's letter, perhaps his greatest written work, initially received little attention. Over a month passed before either the black press or national media mentioned it. And not until mid-May 1963 did a New York magazine present excerpts from it," 109. Oates said King's "lawyers smuggled it out page by page and [King's aid Wyatt] Walker and others typed it in a fever of excitement at the Gaston Motel." *Let the Trumpet Sound*, 230. Wright recalled that England told him not to publish the letter until the *New York Times* had done so, for fear that any prior publication might cause the *Times* not to run the letter. In fact, the letter was published by several small publications before the *Times* printed it. The Ministers and Missionaries Board published it in pamphlet form. Wright, interview.

44. Martin England, Interview 3 and Interview 4; Wright, interview.

45. Martin England, Interview 3; Wright, interview; "J. Martin England," 14; Proctor, "A Story of Two Martins," 11.

46. Martin England, Interview 3 and Interview 4.

47. Ibid.; Mabel England, Interview 2; Wright, interview.

48. Martin England Journal, 2 October 1971, Martin England personal files, in possession of the family of Martin and Mabel England.

49. Mabel England, Interview 2; Moore, *His Heart is Black*, 65-66; Foy D. Valentine, interview by Daniel B. McGee, 25 May 1976, Interview 2, and interview by Thomas L. Charlton and the author, Interview 14, 4 December 1989, both in Texas Collection.

50. Turner, "Way Up Is the Way Out," 9; Trentham, "One Father—One Blood," 18.

51. "Confessions of an Ex-Southern Liberal," 32-33, 34, 39; Lee, *Where Christian Ideas Take Shape in People*, 112-13, 126.

52. Langley, "Into All the World," 63. Willow Meadows Church became a pathbreaking congregation in the 1970s in connection with the issue of women in ministry, See chapter 5.

53. Martin England, Interview 4; Marney, "Dayton's Long Hot Summer," 134, 138-39; Valentine, Interview 14; Valentine, Interview 2.

54. Moore, *His Heart is Black*, 68-69; McClernon, Interview 1; Finlator, interview; Evans to the author, 18 September 1995; Carey, *Carlyle Marney*, 12. Carey referred to such churches as "isolated islands in a large sea of fundamentalism." See Martin England's comments on a Southern Baptist minister named Z.W. Rowtan, another person who was influenced by both Walt Johnson and Carlyle Marney, providing further links between the two in the Southern Baptists dissident family tree. Interview 4.

55. Carey, *Carlyle Marney*, 12; "J. Martin England," 14.

56. Moore, *His Heart is Black*, 23; Ken Sehested, Decatur, Ga., to the author, Waco, Tex., 6 October 1986, author's files.

57. Martin England, Interview 4; Seymour, interview; Seymour, *"Whites Only,"* 70, 114; Robert E. McClernon, Durham, N.C., to the author, Waco, Tex., 13 March 1990, author's files.

58. Martin England, Interview 4; Bryan, *Dissenter in the Baptist Southland*, 96, 173. Another Southern Baptist from the Carolinas who became a U.S. senator was Strom Thurmond, who led the segregationist "Dixiecrat" revolt within the Democratic Party in 1948 as governor of South Carolina. See Rosenberg, "Southern Baptist Response to the Newest South," 151.

59. Carr, interview.

60. McClernon, Interview 1; Julius Corpening, interview by the author, 18 April 1986, Texas Collection; Marney, "Priest at Every Elbow," 68.

61. Martin England, Interview 4.

62. Ibid.

63. Campbell, *Brother to a Dragonfly*, 201; Connelly, *Will Campbell*, 43, 81, 100-1, 140. One of Campbell's realizations concerned his sense that country music was a crucial window into identity of white working-class southerners, something he said qualifies it to be considered "religious" music, 146.

64. Campbell, *Brother to a Dragonfly*, 96, 200; Connelly, *Will Campbell*, 42-43.

65. Valentine, Interview 14; Moore, *His Heart is Black*, 21-22, 31; Ken Sehested, Decatur, Ga., to the author, Waco, Tex., 9 September 1986, author's files.

66. Fletcher, *Southern Baptist Convention*, 224-27; Moore, *His Heart is Black*, 67-70.

67. Ibid., 29, 62, 68-69; Valentine, Interview 14; Perkins, interview; Marney, "Dayton's Long Hot Summer," 139; Farnsley, *Southern Baptist Politics*, 29-30; Sehested to the author, 9 September 1986.

68. Valentine, Interview 14.

69. Ibid.; Valentine, Interview 2.

70. Valentine, Interview 14.

71. Seymour, interview; Maston, Interview 1. Colgate-Rochester later merged with Crozer, England's and Martin Luther King Jr.'s seminary. T.B. Maston's claim that W.T. Conner had been a member of the Ku Klux Klan does not seem to square with the image one normally associates with a southerner who was educated in the North.

72. "Holding Fast the Word of Life," 10; Campbell, "Jesus in the Brush Arbor," 229; Findlay, *Church People in the Struggle,* 25.

73. Kratt, *Marney,* 76.

74. Ibid., 86, from McClernon's funeral sermon for Marney at Myers Park Baptist Church, Charlotte, N.C., 5 July 1978.

75. Proctor, "A Story of Two Martins," 11.

76. McClernon, Interview 2.

77. Albert Blackwell, "Eulogy for J. Martin England," First Baptist Church, Greenville, S.C., 6 January 1989, 1, 3, files of Office of the Chaplain, Furman University.

78. From a sermon by Marney titled "In the Meantime," in *Marney,* 90.

## 4. An Appetite for Justice

"Stand Up, Stand Up for Jesus," words by George Duffield Jr., 1858, *The Broadman Hymnal,* 31.

1. For the South's supposed militarism and its connections to religion, see Woodward, *Origins of the New South,* 159-60; Reed, *Enduring South,* 43-46; Wyatt-Brown, *Honor and Violence in the Old South,* 27-28, 30-31. May, "Dixie's Martial Image," 213-34, questioned the completeness of the South's militarism, in comparison especially with that of the western United States, which he said ranked more highly in several categories of militarism that did that of the South. may acknowledged the accuracy of many measures of this phenomenon in southern life, however. Montell, *Killings,* disputed some of the stereotypes about southern violence. For an example of an argument that carries the notion of southern militancy to the point of an extreme form of regional stereotyping, see Richard E. Nisbett's award-winning "Violence and U.S. Regional Culture," 441-49, which is largely based, historiographically, on the debatable assumptions of Grady McWhiney, *Cracker Culture.* Despite the flaws in his article's caricature of the South, Nisbett accurately noted that many areas of the West that are associated with violence and militancy were initially settled by southerners, therefore calling into question May's reading of the relative militancy of the South and the West, 441.

2. Blackwell, "Eulogy for J. Martin England," 1, 3.

3. Eighmy, *Churches in Cultural Captivity,* 98-100, 114-15, 141-42, 145-47.

4. Manis, *Southern Civil Religions in Conflict,* 29-30.

5. Eighmy saw the peace section, and other elements in the statement that

evoke language of the social gospel, as evidence of the influence of liberal Christianity on Southern Baptists. He said that this is evidence that "social Christianity . . . remained an important intellectual force among Southern Baptists in contrast to the fundamentalist tradition that made personal evangelism the church's sole mission." *Church's in Cultural Captivity,* 131. He sited the absence of any mention of evolution or creation from the Faith and Message statement as evidence that the fundamentalists' prompting the issuance of the statement did not constitute a "complete" victory, 129. The revised statement, approved by the SBC in 1963, Section XVI of *The Baptist Faith and Message,* "Peace and War," affirmed the traditional Southern Baptist view of the centrality of evangelism in the work of churches: "The true remedy for the war spirit is the gospel of our Lord. The supreme need of the world is the acceptance of His teachings in all the affairs of men and nations, and the practical application of His law of love." Baptist Sunday School Board, *Baptist Faith and Message,* 18-19.

6. Eighmy, *Churches in Cultural Captivity,* 98-100, 114-15, 141-42, 145-47. He referred to this decision as a missed "rare opportunity to give practical expression to [Baptists'] historic stand for freedom of conscience," 100.

7. Ibid., 145-47. Eighmy pointed out that Dawson's commitment to the idea of separation of church and state did not require him to keep silent on public issues. Dawson, in fact, became the first executive director of the Baptist Joint Committee on Public Affairs. Ibid. Walt Johnson had a similar enthusiasm for the peacemaking possibilities of a United Nations-type organization, but believed that the essential cause of war was "modern business[,] . . . essentially a system of organized covetousness covering the earth with rivalries and tearing mankind to pieces, in antagonistic cartels and classes and nations and empires." Walt N. Johnson, "At the Bottom of the Human Heart," *The Next Step in the Churches,* February 1945, 1-2.

8. Sara Lowrey, interview by Daniel B. McGee, 2 August 1972, Texas Collection. At the time of McGee's interview, Lowrey, who was then in her mid-seventies, was involved in anti-Vietnam War activities and working on behalf of George McGovern's presidential campaign.

9. Martin, "God's Angry Man," 227.

10. Hill, introduction to Eighmy, *Churches in Cultural Captivity,* xii-xiii.

11. Walt N. Johnson, "Does Jesus Have a Planetary Plan for Us?" *The Next Step in the Churches,* August 1935, 3-4.

12. Eighmy, *Churches in Cultural Captivity,* 114; Wyatt-Brown, *Honor and Violence in the Old South,* 25-30.

13. Mabel England, Interview 2.

14. Parham, "A Reconciler from 'Dixie,'" 6, 7; Martin England, Interview 2.

15. Owen, "Friends and Enemies of Koinonia Farm," 15; Chancey, "Koinonia in the 90s," 893.

16. Dekar, *For the Healing of the Nations,* 261, 265-66; Martin England, Interview 3.

17. Martin England, Interview 3; Lawrence Scott, Peace Action Center in Wash-

ington, D.C., to Martin England, 14 November 1963. All correspondence and manuscript materials, including England's personal journal, are from Martin England personal files, in possession of the family of Martin and Mabel England, unless otherwise noted.

18. Martin England, Interview 4.

19. England, Journal, 30 November 1953.

20. Ibid.

21. Ibid., 8 December 1953.

22. Martin England, "Jesus or the Chief?" sermon manuscript, 18 October 1967.

23. Martin England, "Arithmetic for Christians," manuscript, 1967, 1-3, 5-9. See also "Economics for Head Hunters," in which England compared the Naga tribe's practice of sacrificing heads of their prey to appease their gods with the war-making conduct of more "advanced" nations.

24. Untitled manuscript, n.d., on back of papers dated 1970. England, like Walt Johnson, was an exceedingly frugal person who wrote notes and manuscripts on the most remarkable assortment of scrap paper. England's feelings about avoiding waste had philosophical origins as well as or more than ecological: "We ourselves fear being rejected, cast aside, thrown away. I think I can never accept waste gladly." In England's mind, the links between global stewardship, the responsibility people have for one another, and peacemaking were powerful. See Journal, 15 July 1974 and 30 April 1976.

25. Martin England, "War's Alternative," 297.

26. England, Journal, 6 November 1972.

27. Ibid., 1 July 1978. England said that Marney added, "The blacks were mostly professional people, teachers and staff in the nearby black college, lawyers, doctors."

28. McClernon, Interview 2; Proctor, "Story of Two Martins," 10-11; Blackwell, "Eulogy for J. Martin England," 2-3.

29. England, Journal, 21 August 1972 and 21 September 1972.

30. Ibid., 24 May 1974.

31. Ibid., 3 February 1972.

33. England, draft letter to unspecified list of "friends," 1 May 1976; England, Journal, 4 January 1975. His journal entry for 17 November 74 says, "Sailed from New York 41 years ago," to begin service as a foreign missionary to Burma.

34. Blackwell, "Eulogy for J. Martin England," 5-6.

35. Martin England, Interview 4.

36. Finlator, interview; Bryan, *Dissenter in the Baptist Southland*, 96; Sehested, interview.

37. Finger, "Preaching the Gospel, South of God," 917.

38. Ibid., 918, 919.

39. George W. Cornell, Associated Press, "Graham Faces 'Integrity Issue'," *Durham* [N.C.] *Morning Herald*, 22 May 1982, 8A; "Graham in Moscow: What Did He Really say?" *Christianity Today*, 18 June 1982, 10-12.

40. "Campbell on the SBC," 969. Connelly, *Will Campbell*, 126.

41. Peterson, "Hunger and the Christian Tradition," 6; Hodge, "Sanctuary," 20-22.

42. "Lifestyle Conversion," 1.

43. Campbell, "He Ate Yesterday," 10.

44. "It Used to Be Called 'Frugal' Living," 2.

45. "Southern Baptists Have Heard the Cries of Hungry People" 2; Carter, "Who Cares for the Least of These?" 32-33.

46. *Seeds,* January 1982; Sehested, "Why I Am (Still) a Baptist," 12-13.

47. *Baptist Peacemaker,* April 1982, 9; Glen Stassen to *Baptist Peacemaker* readers, March 1995, correspondence files of Baptist Peace Fellowship of North America. BPFNA materials are in the Southern Baptist Historical Library and Archives in Nashville. Harold Stassen was one of the U.S. signers of the United Nations charter. See Associated Press, "Stassen: Wives Broke U.N. Impasse," [New Orleans] *Times Picayune,* 19 June 1995, A-3, which describes Stassen's memories of the role his wife, Esther Stassen, played in helping keep U.N. charter negotiations from bogging down through her relationship with spouses of Soviet representatives. See also Dekar, *For the Healing of the Nations,* 267; Sehested, interview.

48. Sehested, interview.

49. Ibid.

50. According to Sehested, practically every Southern Baptist congregation that had "what I would consider genuine biblical vitality to its ministry and community life has suffered some major trauma that has turned it around," that is, turned it away from the prevalent Southern Baptist tendency toward triumphalism. Of such congregations, Oakhurst Baptist Church was the archetype, in Sehested's mind. It went through an agonizing process of deciding to stay in an increasingly racially mixed neighborhood of Decatur, instead of moving to an all-white neighborhood, as many other urban congregations did and many Oakhurst members favored. The congregation began to construct a new building, which it had to abandon, moving back into its old facilities because of decreasing membership. Sehested said Oakhurst's experiences represented a "modern story of religious shame" in a "denomination which only honors growth, bigger bottom lines and bigger buildings." See Knight, *Struggle for Integrity,* regarding the Oakhurst Baptist Church story.

51. Sehested, interview.

52. Ibid.; James Gamble, 12 August 1985, and Lester Meriwether, 1 July 1987, to Ken Sehested, correspondence files of Baptist Peace Fellowship of North America.

53. Dan Martin and Marv Knox, "Baptist Peacemakers Eye Alternative Strategies," *Baptist Standard,* 18 August 1982, 12.

54. Sehested, interview; Dekar, *For the Healing of the Nations,* 268.

55. Sehested, interview.

56. Ibid.

57. Ibid.

58. Ibid.

59. "Peace Group Plans Urban Gang Summit," 314, Sehested, interview.

60. Sehested, "Why I Am (Still) a Baptist," 12-13; Sehested, interview.

61. McClernon, "When Every Explanation is Silent"; McClernon, "The Road Less Traveled By"; "A Brother in Christ," to McClernon, 7 October 1982; McClernon to membership of Watts Street Baptist Church, 21 April 1987; all in files of Watts Baptist Church, Durham, N.C.; Sehested, interview.

62. Douglass Creed Sullivan-Gonzales, interviews by Jaclyn Jeffrey, 21 March 1987 and 6 January 1988, Interviews 2 and 7, Texas Collection.

63. Childress, "A Time to Stand," 3; Miriam Davidson, "Sanctuary Movement under Fire," *Christian Science Monitor,* 22 October 1985, 18-19; Elizabeth Ferris, "Give Us *Some* of Your Tired, Your Poor," *Houston Post,* 19 May 1986, B-3.

64. Charles M. Tindell, interview by the author and Jaclyn Jeffrey, 9 April 1986, Texas Collection; Moltmann, *Theology of Hope,* 16; Golden and McConnell, *Sanctuary,* 135-37; Gordon Cosby, Washington D.C., to Martin England, Somerville, N.J., 11 February 1956. At the time of his interview, Tindell and his wife, Diane Tindell, were involved in the home schooling movement, which advocated pulling children out of the public schools and educating them at home, an idea of questionable legality at the time and one often associated with conservative evangelical families.

65. "History and Theology," Reconcilers Fellowship, n.d., files of Reconcilers Fellowship.

66. Jimmy Dorrell, interview by the author, 23 November 1988, Interview 1, 23 May 1990, Interview 2, 1 August 1990, Interview 3; Carolyn Louise Whaley, interview by the author, 20 February 1990; Nancy Gatlin, interview by the author, 22 July 1991, Interview 2; Jerry P. Sams, interview by the author, 29 July 1991; all in Texas Collection; "A Statement of Faith and Calling," Reconcilers Fellowship, 26 June 1989, 1-2, 3, files of Reconcilers Fellowship; "Out of Many, One," *Waco Tribune-Herald,* 8 October 1988, 1C-2C. Ken and Nancy Hastings Sehested had a communal living arrangement in Atlanta, and practiced the common purse with several other families, members of which were community and reform-movement organizers. Sehested, interview.

67. Jimmy Dorrell, Interview 1, 23 November 1988, Interview 2, 23 May 1990, Interview 3, 1 August 1990; Lisa Harris, interview by the author, 18 July 1991, Interview 2, all in Texas Collection; Nancy Gatlin, Interview 2; Tindell, interview. The expression "intentional community" refers to a religious group that has a common life apart from the usual connections maintained by members of traditional churches. An intentional community requires those who wish to attain full membership in it to consent to a system of spiritual guidance overseen by the senior members of the community, a program of personal accountability that regulates personal and group behavior, and a determination to conduct one's personal lifestyle in a "sacrificial" manner, that is, to shun the values of modern society and embrace those that coincide more closely to what the members believe to be the requirements of the gospel. Koinonia and Jubilee are examples of intentional communities.

68. Nancy Gatlin, Interview 2; Joe Gatlin, interview by the author, 16 November 1988, Interview 1; Dail Sams, interview by the author, 29 July 1991; Marney Swabb, interview by the author, 21 May 1990; all in Texas Collection.

69. Marney, "An Ethnic of Parsimony."

70. Walt N. Johnson, "Does Jesus Have a Planetary Plan for Us?" *The Next Step in the Churches,* August 1935, 3.

71. M.A. Huggins, "Walt N. Johnson: Christian, Seer, Pioneer," 1. Huggins said Johnson, along with E.M. Poteat and a few others, intentionally adopted lifestyles of virtual poverty. Ibid., 2-3. Johnson said that Robert Moore, president of Mars Hill College, and one of the people Huggins mentioned, "is a Gandhi among Southern Baptist educators" because he refused to accept salary larger than that of the professors at the college. *The Next Step in the Churches.* June 1931, 3. Part of Johnson's cautious admiration for Joseph Stalin in the early 1930s, like his admiration for Gandhi, was based on Stalin's supposed plain lifestyle. Ibid., January 1932, 3, and that Christians should not be afraid to "commonize," that is, they should use New Testament teachings to permeate every aspect of the current economic situation. Ibid., July 1935, 1.

72. Sehested, interview.

73. See especially the report of the Social Service Commission to the 1930 SBC, Southern Baptist Convention, *Annual* (Nashville: Southern Baptist Convention, 1930), 222.

74. Eighmy, *Churches in Cultural Captivity,* 43, 45-46, 68-69, 101-2, 117-19, 187-88.

75. Rosenberg, *Southern Baptists,* 1, 6; Perkins, interview. Perkins worked to organize pulpwood cutters in Mississippi, an effort for which Martin England expressed hopes. Journal, 15 January 1973. Neither Perkins nor his father thought much of Foy Valentine's leadership, despite his high reputation for ethical positions on the questions of the day.

76. Sehested, interview, quoting Walker Knight.

77. Sehested, "Why I Am (Still) a Baptist," 13; Blackwell, "Eulogy for J. Martin England," 7.

78. Joe Gatlin, interview by the author, 25 June 1991, Interview 2, Texas Collection; Nancy Gatlin, Interview 2.

## 5. Community and Faithfulness

"We've a Story to Tell," words by H. Ernest Nichol, 1896, *Baptist Hymnal,* ed. William J. Reynolds (Nashville: Convention Press, 1975), 281.

1. Fletcher, *Southern Baptist Convention,* 131-32, 203-5, 249-50.

2. Ibid., 133-34, 227-28, 250-51.

3. *Encyclopedia of Southern Baptists, s.v.* "Lottie Moon," "Annie Armstrong," "Woman's Missionary Union."

4. Ibid.; *Encyclopedia of Southern Baptists, s.v.* "Girls' Auxiliary."

5. Fletcher, *Southern Baptist Convention,* 131-32, 203-5, 292; Martin, "Hidden Work," 8-10, 162, 167-68.

6. Scott, "Women, Religion, and Social Change in the South," 103, 105; Anders and Metcalf-Whittaker, "Women as Lay Leaders and Clergy," 203-5.

7. Morrison, "Persistence in Honoring Self," 2, 4-5; Teresa Belt Rose, interview by Elizabeth J. Griffin, 12 May 1981, Interview 2; Jann Aldredge Clanton, interview by Rosalie Beck, 25 September 1986, Interview 3, Texas Collection. For connections between women's involvement in the civil rights and other protest and reform movements and the women's movement, see Evans, *Born for Liberty.*

8. Rauschenbusch, *Christianity and the Social Crisis,* 150.

9. Martin England, Interview 2. In telling the story of Jordan's turning down his military commission, England could not recall whether Jordan's mother was still living at the time, "But whether or not she was, her influence was moving in heavily on Clarence. And the next fall he did go to seminary."

10. Williamson, *A Rage for Order,* 183-85, 198-299, e.g. The reform aims of women and blacks have often seemed to be at odds. See Wheeler, *New Women of the New South,* 102ff., for an analysis of a contrasting exploitation of racial phobias, that of woman suffrage activists in the South who employed racist imagery in an attempt to gain the vote, saying that their support could help white male voters prevent the rise to political power of "unsavory" elements in northern and southern society.

11. Bellinger, "More Hidden than Revealed," 148-49; Fletcher, *Southern Baptist Convention,* 203-5.

12. Addie Davis, "Return from Exile—Twenty years Later," in "Voices of Hope from the Exile," Proceedings, Women in Ministry, SBC, 1985, 1-2, SBWIM Archives; Bellinger, "More Hidden than Revealed," 130; "Pilgrimage toward Equity in Ministry, SBC," 1; Carr, interview.

13. Carr, interview; Davis, "Return from Exile," 2.

14. Fletcher, *Southern Baptist Convention,* 225-26, 292.

15. The other, Susan Sprague, was ordained in 1975 by the Willow Meadows Baptist Church of Houston. Fletcher, *Southern Baptist Convention,* 226.

16. Martha L. Gilmore, interview by the author, 29 July 1977, Interview 1, Texas Collection; Elizabeth B. Barnes, "Women in Ministry: On the Way into the Far Country," Proceedings of the 1984 Conference for Women in Ministry, Southern Baptist Convention, ed. Lela M. Hendrix, 7-8, SBWIM Archives.

17. Martha L. Gilmore, interview by the author, 26 September 1977, Interview 2, Texas Collection.

18. Martha L. Gilmore, interview by the author, 26 November 1977, Interview 3, Texas Collection.

19. Martha L. Gilmore, interview by the author, 30 January 1978, Interview 4, Texas Collection; Morrison, "Persistence in Honoring Self," 54.

20. Martha L. Gilmore, interview by the author, 14 August 1978, Interview 6, and 30 January 1980, Interview 8, Texas Collection.

21. For two succinct presentations of the viewpoint that scriptural views of women

should not be taken as license to try to impose ancient social constructs on modern people, see Stagg, "Hermeneutics and Women," 1, 8; and Jones, "Women's Ordination and the Pretense of Inerrancy," 3. Stagg said that there is much support in Christian Scriptures for the liberation of women from traditional roles: "The evidence is massive in the four Gospels that Jesus affirmed the full worth, dignity, freedom, and responsibility of women," 1.

22. Martha L. Gilmore, interview by the author, 13 July 1978, Interview 5, Texas Collection.

23. Ibid.

24. Ibid.

25. Gilmore, Interview 6. Former Southern Seminary professor Kenneth Chafin extended the interpretation of the disparity between men's and women's treatment beyond the process of ordination: "The best students I have...are women. They've got better minds and better backgrounds. They are better at preparing sermons than anyone else I have in class. And yet the most ill-prepared, uncommitted, limited man I have has a better chance for ministry in our denomination than some of the most brilliant people I teach." Quoted by Will C. Campbell, "On Silencing Our Finest," 2. In 1995, all the preaching awards at Southern Seminary were won by women, one week after the seminary's trustees voted to hire only faculty members who opposed ordination of women. "Women Win Preaching Awards," 3.

26. "Women Win Preaching Awards," 3.

27. Ibid.

28. Ibid.; "Women Deacons, Minister Okayed," *Baptist Standard,* 25 August 1977, 4.

29. Gilmore was the fourth Southern Baptist woman in Texas to be ordained to the ministry, but two had left the state by the time of her ordination. "Women Deacon, Minister Okayed," 3.

30. Martha L. Gilmore, interview by the author, 15 March 1979, Interview 7, Texas Collection, Baylor University, Waco, Tex.

31. Gladys Lewis was also the first woman member of the board of trustees of Southwestern Baptist Theological Seminary. See Gladys Lewis, interview by the author, 22 November 1985, Interview 1, 5 December 1986, Interview 2, Texas Collection.

32. Bellinger, "More Hidden than Revealed," 130-31; Gilmore, Interview 7.

33. Gilmore, Interview 7; Turner, "Guest Editorial," 2.

34. Gilmore, Interview 8; Jim Jones, "Methodist Wife Costs Baptist Job," *Fort Worth Star-Telegram,* 25 April 1985, 1-2A; Debbie Hutchinson, "Baptist Women Urged to Protest," *Waco Tribune-Herald,* 27 April 1985, 1-2C.

35. "Profile: Cathy Cole," 6; "Profile: Deborah Whisnand Stinson," 4; Bellinger, "Women Mourners into Women Messengers," 3; Hill, "What's a Mama to Say?" 7; Butler, "Profile: Marsha Moore," 4; Butler, "Profile: Pat Bailey," 4; Sally Murphey Morgan, "Women in Ministry Testimony," 13 June 1987, in "Living toward a Vision of Shalom," Proceedings of the 1987 meeting of Southern Baptist Women in Minis-

try, ed. Libby S. Bellinger, SBWIM Archives, 8; Weaver-Williams, "Visions of a New Humanity," Ibid., 15; Hargus, "Profile: Joyce Martin," 4; Kneece, "This Is My Story. . . ," 7; Morrison, "Persistence in Honoring Self," 42-44; "Southern Baptist Women in Ministry Office Candidate Biographical Sketch, 1985-1986," Carolyn Blanche Wooten Isley, Karen Conn Mitcham, Gina Roberts, SBWIM Archives; Betty Winstead McGary, interview by Rosalie Beck, 9 July 1986.

36. In 1975, there were about 20 ordained women in the SBC; in 1979, about 75. By 1980, there were about 110, and in 1981, about 150. In 1988, there were an estimated 525 ordained Southern Baptist women ministers, almost half of whom were ordained in and had positions in Virginia, North Carolina, and Kentucky. At that point, it was estimated that 55 women had full-time pastoral positions in Southern Baptist churches out of a total of almost 33,000 such jobs. Anders, "A Chronology: Pilgrimage toward Equity in Ministry, SBC," insert; Anders, "Has a Generation Really Passed?" 5; Morrison, "Persistence in Honoring Self," 5.

37. Women Ministers Organize by States," 3; Burke Watson, "City Baptists Receptive to Women's Ordination, but Elsewhere. . . ," *Houston Chronicle,* 26 November 1983, 6-3; Wright, "SBC Women Ministers Break Their Silence," 998-99; Stewart, "Three Women Fill North Carolina Pulpits," 3.

38. Bellinger, "More Hidden than Revealed," 130-32; Pearce, "A History of Women in Ministry, SBC," 10; McGary, interview.

39. Although weighted toward the East Coast, the original invitation list for "Theology Is a Verb" included pastors and laypeople from "alternative" congregations from the Deep South and from Texas. It constitutes a veritable who's who of dissent in the early days of the fundamentalist resurgence in the SBC. See Women in Ministry Project Files, Institute for Oral History.

40. Bellinger, "More Hidden than Revealed," 131; "Pilgrimage toward Equity," 1; Pearce, "History of Women in Ministry, SBC," 9, 10; "Prescott Memorial Baptist Church, Memphis, Calls Nancy Hastings Sehested as Pastor," 5.

41. Bellinger, "More Hidden than Revealed," 131, 137, 147-48.

42. Ibid., 133-34, 140, 147; "Folio," June 1983, 4. A full run of *Folio* can be found in the SBWIM Archives.

43. "Resolution No. 3: 'On Women,'" 5; "Presidents [sic] Views," Ibid., 4-5; Rosser, "Why Did the SBC Approve a Resolution that Violates and Destroys the Authority and Integrity of Scripture?" Ibid., 6, 11; Stephens, "Baptists Don't Need Two Service Lists," 8.

44. Davis, "Return from Exile," 2; Southern Baptist Convention, *Southern Baptist Annual* (Nashville: Southern Baptist Convention, 1984), 404; Bellinger, "More Hidden than Revealed," 135, 136.

45. Ammerman, *Baptist Battles,* 93-94.

46. Taylor, "Profile: Nancy Sehested," 6; Nancy Hastings Sehested, interview by Rebecca Sharpless, 20 August 1986, Interview 1, Texas Collection; Ammerman, *Baptist Battles,* 94.

47. Bellinger, "More Hidden than Revealed," 149.

48. "On Campus," 4.

49. Lawson, "Women in Ministry Called Critical Issue," 6; Hobbs, "Women in Ministry," 3-4. In addition to its usual coverage of news of women in Southern Baptist life who had paid ministerial positions, in the mid-1980s *Folio* began to run articles on ways women could enhance their employment prospects and keep their wits about them in the process of looking for or holding ministerial jobs. See e.g., Allen, "Rewriting Your Resume," 6; Oates, "Managing Stress," 5; Dorman, "Southern Baptists and Placement," 12. Cf. Ashli Cartwright Peak, "President's Report," 13 June 1987, SBWIM Archives, wherein she cautioned Southern Baptist women in ministry to avoid being too focused on getting power and recognition for their work, 6-7.

50. Leonard, "Good News at Wolf Creek," 1.

51. McBeth, "Women in Ministry," 3; Steve Maynard, "Ordained Southern Baptist Women Break through Barriers," *Houston Chronicle,* 26 July 1986, 6-1, 6-6.

52. Mobley, "One Woman's Story," 6. Nancy Hastings Sehested quoted Carlyle Marney in assessing the departure of talented Southern Baptist women from the denomination that Southern Baptists' "greatest contribution . . . to the wide Christian community is the people we run off." "Women and Ministry in the Local Congregation," 75.

53. "Co-editor Leaves Folio," 2. Cobb made an unsuccessful run for the Kentucky House of Representatives in 1988. Cobb, "Publisher's Column," 2; "Southern Baptist Women in Ministry Office Candidate Biographical Sketch, 1985-1986," Carolyn Blanche Wooten Isley, SBWIM Archives.

54. Bellinger, "Reflections on the Southern Baptist Alliance Meeting," 3; "Activities of and Actions Taken by SBWIM Steering Committees from 1983-1987," addendum for 1988, June 1988, SBWIM Archives; "SBA Gives Grant to Women in Ministry," 1; Johnson, "Name Calling," 5; "Church Calls Women Pastor: Loses Building," 1, concerning the case of the Jefferson Street Baptist Chapel in Louisville, which was evicted from property belonging to the Long Run Baptist Association after it called Johnson as pastor in August 1991. First Baptist Church of Williamsburg, Ky., was "disfellowshipped" by Mount Zion Association in 1991 for ordaining women as deacons. Autry, "Baptist Principles Led Churches to Take Stands for Women," 1, 5. Galveston Baptist Association removed Raye Nelle Dyer, director of the Baptist Student Union at the University of Texas Medical Branch, because she sought ordination to the ministry. "Raye Nelle Dyer Fired," 3. See also, "No Women Clergy," 1104; and "Baptist Church Expelled for Female Deacon," 893.

55. Bellinger, "Going Home by a Different Way," 56, 57.

56. "Minutes: Southern Baptist Women in Ministry, Executive Board Meeting," 19-20, October 1990, SBWIM Archives, 2; "Harvell's Motivations behind the Motion," 7.

57. Siler, "God-Talk," 3, 12. Siler was pastor of the Pullen Memorial Memorial Baptist Church in Raleigh, a congregation that was part of the dissenting network, as were several churches served by Roger Paynter, who was elected to the SBWIM

Steering Committee in 1989. "Minutes of the Seventh Annual Meeting, Southern Baptist Women in Ministry Business Meeting," 10 June 1989, SBWIM Archives, 2. Paynter and Stephen Shoemaker, who served "alternative" churches in Kentucky and Texas, were included in a response piece *Folio* published, "What Our Brothers Are Saying," 8-9.

## 6. The "Return" of Southern Baptist Fundamentalists

"Rise Up, O Men of God," words by William P. Merrill, 1911, *Baptist Hymnal,* 141.

1. Gilmore, Interview 7; Winston, "The Southern Baptist Story," 13-15. In one of the greatest ironies in the history of the dissident network, Paul Pressler was best man in Jerry and Martha Gilmore's wedding.

2. Bailey, *Southern White Protestantism,* 65-66; Fletcher, "Southern Baptists in Higher Education," 4. On what was in large part the other end of the political and theological spectrum, and the other end of the twentieth century, C.R. Daley called for a split in the SBC along the lines Martin had called for in the twenties. Daley was longtime publisher of the Kentucky Southern Baptist newsjournal, a staunch advocate of civil rights for African Americans, and someone with ties to various people in the progressive dissident network. See Hefley, *The Truth in Crisis,* 230. Hefley's book is a careful account of the fundamentalist resurgence by someone in sympathy with it. He described, by the way, Daley's academic rivalry with John Birch during their time together as undergraduates at Southern Baptist-related Mercer University in Georgia, 44.

3. Hankins, *God's Rascal,* 30, 36-37; Russell, *Voices of American Fundamentalism,* 25, 43; Fletcher, "Southern Baptists in Higher Education," 4, 5; Marsden, *Fundamentalism and American Culture,* 210.

4. Russell, *Voices,* 43; Marsden, *Fundamentalism and American Culture,* 210; Rosenberg, *Southern Baptists,* 185. Hankins described Norris's views of the Ku Klux Klan in *God's Rascal,* 48, 50, 165-66.

5. Ammerman, *Baptist Battles,* 70; Martin, "Hearts and Minds," 160, 164; Martin, "God's Angry Man," 153; Jarboe, "War for Thee University," 189-91.

6. Ken Camp, "Criswell Raps 'Shared Ministry,'" *Baptist Standard,* 26 February 1986, 8; Gilmore, Interview 1; McBeth, "J. Frank Norris," 3; Martin, "Hearts and Minds," 164; Rosenberg, *Southern Baptists,* 184, 185-88. Martha Gilmore's father felt very strongly about what he saw as the evil Norris visited on Baptist life, likening him to Hitler, during her childhood: "[Y]ou would fight if anybody called you 'Norris.'" Interview 1.

7. Farnsley, *Southern Baptist Politics,* 19-22; McCall, "Schismatics/Heretics," *Baptist Standard,* 19 October 1977, 16; Morgan, *New Crusades,* 129-30.

8. Ammerman, "North American Protestant Fundamentalism," 49ff.; Ammerman, *Baptist Battles,* 3-12, 70, 238ff.; Jarboe, "War for Thee University," 189-

90; Jim Jones, "Dilday's Firing Stirs Up Interest in Fellowship," *Fort Worth Star-Telegram*, 1 May 1994, 8C; Jim Jones, "Baylor Plans for Growth of Seminary," *Fort Worth Star-Telegram*, 21 May 1994, 27A.

9. Farnsley, *Southern Baptist Politics*, 132; see Morgan, *New Crusades*, 165 for instance, concerning alliances between Patterson and Pressler and Colorado beer magnate Joseph Coors.

10. "Southern Baptist Tension," 97; Leonard, "Southern Baptists and a New Religious Establishment," 775-76; Stan Hastey, "SBC Battle Changing Political Land-scape," *Baptist Standard*, 2 December 1987, 13; Montoya, "Trading Principles for Power in the SBC," 39.

11. Leonard, *God's Last and Only Hope*, 59-60, 133, 179; Rosenberg, *Southern Baptists*, 186.

12. Gary North, "Firestorm Chat," taperecorded interview with Paul Pressler, Religion and Culture Project Files, Institute for Oral History. Pressler's most notori-ous comment referred to the fact that the fundamentalist party was "going for the jugular" in its quest to gain control of the SBC. Tom Miller, "Pressler: 'Going for Jugular' to Control SBC," *Baptist Standard*, 24 September 1980, 4.

13. Leonard, *God's Last and Only Hope*, 118-19, 128-29, 137; Hefley, *Truth in Crisis*, 114-15, 147.

14. David Wilkinson, "Larry Baker Elected to Succeed Valentine," *Baptist Stan-dard*, 21 January 1987, 8, 20; Morgan, *New Crusades*, 114, 116-17, 190-91.

15. Allen, "History of Baptists Committed," 93-94; Neely, "History of the Alli-ance of Baptists," Ibid., 104-6; Ammerman, "New South and the New Baptists," 488; Leonard, "Southern Baptists and a New Religious Establishment," 775.

16. Samuel S. Hill Jr. said the wonder is how long the SBC held together, with such disparate streams of cultural and intellectual heritage as those represented by the Charleston and Sandy Creek and other traditions in Southern Baptist life. *One Name But Several Faces*, 15, 16-18, 20.

17. Leonard, *God's Last and Only Hope*, 178.

18. Ibid., 160; Leonard, "Southern Baptists and a New Religious Establishment," 776; Ammerman, "New South and the New Baptists," 487.

19. Leonard, *God's Last and Only Hope*, 133, 170.

20. Ammerman, *Baptist Battles*, 238-39.

21. Ibid., 61, 160-61; Dan Martin, "Nominee Vows Pro-Life, Racial Justice Stands," *Baptist Standard*, 14 September 1988, 3; Leonard, *God's Last and Only Hope*, 170.

22. George W. Cornell, Associated Press, "Support Grows for Death Penalty," [New Orleans] *Times-Picayune*, 4 December 1993, D-10. Land's first letter asking to be removed from affiliation with the Peace Fellowship cited lack of time to attend to his duties. When the fellowship continued to use a letterhead with Land's name on it, he wrote another letter complaining about the slowness of response to his request and commenting on the adverse reaction he was getting from people who did not appreciate what the Peace Fellowship was doing and the association of his name

with it. Richard Land to Ken Sehested, Memphis, 12 August 1990 and 15 October 1990, Baptist Peace Fellowship of North America Archives.

23. Leonard, *God's Last and Only Hope*, 151-52, 161; Southern Baptist Convention, *SBC Annual* (Nashville: Southern Baptist Convention, 1984), 65.

24. Some moderates believed the Scriptures were inerrant, but they did not believe they needed to take the next step and advocate the removal from positions of responsibility of people who did not accept that concept. Thus, all fundamentalists were biblical literalists, but not all literalists were fundamentalists. See "Rogers Will Appoint Only Inerrantists," *Baptist Standard*, 24 June 1987, 5.

25. Robert Galveston Bratcher, interview by the author, 17 April 1985, Interview 2, Texas Collection. At one point in the dispute with Taylor, Bratcher used one of Taylor's own books, a Greek New Testament grammar that had been published in Portuguese, to prove his point: "I quoted his own grammar to him and of course, that's pretty devastating." Bratcher later realized he had offended the senior New Testament authority in Brazil, and in fact had clashed with him on several other matters of translation and interpretation of Scripture, probably earning an impression as an impertinent upstart." Bratcher, Interview 2.

26. Robert Galveston Bratcher, interview by the author, 14 April 1986, Interview 3, Texas Collection. On the same page of the issue of the Texas Baptist newsjournal that reported on the events following the CLC seminar appeared a short article depicting some of the "damage control" in which Bailey Smith engaged after his widely publicized remarks, trying to depict himself as being someone who was not anti-Semitic. "Smith, Family Observe Passover," *Baptist Standard*, 22 April 1981, 5. See the letters to the editor in that issue, which called Bratcher's statements "liberal and narrow," a "stumbling block" to young people, and "the atheists' view of the Bible." Oliver W. Sumerlin, Mrs. J.O. Lindsey, letters, Ibid., 2. Editor Presnall H. Wood's response was that "Bratcher's remarks are unacceptable and regrettable." Ibid. See also "Israel Dismayed at Smith Remarks," *Baptist Standard*, 1 October 1980, 8; "Criswell Expressed 'Regret' at Statement," Ibid., 9; "Smith Sets Meeting to State Love for Jews," *Baptist Standard*, 26 November 1980, 3. Cf. "Jews Angered, but Smith Stands by Remarks," *Baptist Standard*, 24 September 1980, 3.

27. "Bratcher Clarifies, Apologizes," *Baptist Standard*, 24 September 1980, 3; Robert Galveston Bratcher, interview by the author, 14 April 1986, Interview 4, Texas Collection; Valentine, Interview 14. See also Robert G. Bratcher, "Translator Translated," 1978, Vertical Files, Special Collections, Denny Library.

28. Bratcher, Interview 4.

29. Valentine, Interview 14.

30. Bratcher, "Translator Translated," 13, 15-16; Bratcher, Interview 1, Interview 3, and Interview 4.

31. Valentine, Interview 14. Valentine added, "They fired him anyway, but they were hypocrites about it. They gave him a job with a branch office they had of some other kind . . . I lost respect for [the ABS] out of that having pretended that he was gone. They'd say, 'He's no longer with us.' But he was down there doing something

else in another building." Ibid. Actually, Bratcher went to work for another organization, the United Bible Societies, which had ties to the ABS, but was not "a branch office" of it. Bratcher, Interview 4.

32. Valentine, Interview 14.

33. Bratcher, Interview 4.

34. Ibid. In 1998, Patterson was elected president of the Southern Baptist Convention.

35. Lemley, "Marshall Leaves SBTS," 1; "Southern Seminary Undergoes Changes," 3; Jack U. Harwell, "Fallout Ripples across Baptist Waters in Wake of Firing at Southern Seminary," *Baptists Today*, 4 May 1995, 5; Jim Newton, Home Missions [SBC] News Service, "HMB Trustees Reaffirm Ordination Policy," *Baptist Standard*, 21 March 1984, 5; Starling, "Women in Ministry Respond to Home Mission Board Vote," 3, 7; "New Administration Closes Southeastern Women's Center," 12.

36. "Survey Shows 2,100 Pastors Fired during Past 18 Months," *Baptist Standard*, 30 November 1988, 5.

37. Sehested, "An Open Letter to the Home Mission Board of the Southern Baptist Convention," 1.

38. Ken Sehested, interview. Sehested said that Ralph Elliot told him in the mid-1980s that he felt sorry for the beleaguered leaders of Southern Baptist seminaries but that they were among the people who "hounded" him a generation earlier, as they were then being hounded by the fundamentalist Baptists who were well on their way to taking over leadership of the SBC. Ibid.

39. Gilmore, Interview 8; "Former HMB Chairman Now a Methodist," *Baptist Standard*, 2 July 1986, 11; Glenda Fontenot, interview by the author, New Orleans, taperecorded, 23 June 1995.

40. Valentine, Interview 14.

41. A similar resolution was defeated in 1990. The sincerity and purposefulness of the 1995 resolution were questioned by a number of observers, including representatives of the predominantly African American National Baptist Convention. "Black Baptist Rejects Apology by SBC," 879-80.

42. Ammerman, "SBC Moderates and the Making of a Postmodern Denomination," 898, 899; Herb Hollinger, "Fellowship to Study Becoming Denomination," *Baptist Standard*, 2 August 1995, 3-4. To Ken Sehested, "The CBF is 'SBC Lite.'" In his view, the CBF had castigated the Alliance of Baptists for making moves toward a split from the SBC three years before, until some of the former SBC leaders who helped organize the CBF began to find themselves "suffering applause deprivation" and to move CBF more toward becoming a denomination itself, not just a subset of Southern Baptist life. Sehested, interview.

43. See Farnsley, *Southern Baptist Politics*, 133.

44. Bob Allen, "SBC Takes Next Step toward Reorganization," *Baptist Standard*, 28 February 1996; Marv Knox, "Politics Steps Up to the Pulpit," *Baptist Standard*, 23 October 1996, 1, 6; Marv Knox, "Congregations Enter Church-State Fracas," Ibid., 7.

## 7. *Conclusion*

"There Is Power in the Blood," words by Lewis E. Jones, 1899, in *Baptist Hymnal,* 159.

1. "Fontenot Chosen as New President of the Baptist Peace Fellowship," 20; Glenda Fontenot, interview; Will Campbell to Ken Sehested, Memphis, 6 August 1988, files of the Baptist Peace Fellowship of North America.

2. The moderates might have been better off if their forebears had accepted Thomas T. Martin's suggestion in 1925 that the convention split along the lines of modernist and literalist belief. For one thing, they might have kept control of the Southern Baptist Theological Seminary.

3. Gaustad, *Dissent in American Religion,* 1, 2.

4. Goodwyn, *Democratic Promise.*

# Bibliography

## Abbreviations

IOH     Institute for Oral History, Baylor Univ., Waco, Tex.
NCBHC  North Carolina Baptist Historical Collection, Z. Smith Reynolds Library, Wake Forest Univ., Winston-Salem, N.C.
SBC     Southern Baptist Convention
SBHLA  Southern Baptist Historical Library and Archives, Nashville, Tenn.
SBWIM  Southern Baptist Women in Ministry
SEBTS  Special Collections, Denny Library, Southeastern Baptist Theological Seminary, Wake Forest, N.C.
TC     The Texas Collection, Baylor Univ., Waco, Tex.
WMU   Woman's Missionary Union, Birmingham, Ala.

## Primary Material

Author's correspondence Files. Humanities Division, Lyon College, Batesville, Ark.

Baptist Historic Files. SBHLA.

Baptist Peace Fellowship of North America Archives. SBHLA.

Baptist Press Release Files. SBHLA.

Baptist Sunday School Board. *The Baptist Faith and Message.* Nashville: Sunday School Board of the Southern Baptist Convention, 1963.

Binkley, Olin T. Reminiscences and Memoirs Regarding Walter Nathan Johnson. 1964. SEBTS.

Carpenter, L.L. Reminiscences and Memoirs Regarding Walter Nathan Johnson. 1964. SEBTS.

Carver, William Owen. Papers. SBHLA.

*Christian Frontiers* Files. SBHLA.

England, Martin and Mabel. Correspondence and journals.

————. Materials concerning. Office of the Chaplain. Furman Univ., Greenville, S.C.

Gardner, Brother Dave. *"Ain't That Weird?"* RCA Victor, LPM-2335, 1961.

Grigg, W.R. Reminiscences and Memoirs Regarding Walter Nathan Johnson. 1964. SEBTS.

Huggins, M.A. Reminiscences and Memoirs Regarding Walter Nathan Johnson. 1964. SEBTS.

Johnson, Walter Nathan. "Letters from the Lighted Couch." Unpublished novel, n.d. NCBHC.

————. Papers. NCBHC.

————. "The Lighted Couch." Unpublished novel, n.d. NCBHC.

————, ed. *LCV Quarterly Communication,* 1948-51.

————, ed. *The Next Step in the Churches,* 1923-48.

Martin England Testimonial. Tape recording. 10 Feb. 1986. First Baptist Church, Greenville, S.C.

McKinney, B.B., ed. *The Broadman Hymnal.* Nashville: Broadman Press, 1940.

Race Relations and Southern Baptists Files. SBHLA.

Reconcilers Fellowship. Doctrinal Statements, Minutes, Membership Communications. Waco, Tex.

Religion and Culture Project Files. IOH.

Reynolds, William J., ed. *The Baptist Hymnal.* Nashville: Convention Press, 1975.

Southern Baptist Convention. *Annual.* Nashville: Southern Baptist Convention, 1906.

————. *Annual.* Nashville: Southern Baptist Convention, 1930.

————. *Southern Baptist Annual.* Nashville: Southern Baptist Convention, 1947.

————. *Southern Baptist Annual.* Nashville: Southern Baptist Convention, 1954.

————. *Southern Baptist Annual.* Nashville: Southern Baptist Convention, 1984.

Southern Baptist Women in Ministry Archives. WMU.

State Baptist Convention of North Carolina. *North Carolina Baptist Annual.* Raleigh: State Baptist Convention, 1952.

Taylor, Joseph Judson. Papers. SBHLA.

Watts Street Baptist Church. Correspondence and notes. Durham, N.C.

Women in Ministry Project Files. IOH.

## Interviews, Memoirs, and Sermons

Barnes, Elizabeth B. "Women in Ministry: On the Way into the Far Country." In "Voices of Hope from the Exile," Proceedings of the 1984 Conference of Women in Ministry, SBC, ed. Lela M. Hendrix. SBWIM Archives, WMU.

Bellinger, Elizabeth Smith. "Going Home by a Different Way." In *A Costly Obedience: Sermons by Women of Steadfast Spirit,* ed. Elizabeth Smith Bellinger. Valley Forge, Pa.: Judson Press, 1994.

————. Interview by Rosalie Beck. 14 May 1990. Interview 2. TC.

———. "Living toward a Vision of Shalom." In Proceedings of the 1987 meeting of Southern Baptist Women in Ministry. SBWIM Archives, WMU.

Bratcher, Robert Galveston. Interview by author. 17 April 1985. Interview 2. TC.

———. Interview by author. 14 April 1986. Interview 3. TC.

———. Interview by author. 14 April 1986. Interview 4. TC.

Campbell, Will D. *Brother to a Dragonfly.* New York: Seabury Press, 1977.

Carr, Warren T. Interview by author. 18 April 1986. TC.

Carter, Jimmy. *Turning Point: A Candidate, a State, and a Nation Come of Age.* New York: Times Books, 1992.

Clancy, Walter B. "Jesus in the Brush Arbor: An Interview with Will Campbell." *New Orleans Review* 4 (1974): 228-31.

Clanton, Jann Aldredge. Interview by Rosalie Beck. 25 Sept. 1986. Interview 3. TC.

———. Interview by Rosalie Beck. 6 July 1989. Interview 3. TC.

Claypool, John R. "If I Go Down into Hell." In *Baptists See Black,* ed. Wayne Dehoney. Waco, Tex.: Word Books, 1969.

Corpening, Julius. Interview by author. 18 April 1986. TC.

Criswell, W. A. "The Church of the Open Door." In *Baptists See Black,* ed. Wayne Dehoney. Waco, Tex.: Word Books, 1969.

Davis, Addie. "Return from Exile--Twenty Years Later." In "Voices of Hope from the Exile," Proceedings of the 1984 Conference of Women in Ministry, SBC, ed. Lela M. Hendrix. SBWIM Archives, WMU.

Dehoney, Wayne. "To Tell It Like It Is!" In *Baptists See Black,* ed. Wayne Dehoney. Waco, Tex.: Word Books, 1969.

Dorrell, Jimmy. Interview by author. 23 Nov. 1988. Interview 1. TC.

———. Interview by author. 23 May 1990. Interview 2. TC.

———. Interview by author. 1 Aug. 1990. Interview 3. TC.

England, Mabel C. Interview by author. 26 July 1984. Interview 1. TC.

———. Interview by author. 16 Aug. 1984. Interview 2. TC.

England, Martin. Interview by author. 27 July 1984. Interview 1. TC.

———. Interview by author. 27 July 1984. Interview 2. TC.

———. Interview by author. 15 Aug. 1984. Interview 3. TC.

———. Interview by author. 25 Sept. 1984. Interview 4. TC.

Finger, Bill. "Preaching the Gospel, South of God: An Interview with Carlyle Marney." *Christian Century,* 4 October 1978, 914-20.

Finlator, William W. Interview by author. 12 Sept. 1984. TC.

Fontenot, Glenda. Interview by author. 13 June 1995. Author's collection.

Gatlin, Joe W. Interview by author. 16 Nov. 1988. Interview 1. TC.

Gatlin, Nancy. Interview by author. 22 Dec. 1988. Interview 1. TC.

———. Interview by author. 22 July 1991. Interview 2. TC.

Gilmore, Martha. Interview by author. 29 July 1977. Interview 1. TC.

———. Interview by author. 26 Sept. 1977. Interview 2. TC.

———. Interview by author. 26 Nov. 1977. Interview 3. TC.

———. Interview by author. 8 July 1978. Interview 4. TC.

————. Interview by author. 13 July 1978. Interview 5. TC.

————. Interview by author. 14 Aug. 1978. Interview 6. TC.

————. Interview by author. 15 March 1979. Interview 7. TC.

————. Interview by author. 30 Jan. 1985. Interview 8. TC.

Harris, Lisa. Interview by author. 18 July 1991. TC.

Hendricks, Garland A. Interview by author. 12 March 1987. TC.

Langley, Ralph H. "Into All the World . . . of the Inner City." In *Baptists See Black,* ed. Wayne Dehoney. Waco, Tex.: Word Books, 1969.

Lee, G. Avery. "Confessions of an Ex-Southern Liberal . . . Who Is Still Both." In *Baptists See Black,* ed. Wayne Dehoney. Waco, Tex.: Word Books, 1969.

Lewis, Gladys. Interview by author. 22 Nov. 1985. Interview 1. TC.

————. Interview by author. 5 Dec. 1986. Interview 2. TC.

Lowrey, Sara. Interview by Daniel B. McGee. 2 Aug. 1972. TC.

Marney, Carlyle. "Dayton's Long Hot Summer." In *D-Days at Dayton: Reflections on the Scopes Trial,* ed. Jerry R. Tompkins. Baton Rouge: Louisiana State Univ. Press, 1965.

————. "An Ethic of Parsimony." Theological Cassettes, vol. 9, August 1978, Divinity School Library, Duke Univ., Durham, N.C.

————. "In the Meantime." In *Marney,* ed. Mary Kraft. Charlotte, N.C.: Myers Park Baptist Church, 1979.

————. "The Priest at Every Elbow." In *Church in the World,* ed. Bruce Evans. Baton Rouge, La.: Fellowship Baptist Church, 1965.

Maston, T.B. Interview by Rufus B. Spain. 1 June 1977. Interview 1. TC.

McAteer, Ed. Interview by author and Larry Braidfoot. 28 October 1988. Interview 3. TC.

McClernon, Robert E. Funeral sermon for Carlyle Marney. In *Marney,* ed. Mary Kraft. Charlotte, N.C.: Myers Park Baptist Church, 1979.

————. Interview by author. 17 April 1985. Interview 1. TC.

————. Interview by author. 13 March 1986. Interview 2. TC.

————. "The Road Less Traveled By." Typescript. 28 Aug. 1985. Watts Street Baptist Church, Durham, N.C.

————. "When Every Explanation is Silent." Typescript. 29 Jan. 1978. Watts Street Baptist Church, Durham, N.C.

McGary, Betty Winstead. Interview by Rosalie Beck. 9 July 1986. TC.

Monroe, James L. "A Southerner's Dilemma." In *Baptists See Black,* ed. Wayne Dehoney. Waco, Tex.: Word Books, 1969.

Morgan, Sally Murphey. "Women in Ministry Testimony." In Proceedings of the 1987 meeting of Southern Baptist Women in Ministry. SBWIM Archives, WMU.

North, Gary. "Firestorm Chat: An Interview with Paul Pressler." Tape recording. Religion and Culture Project Files, IOH, n.d.

Orrick, Bailis William. Interview by Rufus B. Spain. 11 July 1975. Interview 1. TC.

Paynter, Roger A. Interview by author. 5 March 1995. Author's collection.

Perkins, Perry. Interview by author. 1 July 1995. Author's collection.

Ramsey, Brooks. "Partial Christians and an Impartial God." In *Baptists See Black,* ed. Wayne Dehoney. Waco, Tex.: Word Books, 1969.

Rose, Teresa Belt. Interview by Elizabeth J. Griffin. 12 May 1981. Interview 2. TC.

Sams, Dail. Interview by author. 29 July 1991. TC.

Sams, Jerry P. Interview by author. 29 July 1991. TC.

Sehested, Ken. Interview by author. 1 Dec. 1995. Author's collection.

Sehested, Nancy Hastings. Interview by M. Rebecca Sharpless. 20 Aug. 1986. Interview 1. TC.

Seymour, Robert E. Interview by author. 13 March 1986. TC.

———. *"Whites Only": A Pastor's Retrospective on Signs of the New South.* Valley Forge, Pa.: Judson Press, 1991.

Sherman, Cecil E. "The Way Things Are." In *Baptists See Black,* ed. Wayne Dehoney. Waco, Tex.: Word Books, 1969.

Siler, M. Mahan. "God-Talk: A Sermon." *Folio,* Spring 1987, 3, 12.

Smith, Oscar Blake. Interview by Thomas L. Charlton. 27 October 1972. Interview 4. TC.

Stinson, Deborah. Interview by Rosalie Beck. 23 June 1990. Interview 4. TC.

Strickland, Otis. Interview by Glenn O. Hilburn. 21 Aug. 1972. Interview 1. TC.

Sullivan-Gonzalez, Douglass Creed. Interview by Jaclyn Jeffrey. 26 March 1987. Interview 2. TC.

———. Interview by Jaclyn Jeffrey. 6 Jan. 1988. Interview 7. TC.

Swabb, Marnie. Interview by author. 21 May 1990. TC.

Tindell, Charles Morris Jr. Interview by author and Jaclyn Jeffrey. 9 April 1986. Interview 1. TC.

Trantham, Charles A. "One Father--One Blood." In *Baptists See Black,* ed. Wayne Dehoney. Waco, Tex.: Word Books, 1969.

Turner, Paul. "The Way Up Is the Way Out." In *Baptists See Black,* ed. Wayne Dehoney. Waco, Tex.: Word Books, 1969.

Valentine, Foy D. Interview by Daniel B. McGee. 25 May 1976. Interview 2. TC.

———. Interview by Thomas L. Charlton and Daniel B. McGee. 8 March 1980. Interview 6. TC.

———. Interview by Thomas L. Charlton and author. 4 Dec. 1989. Interview 14. TC.

Weaver-Williams, Lynda. "Visions of a New Humanity." In Proceedings of the 1987 meeting of Southern Baptist Women in Ministry. SBWIM Archives, WMU.

Whaley, Carolyn Louise. Interview by author. 20 Feb. 1980. TC.

Wright, Dean. Telephone interview by author. 16 Nov. 1994. Author's collection.

Zhang, C.K. Interview by author and Gerald Fielder. 2 Feb. 1989. Interview 14. TC.

## *Secondary Material*

Ahlstrom, Sydney E. *A Religious History of the American People.* New Haven: Yale Univ.Press, 1972.

Allen, Bob. "SBC Takes Next Steps toward Reorganization." *Baptist Standard,* 28 Feb. 1996, 3.

Allen, Jimmy. "The History of Baptists Committed." In *The Struggle for the Soul of the SBC: Moderate Responses to the Fundamentalist Movement,* ed. Walter B. Shurden. Macon, Ga.: Mercer Univ. Press, 1993.

Allen, Nancy Drown. "Rewriting Your Resume." *Folio,* winter 1985, 6.

Ammerman, Nancy Tatom. *Baptist Battles: Social Change and Religious Conflict in the Southern Baptist Convention.* New Brunswick, N.J.: Rutgers Univ. Press, 1990.

———. "The New South and the New Baptists." *The Christian Century,* 14 May 1986, 486-88.

———. "North American Protestant Fundamentalism." In *Fundamentalisms Observed,* ed. Martin E. Marty and R. Scott Appleby. Chicago: Univ. of Chicago Press, 1991.

———. "SBC Moderates and the Making of a Postmodern Denomination." *Christian Century,* 22-29 Sept. 1993, 898-99.

———, ed. *Southern Baptists Observed: Multiple Perspectives on a Changing Denomination.* Knoxville: Univ. of Tennessee Press, 1993.

Anders, Sarah Frances. "A Chronology: Pilgrimage toward Equity in Ministry, SBC." *Folio,* 1983, insert, n.p.

———. "Has a Generation Really Passed?" *Folio,* Summer 1989, 5.

———, and Marilyn Metcalf-Whittaker. "Women as Lay Leaders and Clergy: A Critical Issue." In *Southern Baptists Observed: Multiple Perspectives on a Changing Denomination,* ed. Nancy Tatom Ammerman. Knoxville: Univ. of Tennessee Press, 1993.

Appleby, R. Scott. Review of *Southern Baptist Politics: Authority and Power in the Restructuring of an American Denomination,* by Arthur Emery Farnsley II. *Journal of American History* 82 (Sept. 1995): 835-36.

Autry, Renee Smith. "Baptist Principles Led Churches to Take Stands for Women." *Folio,* fall 1994, 1, 5.

Bailey, Anne Lowrey. "Encyclopedia of the South Links Legend and Reality." *Chronicle of Higher Education,* 3 Aug. 1988, A-6.

Bailey, Kenneth K. *Southern White Protestantism in the Twentieth Century.* New York: Harper & Row, 1964.

Baker, Robert A. *Relations between Northern and Southern Baptists.* Fort Worth: Seminary Hill Press, 1948.

———. *The Southern Baptist Convention and Its People, 1607-1972.* Nashville: Broadman Press, 1974.

Balmer, Randall. *Mine Eyes Have Seen the Glory: A Journey into the Evangelical Subculture in America.* New York: Oxford Univ. Press, 1989.

"Baptist Church Expelled for Female Deacon." *Christian Century,* 22-29 Sept. 1993, 893.

Barnes, W.W. *The Southern Baptist Convention, 1845-1953.* Nashville: Broadman Press, 1954.

Bedell, George C., Leo Sandon, Jr., and Charles T. Wellborn. *Religion in America.* 2d ed. New York: Macmillan, 1982.

Bellinger, Libby. "More Hidden than Revealed: The History of Southern Baptist Women in Ministry." In *The Struggle for the Soul of the SBC: Moderate Responses to the Fundamentalist Movement,* ed. Walter B. Shurden. Macon, Ga.: Mercer Univ. Press, 1993.

———. "Reflections on the Southern Baptist Alliance Meeting." *Folio,* summer 1987, 3.

———. "Women Mourners into Women Messengers." *Folio,* autumn 1986, 3.

"Black Baptist Rejects Apology by SBC." *Christian Century,* 27 Sept.-4 October 1995, 879-80.

Boles, John B. *The Great Revival, 1787-1805: The Origins of the Southern Evangelical Mind.* Lexington: Univ. Press of Kentucky, 1972.

———. *The South through Time: A History of an American Region.* Englewood Cliffs, N. J.: Prentice Hall, 1995.

"Bratcher Clarifies, Apologizes." *Baptist Standard,* 24 Sept. 1980, 3.

Bratcher, Robert G. "The Translator Translated." Vertical Files, Denny Library, Southeastern Baptist Theological Seminary, Wake Forest, N.C., 1978.

Bronner, Simon J. "Storytelling." In *Encyclopedia of Southern Culture,* ed. Charles Reagan Wilson and William Ferris. Chapel Hill: Univ. of North Carolina Press, 1989.

Brown, Lavonn D. "A History of Representative Southern Baptist Preaching from the First World War to the Depression, 1914-1929." Th.D. thesis, Southwestern Baptist Theological Seminary, 1964.

Bryan, G. McLeod. *Dissenter in the Baptist Southland: Fifty Years in the Career of William Wallace Finlator.* Macon, Ga.: Mercer Univ. Press, 1985.

Burkhalter, Frank E. "Seventy-five Million Campaign." In *Encyclopedia of Southern Baptists,* ed. Norman Wade Cox. Nashville: Broadman, 1958.

Butler, Cathy. "Profile: Pat Bailey." *Folio,* summer 1987, 4.

———. "Profile: Marsha Moore." *Folio,* spring 1987, 4.

Camp, Ken. "Criswell Raps 'Shared Ministry.'" *Baptist Standard,* 26 Feb. 1986, 8.

"Campbell on the SBC." *Christian Century,* 5 Nov. 1986, 969.

Campbell, Will D. "He Ate Yesterday." *Seeds,* October 1982, 10.

———. "On Silencing Our Finest." *Folio,* winter 1985, 2.

Carey, John J. *Carlyle Marney: A Pilgrim's Progress.* Macon, Ga.: Mercer Univ. Press, 1980.

Carter, Jimmy. "Who Cares for the Least of These?" *Seeds,* Special Edition, 1982, 32-33.

Chancey, Andrew S. "A Demonstration Plot for the Kingdom of God: The Establishment and Early Years of Koinonia Farm." *Georgia Historical Quarterly* 75 (summer 1991): 321-31.

———. "Koinonia in the '90s." *Christian Century,* 14 October 1992, 892-93.

————. "Race, Reform, and Religion: Koinonia's Challenge to Southern Society, 1942-1992." Ph.D. diss., Univ. of Florida, forthcoming.

Childress, Kyle. "A Time to Stand." *PeaceWork,* Sept. 1985, 3.

"Church Calls Woman Pastor: Loses Building." *Folio,* winter 1991, 1.

"Church Expelled for Ordaining Gay Man." *Christian Century,* 25 October 1995, 983.

Cobb, Reba Sloan. "Publisher's Column." *Folio,* spring 1989, 2.

"Co-editor Leaves Folio." *Folio,* summer 1987, 2.

Connelly, Thomas L. "Campbell, Will." In *Encyclopedia of Southern Culture,* ed. Charles Reagan Wilson and William Ferris. Chapel Hill: Univ. of North Carolina Press, 1989.

————. *Will Campbell and the Soul of the South.* New York: Continuum, 1982.

Cornell, George W. "Graham Faces 'Integrity Issue.'" *Durham* [N.C.] *Morning Herald,* 22 May 1982, 8A.

————. "Support Grows for Death Penalty." *Times-Picayune,* 4 Dec. 1993, D-10.

Cotes, Haddon Eugene. "Southern Baptist Preaching." In *Encyclopedia of Southern Baptists,* Vol. III., ed. Davis Collier Woolley. Nashville: Broadman, 1971.

"Criswell Expressed 'Regret' at Statement." *Baptist Standard,* 1 October 1980, 9.

Cullom, W.R. "Johnson, Walter Nathan." In *Encyclopedia of Southern Baptists,* ed. Norman Wade Cox. Nashville: Broadman, 1958.

Davidson, Miriam. "Sanctuary Movement Under Fire." *Christian Science Monitor,* 22 October 1985, 18-19.

Degler, Carl. *Place over Time: The Continuity of Southern Distinctiveness.* Baton Rouge: Louisiana State Univ. Press, 1977.

Dekar, Paul R. *For the Healing of the Nations: Baptist Peacemakers.* Macon, Ga.: Smith & Helwys, 1993.

Dobbins, Gaines S. "Toy, Crawford Howell." In *Encyclopedia of Southern Baptists,* ed. Norman Wade Cox. Nashville: Broadman, 1958.

————. "Whitsitt, William Heth." In *Encyclopedia of Southern Baptists,* ed. Norman Wade Cox. Nashville: Broadman, 1958.

Dorman, Charles T. "Southern Baptists and Placement." *Folio,* summer 1986, 12.

Eighmy, John L. *Churches in Cultural Captivity.* Ed. Samuel S. Hill. Knoxville: Univ. of Tennessee Press, 1987.

"Embattled Fellowship Farm." *Time,* 17 Sept. 1956, 79.

England, Martin. "War's Alternative: Drastic and Dramatic Sharing." *Foundations* 15 (October-Dec. 1972): 297.

Evans, Sara M. *Born for Liberty: A History of Women in America.* New York: Free Press, 1989.

Farnsley, Arthur Emery. *Southern Baptist Politics: Authority and Power in the Restructuring of an American Denomination.* Univ. Park: Pennsylvania State Univ. Press, 1994.

Fasol, Al. "A History of Representative Southern Baptist Preaching, 1930-45." Th.D. thesis, Southwestern Baptist Theological Seminary, 1975.

Ferris, Elizabeth. "Give Us *Some* of Your Tired, Your Poor." *Houston Post,* 19 May 1986, B-3.

Findlay, James. *Church People in the Struggle: The National Council of Churches and the Black Freedom Movement, 1950-1970.* New York: Oxford Univ. Press, 1993.

Fletcher, Jesse C. *The Southern Baptist Convention: A Sesquicentennial History.* Nashville: Broadman & Holman, 1994.

———. "Southern Baptists in Higher Education—Part 2." *Southern Baptist Educator,* October 1995, 4-5.

Flynn, Robert. "Genesis, Jeremiah, and Gospels." In *Communion: Contemporary Writers Reveal the Bible in Their Lives,* ed. David Rosenberg. New York: Anchor/Doubleday, 1996.

Flynt, J. Wayne. *Dixie's Forgotten People: The South's Poor Whites.* Bloomington: Indiana Univ. Press, 1980.

———. "Feeding the Hungry and Ministering to the Broken Hearted: The Presbyterian Church in the United States and the Social Gospel, 1900-1920." In *Religion in the South,* ed. Charles Reagan Wilson. Jackson: Univ. Press of Mississippi, 1985.

"Folio." *Folio,* summer 1983, 4.

"Fontenot Chosen as New President of the Baptist Peace Fellowship." *Baptist Peacemaker,* fall-winter 1994, 20.

"Former HMB Chairman Now a Methodist." *Baptist Standard,* 2 July 1986, 11.

Fuller, Millard. *No More Shacks! The Daring Vision of Habitat for Humanity.* Waco, Tex.: Word Books, 1986.

"Fundamentalist Students Assail Baylor U. Policies." *Chronicle of Higher Education,* 9 Jan. 1985, 16.

Gaustad, Edwin Scott. *Dissent in American Religion.* Chicago History of American Religion. Chicago: Univ. of Chicago Press, 1973.

Gilmore, Walter M. "Schools of Applied Stewardship." *Biblical Recorder,* 24 October 1924, 4.

Gines, Sandra. "Out of Many, One." *Waco Tribune-Herald,* 8 October 1988, 1C-2C.

Ginger, Ray. *Six Days or Forever? Tennessee v. John Thomas Scopes.* London: Oxford Univ. Press, 1958.

Golden, Renny, and Michael McConnell. *Sanctuary: The New Underground Railroad.* Maryknoll, N.Y.: Orbis Books, 1986.

Goodwyn, Lawrence. *Democratic Promise: The Populist Movement in America.* New York: Oxford Univ. Press, 1976.

"Graham in Moscow: What Did He Really Say?" *Christianity Today,* 18 June 1982, 10-12.

Grantham, Dewey W. *Southern Progressivism: The Reconciliation of Progress and Tradition.* Knoxville: Univ. of Tennessee Press, 1983.

Green, John C. "Pat Robertson and the Latest Crusade: Religious Resources and the 1988 Presidential Campaign." *Social Science Quarterly* 74 (March 1993): 157-68.

Grice, Homer L. and R. Paul Caudill. "Graves-Howell Controversy." In *Encyclopedia of Southern Baptists*, ed. Norman Wade Cox. Nashville: Broadman, 1958.

Handy, Robert T., ed. *The Social Gospel in America, 1870-1920.* New York: Oxford Univ. Press, 1966.

Hankins, Barry. *God's Rascal: J. Frank Norris and the Beginnings of Southern Fundamentalism.* Lexington: Univ. Press of Kentucky, 1996.

Hargus, Relma. "Profile: Joyce Martin." *Folio*, winter 1991, 4.

Harper, Keith. *The Quality of Mercy: Southern Baptists and Social Christianity, 1890-1920.* Tuscaloosa: Univ. of Alabama Press, 1996.

Harvey, Paul. *Redeeming the South: Religious Cultures and Racial Identities among Southern Baptists, 1865-1925.* Chapel Hill: Univ. of North Carolina Press, 1997.

Harvey, Van A. "Atonement." In *A Handbook of Theological Terms*, ed. Harvey. New York: Macmillan, 1964.

"Harwell's Motivations behind the Motion." *Folio*, winter 1995, 7.

Harwell, Jack U. "Fallout Ripples across Baptist Waters in Wake of Firing at Southern Seminary." *Baptists Today*, 4 May 1995, 5.

Hastey, Stan. "SBC Battle Changing Political Landscape." *Baptist Standard*, 2 Dec. 1987, 13.

Hays, Brooks, and John E. Steely. *The Baptist Way of Life.* 2d rev. ed. Macon, Ga.: Mercer Univ. Press, 1981.

Hefley, James Carl. *The Truth in Crisis: The Controversy in the Southern Baptist Convention.* Dallas: Criterion Publications, 1986.

Hill, Davis C. "Southern Baptist Thought and Action in Race Relations, 1940-1950." Th.D. thesis, Southern Baptist Theological Seminary, 1952.

Hill, Diane Eubanks. "What's a Mama to Say?" *Folio*, winter 1986, 7.

Hill, Samuel S. Jr. Introduction to *Churches in Cultural Captivity*, by John L. Eighmy, ed. Samuel S. Hill. Knoxville: Univ. of Tennessee Press, 1987.

———. *One Name but Several Faces: Variety in Popular Denominations in Southern History.* Athens: Univ. of Georgia Press, 1996.

———. *The South and the North in American Religion.* Athens: Univ. of Georgia Press, 1980.

———. "The Story before the Story: Southern Baptists since World War II." In *Southern Baptists Observed: Multiple Perspectives on a Changing Denomination*, ed. Nancy Tatom Ammerman. Knoxville: Univ. of Tennessee Press, 1993.

———, et al. *Religion and the Solid South.* Nashville: Abingdon Press, 1972.

Hobbs, Sara Ann. "Women in Ministry: Predictions for the Next 30 Years." *Folio*, summer 1984, 3-4.

Hodge, Evelyn. "Sanctuary." *Seeds*, Special Edition, 1982, 20-22.

"Holding Fast the Word of Life." *ABC People*, 1993, 10.

Hollinger, Herb. "Fellowship to Study Becoming Denomination," *Baptist Standard*, 2 Aug. 1995, 3-4.

Hughes, Richard B. "The Baptist-Baptists of Pampa." *Texas Observer*, 21 October 1988, 23.

Hunt, W. Boyd. "Atonement." In *Encyclopedia of Southern Baptists,* ed. Norman Wade Cox. Nashville: Broadman, 1958.

Hutchinson, Debbie. "Baptist Women Urged to Protest." *Waco Tribune-Herald,* 27 April 1985, 1-2C.

Ingalls, Zoe. "Baptists' Leaders Defend Drive." *Chronicle of Higher Education,* 25 June 1986, 3.

Isaacs, Rhys. *The Transformation of Virginia, 1740-1790: Communications, Religion and Authority.* Chapel Hill: Univ. of North Carolina Press, 1982

"Israel Dismayed at Smith Remark." *Baptist Standard,* 1 October 1980, 8.

"It Used to Be Called 'Frugal' Living." *Seeds,* March 1981, 2.

Jarboe, Jan. "War for Thee Univ.." *Texas Monthly,* Nov. 1991, 189-91.

"Jews Angered, but Smith Stands by Remarks," *Baptist Standard,* 24 Sept. 1980, 3.

"J. Martin England." *Tomorrow,* March 1989, 14.

Johnson, Cindy Harp. "Name Calling: The Art of Identifying the Intangible." *Folio,* summer 1990, 5.

Johnson, Daniel Calhoun. "Walter N. Johnson: Apostle of Stewardship." Th.M. thesis, Southeastern Baptist Theological Seminary, 1965.

Johnson, Walter N. "The Lawyer and the Preacher." *Biblical Recorder,* 21 Sept. 1910, 1.

Jones, Jim. "Baylor Plans for Growth of Seminary." *Fort Worth Star-Telegram,* 21 May 1994, 27A.

———. "Dilday's Firing Stirs Up Interest in Fellowship." *Fort Worth Star-Telegram,* 1 May 1994, 8C.

———. "Methodist Wife Costs Baptist Job." *Fort Worth Star-Telegram,* 25 April 1985, 1-2A.

Jones, Neal. "Women's Ordination and the Pretense of Inerrancy." *Folio,* summer 1986, 3.

K'Meyer, Tracy E. "What Koinonia Was All About: The Role of Memory in a Changing Community," *Oral History Review* 24 (summer 1997): 1-22.

King, Larry L. *The Old Man and Lesser Mortals.* New York: Delta, 1975.

Kneece, Brenda. "This Is My Story . . . ." *Folio,* summer 1995, 7.

Knight, Walker L. "Race Relations: Changing Patterns and Practices." In *Southern Baptists Observed: Multiple Perspectives on a Changing Denomination,* ed. Nancy Tatom Ammerman. Knoxville: Univ. of Tennessee Press, 1993.

———. *Struggle for Integrity.* Atlanta: Home Mission Board, 1969.

Knox, Marv. "Congregations Enter Church-State Fracas," *Baptist Standard,* 23 October 1996, 7.

———. "Politics Steps Up to the Pulpit," *Baptist Standard,* 23 October 1996, 1, 6.

"Koinonia Farm." *Fellowship of Intentional Communities Newsletter,* Feb. 1955, 3.

Lacy, Edmund Emmett. "A History of Representative Southern Baptist Preaching from 1895 to the First World War." Th.D. thesis, Southwestern Baptist Theological Seminary, 1960.

Lasch, Christopher. *The True and Only Heaven: Progress and Its Critics.* New York: W.W. Norton, 1991.

Lawson, Linda, Baptist Press. "Women in Ministry Called Critical Issue." *Folio*, spring 1984, 6.

Lee, Dallas. *The Cotton Patch Evidence.* New York: Harper & Row, 1971.

Lee, G. Avery. *Where Christian Ideas Take Shape in People: The Unfolding Drama of a Church.* New Orleans: St. Charles Avenue Baptist Church, 1973.

Lemley, Laura. "Marshall Leaves SBTS." *Folio*, winter 1995, 1.

Leonard, Bill J. *God's Last and Only Hope: The Fragmentation of the Southern Baptist Convention.* Grand Rapids, Mich.: Wm. B. Eerdmans, 1990.

———. "Good News at Wolf Creek." *Folio*, summer 1984, 1.

———. "Southern Baptists and a New Religious Establishment." *Christian Century*, 10-17 Sept. 1986, 775-76.

———. "When the Denominational Center Doesn't Hold: The Southern Baptist Experience." *Christian Century*, 22-29 Sept. 1993, 905-10.

Levy, Peter B., ed. *Documentary History of the Modern Civil Rights Movement.* New York: Greenwood Press, 1992.

"Lifestyle Conversion." *Seeds*, Nov. 1980, 1.

Linder, Suzanne. *William Louis Poteat: Prophet of Progress.* Chapel Hill: Univ. of North Carolina Press, 1966.

Lippy, Charles H. *Bibliography of Religion in the South.* Macon, Ga.: Mercer Univ. Press, 1985.

"Maddox Urged Bailey Smith Not to Attend Dallas Briefing." *Baptist Standard,* 3 Sept. 1980, 5.

Manis, Andrew Michael. *Southern Civil Religions in Conflict: Black and White Baptists and Civil Rights, 1947-1957.* Athens: Univ. of Georgia Press, 1987.

Marsden, George M. *Fundamentalism and American Culture: The Shaping of Twentieth-Century Evangelicalism, 1870-1925.* Oxford: Oxford Univ. Press, 1980.

———. "The New Paganism." *Reformed Journal* (Jan. 1988): 3-13.

———. *Understanding Fundamentalism and Evangelicalism.* Grand Rapids, Mich.: Wm. B. Eerdmans, 1991.

Martin, Dan, and Marv Knox. "Baptist Peacemakers Eye Alternative Strategies." *Baptist Standard,* 18 Aug. 1982, 12.

———. "Nominee Vows Pro-Life, Racial Justice Stands." *Baptist Standard,* 14 Sept. 1988, 3.

Martin, Patricia Summerlin. "Hidden Work: Baptist Women in Texas, 1880-1920." Ph.D. diss., Rice Univ., 1982.

Martin, William. "God's Angry Man." *Texas Monthly,* April 1981, 152-235.

———. "Hearts and Minds." *Texas Monthly,* Sept. 1979, 160-64.

———. *With God on Our Side: The Rise of the Religious Right in America.* New York: Broadway Books, 1996.

Marty, Martin E., and R. Scott Appleby, eds. *Fundamentalisms Observed.* Chicago: Univ.of Chicago Press, 1991.

Mather, Juliette. "Armstrong, Annie." In *Encyclopedia of Southern Baptists*, ed. Norman Wade Cox. Nashville: Broadman, 1958.

————. "Woman's Missionary Union." In *Encyclopedia of Southern Baptists,* ed. Norman Wade Cox. Nashville: Broadman, 1958.

Matthews, C. DeWitt. "History of Preaching." In *Encyclopedia of Southern Baptists,* Vol. III., ed. Davis Collier Woolley. Nashville: Broadman, 1971.

May, Robert E. "Dixie's Martial Image: A Continuing Historiographical Enigma." *Historian* 40 (Feb. 1978): 213-34.

Maynard, Steve. "Ordained Southern Baptist Women Break through Barriers." *Houston Chronicle,* 26 July 1986, 6-1, 6-6.

McBeth, Leon. "J. Frank Norris, Father of SBC Fundamentalism." *Biblical Recorder,* 5 Nov. 1983, 3.

————. "Who Was J. Frank Norris?" *Baptist Standard,* 8 Aug. 1990, 12-13.

————. "Women in Ministry: An Assessment." *Folio,* spring 1985, 3.

McCall, Duke K. "Schismatics/Heretics." *Baptist Standard,* 19 October 1977, 16.

McClendon, James Wm., Jr. *Biography as Theology: How Life Stories Can Remake Today's Theology.* Nashville: Abingdon Press, 1974.

McDowell, John Patrick. *The Social Gospel in the South: The Woman's Home Mission Movement in the Methodist Episcopal Church, South, 1886-1939.* Baton Rouge: Louisiana State Univ. Press, 1982.

McWhiney, Grady. *Cracker Culture: Celtic Ways in the Old South.* Tuscaloosa: Univ. of Alabama Press, 1988.

Melvin, Robert Alfred. "The Life and Thought of Walter Nathan Johnson." D.Div. thesis, Vanderbilt Univ. Divinity School, 1975.

Miller, Acker C. "Christian Life Commission." In *Encyclopedia of Southern Baptists,* ed. Norman Wade Cox. Nashville: Broadman, 1958.

Miller, Howard. "Texas." In *Religion in the Southern States: A Historical Study,* ed. Samuel S. Hill. Macon, Ga.: Mercer Univ. Press, 1983.

Miller, Tom. "Pressler: 'Going for Jugular' to Control SBC." *Baptist Standard,* 24 Sept. 1980, 4.

Mobley, Jennie Batson. "One Woman's Story." *Folio,* spring 1986, 6.

Moltmann, Jurgen. *Theology of Hope.* New York: Harper & Row, 1967.

Montell, William Lynwood. *Killings: Folk Justice in the Upper South.* Lexington: Univ. Press of Kentucky, 1986.

Montoya, David K. "Trading Principles for Power in the SBC." *Christian Century,* 17 Jan.1990, 39-40.

Moore, Merrill D. "Stewardship." In *Encyclopedia of Southern Baptists,* ed. Norman Wade Cox. Nashville: Broadman, 1958.

————. "Stewardship Commission of the Southern Baptist Convention." In *Encyclopedia of Southern Baptists,* Vol. III., ed. Davis Collier Woolley. Nashville: Broadman, 1971.

Moore, W.T. *His Heart Is Black.* Atlanta: Home Mission Board of the Southern Baptist Convention, 1978.

Morgan, David T. *The New Crusades,the New Holy Land: Conflict in the Southern Baptist Convention, 1969-1991.* Tuscaloosa: Univ. of Alabama Press, 1996.

Morrison, Karen Lyn. "Persistence in Honoring Self as Seen in the Lives of Ordained Southern Baptist Women." Ph.D. diss., Texas Woman's Univ., 1995.

Neely, Alan , "The History of the Alliance of Baptists," In *The Struggle for the Soul of the SBC: Moderate Responses to the Fundamentalist Movement,* ed. Walter B. Shurden. Macon, Ga.: Mercer Univ. Press, 1993.

"New Administration Closes Southeastern Women's Center." *Folio,* winter 1988, 12.

Newton, Jim, Home Missions [SBC] News Service. "HMB Trustees Reaffirm Ordination Policy." *Baptist Standard,* 21 March 1984, 5.

Nisbett, Richard E. "Violence and U.S. Regional Culture." *American Psychologist* 48 (April 1993): 441-49.

"No Women Clergy." *Christian Century,* 30 Nov. 1983, 1104.

Oates, Stephen B. *Let the Trumpet Sound: A Life of Martin Luther King, Jr.* New York: HarperCollins, 1994.

Oates, Wayne E. "Managing Stress." *Folio,* spring 1986, 5.

"On Campus," *Folio,* June 1983, 4.

Owen, Christopher H. "The Friends and Enemies of Koinonia Farm, 1956-58." Seminar paper, Emory Univ., 1986.

Parham, Robert. "A Reconciler from 'Dixie': Clarence Jordan." *Baptist Peacemaker,* July 1983, 6, 7.

Parmley, Helen. "Evangelicals Plan Anti-Poverty Effort." *Dallas Morning News,* 1 May 1982, 1-A.

"Peace Group Plans Urban Gang Summit." *Christian Century,* 24-31 March 1993, 314.

Pearce, Betty McGary. "A History of Women in Ministry, SBC." *Folio,* summer 1985, 9-10.

Peterson, Tom. "Hunger and the Christian Tradition." *Seeds,* spring 1985, 6-11.

"Pilgrimage toward Equity in Ministry, SBC." *Folio,* summer 1983, 1.

Poteat, E. McNeill, Jr. "The Passing of a Modern Saint." *Biblical Recorder,* 5 July 1952, 5.

"Prescott Memorial Baptist Church, Memphis, Calls Nancy Hastings Sehested as Pastor." *Folio,* fall 1987, 5.

"Presidents [sic] Views." *Folio,* autumn 1984, 4-5.

Proctor, Samuel D. "A Story of Two Martins." *ABC People,* 1984, 11.

"Profile: Cathy Cole." *Folio,* summer 1984, 6.

"Profile: Deborah Whisnand Stinson." *Folio,* summer 1985, 4.

Queen, Edward L. II. *In the South the Baptists Are the Center of Gravity: Southern Baptists and Social Change, 1930-1980.* Brooklyn, N.Y.: Carlson, 1991.

Rauschenbusch, Walter. *Christianity and the Social Crisis.* Ed. Robert D. Cross. New York: Harper & Row, 1964.

"Raye Nelle Dyer Fired from Texas BSU Position over Ordination." *Folio,* winter 1995, 3.

"Reagan Feeling New Heat from New Right." *Baptist Standard,* 11 Feb. 1981, 5.

Reed, John Shelton. *The Enduring South: Subcultural Persistence in Mass Society.* Chapel Hill: Univ. of North Carolina Press, 1986.

"Resolution No. 3: 'On Women.'" *Folio*, autumn 1984, 5.

Robinson, Armstead L., and Patricia Sullivan, eds. *New Directions in Civil Rights Studies*. Charlottesville: Univ. Press of Virginia, 1991.

"Rogers Will Appoint Only Inerrantists." *Baptist Standard*, 24 June 1987, 5.

Rosenberg, Ellen M. "The Southern Baptist Response to the Newest South." In *Southern Baptists Observed: Multiple Perspectives on a Changing Denomination*, ed. Nancy Tatom Ammerman. Knoxville: Univ. of Tennessee Press, 1993.

——. *The Southern Baptists: A Subculture in Transition*. Knoxville: Univ. of Tennessee Press, 1989.

Rosser, Anne P. "Why Did the SBC Approve a Resolution That Violates and Destroys the Authority and Integrity of Scripture?" *Folio*, autumn 1984, 6, 11.

Routh, E.C. "District Association." In *Encyclopedia of Southern Baptists*, ed. Norman Wade Cox. Nashville: Broadman, 1958.

——. "Moon, Lottie." In *Encyclopedia of Southern Baptists*, ed. Norman Wade Cox. Nashville: Broadman, 1958.

Russell, C. Allyn. *Voices of Fundamentalism: Seven Biographical Studies*. Philadelphia: Westminster Press, 1976.

Sauls, H.S. "Associational Missions." In *Encyclopedia of Southern Baptists*, ed. Norman Wade Cox. Nashville: Broadman, 1958.

"SBA Gives Grant to Women in Ministry." *Folio*, spring 1989, 1.

Scott, Anne Firor. "Women, Religion, and Social Change in the South, 1830-1930." In *Religion and the Solid South*, ed. Samuel S. Hill Jr., et al. Nashville: Abingdon Press, 1972.

Sehested, Ken. "Why I Am (Still) a Baptist." *The Witness*, October 1994, 12-13.

Sehested, Nancy Hastings. "An Open Letter to the Home Mission Board of the Southern Baptist Convention." *Folio*, Summer 1989, 1.

——. "Women and Ministry in the Local Congregation." *Review and Expositor* 83 (1986): 71-80.

Shurden, Walter B. "Rebellion: Baptist Style." *The Student*, October 1970, 29-31, 40.

"Smith, Family Observe Passover." *Baptist Standard*, 22 April 1981, 5.

"Smith Sets Meeting to State Love for Jews." *Baptist Standard*, 26 Nov. 1980, 3.

Snider, P. Joel. *The "Cotton-Patch" Gospel: The Proclamation of Clarence Jordan*. Lanham, Md.: Univ. Press of America, 1985.

"Southern Baptist Tension." *Christian Century*, 30 Jan. 1985, 97.

"Southern Baptists Have Heard the Cries of Hungry People." *Seeds*, Special Hunger Day Edition, 1980, 2.

"Southern Seminary Undergoes Changes." *Folio*, summer 1995, 3.

Spain, Rufus B. *At Ease in Zion: Social History of Southern Baptists, 1865-1900*. Nashville: Vanderbilt Univ. Press, 1961.

Spence, Donald P. *Narrative Truth and Historical Truth: Meaning and Interpretation in Psychoanalysis*. New York: W.W. Norton, 1982.

St. Amant, Penrose C. *A Short History of Louisiana Baptists.* Nashville: Broadman Press, 1948.

Stagg, Frank. "Hermeneutics and Women." *Folio,* summer 1985, 1, 8.

Starling, Ginger. "Women in Ministry Respond to Home Mission Board Vote." *Folio,* winter 1986, 3, 7.

"Stassen: Wives Broke U.N. Impasse. *Times-Picayune,* 19 June 1995, A-3.

Stephens, Shirley L. "Baptists Don't Need Two Service Lists." *Folio,* winter 1985, 8.

Stewart, Felicia. "Three Women Fill North Carolina Pulpits." *Biblical Recorder,* 11 Feb. 1984, 3.

Storey, John W. "Battling Evil: The Growth of Religion in Texas." In *Texas: A Sesquicentennial Celebration,* ed. Donald W. Whisenhunt. Austin, Tex.: Eakin Press, 1984.

———. *Texas Baptist Leadership and Social Christianity, 1900-1980.* College Station: Texas A&M Univ. Press, 1986.

Strickland, Phil. "Christian Life Commission, Texas." In *Encyclopedia of Southern Baptists,* Vol. III., ed. Davis Collier Woolley. Nashville: Broadman, 1971.

"Survey Shows, 2,100 Pastors Fired during Past 18 Months." *Baptist Standard,* 30 Nov. 1988, 5.

Sweet, William W. *The Story of Religion in America.* Grand Rapids, Mich.: Baker Book House, 1975.

Taylor, Susan K. "Profile: Nancy Sehested." *Folio,* summer 1985, 6.

Taylor, Wilburn S. "Norris, John Franklyn." In *Encyclopedia of Southern Baptists,* ed. Norman Wade Cox. Nashville: Broadman, 1958.

"Threatening Picture," *Newsweek,* 15 Nov. 1971, 105.

Trentham, Charles A. "Guilt." In *Encyclopedia of Southern Baptists,* ed. Norman Wade Cox. Nashville: Broadman, 1958.

Turner, Helen Lee. "Guest Editorial." *Folio,* winter 1984, 2.

Turner, Paul. "A Quality Life," *Mid-South/Memphis Commercial Appeal,* 1 Feb. 1987, 4-8.

Valentine, Foy D. *A Historical Study of Southern Baptists and Race Relations, 1917-1947.* New York: Arno Press, 1980.

Watson, Burke. "City Baptists Receptive to Women's Ordination, but Elsewhere. . . ." *Houston Chronicle,* 26 Nov. 1983, 6-3.

Weeks, Dorothy Louise. "Girls' Auxiliary." In *Encyclopedia of Southern Baptists,* Vol. III., ed. Davis Collier Woolley. Nashville: Broadman, 1971.

"What Our Brothers Are Saying." *Folio,* autumn 1990, 8-9.

Wheeler, Marjorie Spruill. *New Women of the New South: The Leaders of the Woman Suffrage Movement in the Southern States.* New York: Oxford Univ. Press, 1993.

White, Ronald C. Jr., and C. Howard Hopkins. *The Social Gospel: Religion and Reform in Changing America.* Philadelphia: Temple Univ. Press, 1976.

Wilbanks, C.E. "Matthews, Charles Everett." In *Encyclopedia of Southern Baptists,* ed. Norman Wade Cox. Nashville: Broadman, 1958.

Wilcox, Clyde. *God's Warriors: The Christian Right in Twentieth-Century America.* Baltimore: Johns Hopkins Univ. Press, 1992.

Wilkinson, David. "Larry Baker Elected to Succeed Valentine." *Baptist Standard,* 21 Jan. 1987, 8, 20.

Williamson, Joel. *A Rage for Order: Black/White Relations in the American South since Emancipation.* New York: Oxford Univ. Press, 1986.

Wilson, Charles Reagan. *Baptized in Blood: The Religion of the Lost Cause, 1865-1920.* Athens: Univ. of Georgia Press, 1980.

————. "Moyers, Bill." In *Encyclopedia of Southern Culture,* ed. Charles Reagan Wilson and William Ferris. Chapel Hill: Univ. of North Carolina Press, 1989.

————, ed. *Religion in the South.* Jackson: Univ. Press of Mississippi, 1985.

Winston, Diane. "The Southern Baptist Story." In *Southern Baptists Observed: Multiple Perspectives on a Changing Denomination,* ed. Nancy Tatom Ammerman. Knoxville: Univ. of Tennessee Press, 1993.

"Women Deacons, Minister Okayed." *Baptist Standard,* 25 Aug. 1977, 4.

"Women Ministers Organize by States." *Folio,* winter 1984, 3.

"Women Win Preaching Awards." *Folio,* summer 1995, 3.

Woodward, C. Vann. *Origins of the New South, 1877-1913.* Baton Rouge: Louisiana State Univ. Press, 1951.

Wright, Susan Lockwood. "SBC Women Ministers Break Their Silence." *Christian Century,* 12 Nov. 1986, 998-99.

Wuthnow, Robert. *The Restructuring of American Religion: Society and Faith since World War II.* Princeton, N.J.: Princeton Univ. Press, 1988.

Wyatt-Brown, Bertram. *Honor and Violence in the Old South.* New York: Oxford Univ. Press, 1986.

# Index